CHINESE MEDIA

—A WINDOW TO CHINESE CIVILIZATION AND CULTURE

顾日国　张舍茹　编

华夏文明之窗

中国传媒

铸造符号软实力

外语教学与研究出版社
FOREIGN LANGUAGE TEACHING AND RESEARCH PRESS
北京 BEIJING

图书在版编目（CIP）数据

中国传媒 ：铸造符号软实力 ：英文 / 顾曰国，张舍茹编. -- 北京 ：外语教学与研究出版社，2021.12
（华夏文明之窗）
ISBN 978-7-5213-3302-2

Ⅰ. ①中… Ⅱ. ①顾… ②张… Ⅲ. ①英语－阅读教学－高等学校－教材②传播媒介－中国 Ⅳ. ①H319.4：G

中国版本图书馆 CIP 数据核字（2022）第 011441 号

出 版 人　王　芳
责任编辑　付分钗
责任校对　闫　璟
封面设计　彩奇风
版式设计　涂　俐
出版发行　外语教学与研究出版社
社　　址　北京市西三环北路 19 号（100089）
网　　址　https://www.fltrp.com
印　　刷　北京九州迅驰传媒文化有限公司
开　　本　787×1092　1/16
印　　张　18.5
版　　次　2023 年 10 月第 1 版　2023 年 10 月第 1 次印刷
书　　号　ISBN 978-7-5213-3302-2
定　　价　99.00 元

如有图书采购需求，图书内容或印刷装订等问题，侵权、盗版书籍等线索，请拨打以下电话或关注官方服务号：
客服电话：400 898 7000
官方服务号：微信搜索并关注公众号“外研社官方服务号”
外研社购书网址：https://fltrp.tmall.com

物料号：333020001

记载人类文明
沟通世界文化
www.fltrp.com

CHEN Hanqing (Beijing Institute of Graphic Communication)

XIA Qing (Beijing Institute of Graphic Communication)

XING Ruixue (Beijing Institute of Graphic Communication)

English Copy Editor: Robert W Archbald III (Pedagogical Teacher Training School in Guangzhou)

Web-Based Courseware Production Team

General Director: GU Yueguo (Beijing Foreign Studies University)

Team Leader: WANG Dejun (Beijing Foreign Studies University)

Scripts for Filming: HU Yang (Beijing Foreign Studies University)

Camera Men: QI Yingji, ZHENG Dequan (Beijing Foreign Studies University)

Post Editing: WANG Dejun (Beijing Foreign Studies University)

Presentation Team

Maynor (Lecturer): Peter ALMEDA (American, Beijing Polytechnic College)

Edward (Supervisor): CHEN Hanqing (Beijing Institute of Graphic Communication)

Irene: XIA Qing (Beijing Institute of Graphic Communication)

Angela: XING Ruixue (Beijing Institute of Graphic Communication)

Davis: Bryan Rafael Huezo Cubias (Salvador) (Beijing Institute of Graphic Communication)

《中国传媒》课件制作组

顾　　问　顾曰国
文字作者　张舍茹
课程策划　唐锦兰
制作督导　蒋亦蕾
责任编辑　王德军
脚本设计　王德军　胡　阳
导　　演　胡　阳
演　　员　陈翰卿　[美] Peter ALMEDA
　　　　　[萨尔瓦多] Bryan Rafael Huezo Cubias　夏　青　邢瑞雪
摄　　像　齐英吉　郑德权
视频剪辑　郑德权　齐英吉
美术设计　张　鹏　翟美乐
课件制作　刘雷雷
数字技术　冯　晋　袁劲松
平台支持　曹新龙　王珠泉

Credit Claims

Most figures in this work, including graphics and photographs, are either drawn or taken by the author. However, there are a couple of figures that are screen-captured from anonymous authors on the Web. The publisher welcomes the original authors to make a claim and is ready to accommodate the legitimate credit via mutual agreement.

Preface

Among human beings language is surely the most important and widely used method of communication. The entire range of human complexity, subtlety, ambiguity, anger, concern, confusion, a list too long to include here, is passed from one human to another through language. We acknowledge and appreciate the other forms of human interaction such as music, art, printing, acting, to name just a few, that are in this category. People who can command language are able to communicate with all other human beings, and we know that when the other forms of communication listed above are combined with human language, for example when we combine an artistic piece with a verbal explanation, the impact of the emotional and intellectual exchange is often especially profound.

Language helps to make more precise the idea being conveyed. We know that words and meanings regularly change within cultures and throughout different historical periods. The same can be true of appreciation for objects of art, the implications of music, the purpose of theatrical acting. As times change and social/cultural values and forms alter through the passage of centuries, language about art or music or theater allows us to record those changes and to reconstruct the values that originally brought forth the art, music, or theater. In those cases, written language has the greatest potential to allow us to understand the people of different, earlier times.

Because human beings are so inventive, there are many, many spoken and written languages in the world today, as there have been over past times as well. The Chinese language is surely among these great accomplishments of human beings. Its historical, geographic, and cultural influence has been overwhelming, and continues to be so today. As China's role in the international community continues to expand, the Chinese language will take on even more influence in many corners of the world. All human beings should respect and celebrate the gifts given to mankind by the Chinese language.

The English language has a shorter history as a means of widespread communication, perhaps only a few hundred years. Its pedigree is longer than that, though because it traces its roots as a Germanic language with many influences from Latin, classical Greek and French, all links that preceded it by hundreds of years. Because of historical circumstances, especially the quest of the British people for exploration and world trade from the 16th century on, and because of the Industrial Revolution of the 18th century, English has come to be the single most widely used language in the world today. Many people who do not use English as their first language find it is convenient to communicate with others through the use of English. Indeed, the person who can communicate in English has instant access to fellow human beings all over the world. As stated in this series, English has become "the matter-of-fact *lingua franca*."

It is also the case that these days people all over the world have found new ways to communicate through language. This is so because of the blindingly fast advances in technology. We are able to see and hear each other instantaneously regardless of where we are in the geographic world. We can talk and laugh and share ideas quite easily through the Internet. It can store, examine, change and convey amazing amounts of information, all of it created by human beings and intended for other human beings. Through this technology we can speak and revise our statements, we can make friends and inform others, we can express our ideas and learn new information much more quickly and with greater ease than has ever been possible in the past.

Happily, the new technology does not mean we must abandon the human inventions of the past. The new technology employs all of the contributions of our inherited cultures, and provides them to us often in "real time," meaning we communicate with each other in a matter of seconds, regardless of where our friends are physically. Understanding and respecting our past is now more effortless, and maybe even more important, than it has ever been before. This is so because others around the world also have access to information about our inherited past, and they want to know about our past just as we show interest in their cultural roots.

This new series Windows to Chinese Civilization and Culture has been created in a way that maximizes the latest in technology. It is designed for a web-based delivery of courseware and allows for mobile delivery of these materials. Printed materials, which have been so vitally important in the history of mankind are also included. All of this material is organized to fit in perfectly with the latest effective technology-based teaching methods. What are those methods? They ask the learners to be active in designing the questions they ask. They allow all of the learners to communicate with each other through discussions and a back-and-forth give-and-take of communication so that any of the members pondering a question can contribute to the conversation. When people learn information in this manner, combined with the offerings of the printed texts they truly learn the subject, not in a passive but in an active and an interactive way. Their seminar room is a virtual seminar room because they communicate on-line.

At the same time, the series respects the traditional methods of time-tested education. There is a specialist professor to guide the learners, to offer perspective when it is needed, to keep learners on the right path. The series also continues to respect the use of written textual materials. Of course the subjects it introduces are from the rich, traditional past, as seen for example in the introductions to Chinese painting, printing, ink and paper-making techniques covered as part of this extensive series. The traditional past is used to instruct and encourage the students of the present day.

Moreover, in this series young students who themselves want to learn are ready to welcome new learners into their group. The young students do not pretend to have all of the answers. They don't even pretend to have all of the questions, since they ask their new friends to also provide questions. And they plan their group activities together, just as many students are encouraged to do these days. The series approaches its topics from the learner's point of view. This is an open and easy way to come to enjoy new material.

All of this is accomplished as a way to learn English. The English used in this series is standard, current-day language as it is used by students and professors throughout the world in English-speaking countries. The language level is relaxed, casual and conversational, just as young students would use it. The language spoken by the teachers and professors is more structured and professional, as it would be in real life. But these are modern day instructors, they are relaxed about welcoming new learners into the discussion. They are the type of professors we always want to meet when we are trying to understand new material. If you jump in to this material sincerely you will learn about China's past, maybe things you've heard before and maybe something you never fully understood before, and you will learn how to discuss the particular topic of each section. You will learn the necessary vocabulary in English and the sentence patterns that are most useful when talking about these important topics. Your reading comprehension will expand in a way useful to you and you'll find that other English language texts outside of this series will become easier to understand because of what you have learned from these lessons.

There is provision for translation practice, which is a fun way to demonstrate your English comprehension skills to yourself and to others. You will learn about how to attend a lecture in English and how to listen carefully when serious topics are being presented. You will learn how to write up a summary in English of the material that has been examined.

An unusually creative and forward-looking group of individuals has come together at the Beijing Institute of Graphic Communication to devise this series and present it to you. English language experts from the Foreign Language Teaching and Steering Committee of the Ministry of Education have examined portions of these materials and offered their guidance. The series is funded by the Beijing Institute of Graphic Communication (BIGC), and numerous distinguished faculty at the BIGC lent their expertise to the project. A number of native English speakers participated in the project. You will find a list of these scholars and advisors in the Acknowledgements section. Two professors took the lead in organizing and producing this series and they deserve special thanks for their work: Sheru Zhang and Yueguo Gu. It has been my pleasure to visit the BIGC campus on several occasions and to meet a number of the faculty and also some of the capable students there. In the summer of 2014 my university, Suffolk University in Boston, welcomed Professor Zhang and her delegation of faculty and students to our campus, where I was able to discuss this important series with her.

Ronald Suleski, PhD

Professor and Director
Rosenberg Institute for East Asian Studies
Suffolk University, Boston (Current position)
Fairbank Center for Chinese Studies
Harvard University (Former position)
December 2016

Contents

Acknowledgements

The present work is a part of the Windows to Chinese Civilization and Culture series funded by Beijing Institute of Graphic Communication (BIGC).

In the production of the editions, Professor CHANG Hongmei and LU Lihong offered a lot of advice. BIGC colleagues contributed considerable support for materials and showed great patience in painstaking editing and typing. Many thanks go to them.

The authors are also thankful to BIGC teachers for their invaluable help during trialing of the texts, tasks and teachers' notes, and to BIGC students for their feedback in learning the manuscript.

The revised version of the manuscript was edited, proofread and polished by Robert W. Archbald III (American education expert) for fluency and idiomaticity of English. The authors appreciate very much for his editorial work.

ZHANG Sheru

August 20, 2023

A Note from the Authors

All students, professors, advisors, some places, and exhibitions are fictitious. All the figures mentioned in the work are historically real, unless indicated otherwise. What should be especially declared is that some filmed locations are in the Chinese Printing Museum, and some are in the library of Beijing Institute of Graphic Communication in order to simulate real-life activities.

General Introduction

The Package

Chinese Media: A Window to Chinese Civilization and Culture is a package consisting of

- printed materials traditionally known as a textbook;
- web-based delivery of the courseware bearing the same title;
- mobile delivery of the same courseware materials.

The web-based courseware provides you with audio materials which you may listen to, and video-based lectures which you may watch and enjoy. Furthermore, the web mode enables you to interact with fellow users, teachers and even with the authors via social media tools. The mobile mode is as empowering as the web mode due with the assistance of the mobile technology. It gives you an easier access while you are on the move. It enables you to make the most of your precious time! The printed textbook reminds you of the "good old days", doesn't it? It never runs out of battery! You may lie snug on the sofa, reading! But unfortunately, you cannot listen to, or watch a printed text, or send an instant message around by pressing it! So, the package as a whole has harvested all the advantages from its components while overcoming its separate disadvantages.

Readership

Chinese Media: A Window to Chinese Civilization and Culture is prepared for students with a comparatively higher English level, especially for students who major in related subjects; for students who have passed College English Test Band 4 and graduate students. It also suits Chinese readers who are keen on Chinese media in English; and for foreign readers who hope to understand Chinese media history and development.

Just as Marshall McLuhan, in his now classic masterpiece *Understanding Media: The Extensions of Man* (by Routledge & Kegan Paul, 1964), metaphorizes human use of media as extensions of man's own sensory modalities. Invention of mechanical technologies is exploding, while employment of such technologies is imploding. *Understanding Media* opens with this message:

After three thousand years of explosion, by means of fragmentary and mechanical technologies, the Western world is imploding. During the mechanical ages we had extended our bodies in space. Today, after more than a century of electric technology, we have extended our central nervous system itself in a global embrace, abolishing both space and time as far as our planet is concerned. Rapidly, we approach the final phase of the extensions of man — the technological simulation of consciousness, when the creative process of knowing will be collectively and corporately extended to the whole of human society, much as we have already extended our senses and our nerves by the various media. Whether the extension of consciousness, so long sought by advertisers for specific products, will be "a good thing" is a question that admits of a wide solution. There is little possibility of answering such questions about the extensions of man without considering all of them together. Any extension, whether of skin, hand, or foot, affects the whole psychic and social complex.

McLuhan's observations about media in the Western world are equally applicable to the Chinese media. Oracle bones and bronze vessels are physical media invented in ancient China and employed by the Shang people in particular to inscribe messages. In McLuhan's wording, oracle bone and bronze inscriptions together with the physical media have extended the ancient Shang people's senses for later generations to interact with, and to read their minds.

The English word medium (*pl.* media), as a technical term, refers to one of the means or channels of general communication, information, or entertainment in society, as newspapers, radio, or television as print media. This technical usage is adopted in this textbook. The term Chinese media covers both traditional media and new media, i.e., Chinese newspaper and press, Chinese radio & television, and new media such as internet–based computer, mobile, iPad, websites, platform etc.

In compiling, we have taken the two aspects of Chinese media into consideration. In terms of content, we have the following objects in mind: (1) Providing a historical glance at the development of Chinese media; (2) Sketching a general contour about Chinese media; and (3) Highlighting the insights drawn from scholarly studies by both Chinese and foreign media researchers.

Objectives

There are broad and specific objectives. The broad ones are described already in the ***Readership***. Here are specific objectives. By working through the ***Package***, users should be able to communicate in English about Chinese media from the following aspects:

- the historical outline, from the beginning of traditional media to the media convergence;
- the correlation between media, culture and soft power;
- the evolution of media — newspaper, periodical, media, radio, television, website etc.;
- social media like Weblog, WeChat, and QQ etc.;
- high-tech versus new media and multimedia;
- media convergence — transformation and development.

Design

There are two fundamental principles guiding the ***Package*** design. The first is the ***Principle of 3-M Learning***, that is, the principle of learning via multimodality, multimedia and multiple environments. Natural learning involves multiple sensory organs working seamlessly and harmoniously together. In fact, it takes a whole body to learn. This means that traditionally explicit cognitive-oriented learning is inadequate, and that the implicit, sub-conscious learning through immersion experiences must be given due appreciation. Learning via multimodality has become a default mode in the digital internet age. The era of orthographic only text-based presentation of learning materials has passed. The integration of printed texts, audio and video streams, still images and photographs, hypertext links, etc. has become the dominant model of the day. Learning via multiple environments, a long-dreamed goal of human education is now a reality. The boundaries between class and out-of-class, between campus and off-campus, between learning time and work or leisure time, all these traditional boundaries set up by man according to physical space and time, are rendered immaterial, thanks to digital mobile technology.

The COVID-19 pandemic has tragically affected our societies worldwide. As we are forced under these extraordinary circumstances to spend more time indoors, severely limiting our movements and journeys, telecommunications networks, communications services and the media are standing in to play a major role in economic and social resilience. While our class teaching has been severely hit by the pandemic, the online teaching and learning, including TV and streaming platforms, have been booming as people were confined to their homes. Learning anywhere at any time has become a matter of will — Now it comes true.

The second guiding principle is the ***Principle of Learning by Doing***. The importance of this principle cannot be overemphasized. It is meant to counterbalance the habit of passive reading, and mechanical learning by rote. Passive reading can only lead you to shallow learning at best. Learning by doing leads to deep learning. The most distinctive feature of our design, as part of putting the Principle of Learning by Doing into practice, is the presentation of the materials from the user's perspective rather than from the teacher's. Traditionally the content is presented to the reader through the silent voice of an expert. Between the textbook and the reader/learner there is a teacher in the classroom acting like a bridge guiding the reader/learner to the textbook content. This sage-on-the-stage role of a teacher is no longer existent in our design. The materials are structured in such a way that they flow from learners themselves. There are a group of enthusiasts who are keen on getting Chinese media known to the outside world in English. The enthusiasts organize their own learning activities, e.g., reading groups, seeking advice, doing fieldwork, hands-on practicing, summarizing or commenting, organizing public lectures and forums, etc. The potential users of the ***Package*** are invited to join them and learn by doing things together with them. It's fun!

Task designs and instructions will convince you that the two guiding principles are fully implemented throughout the ***Package***. Your adoption of the two principles as your learning guide will be richly rewarded.

Organization

The ***Package*** is organized into 8 units. Each unit consists of 8 tasks. The unit always begins with a warm-up exercise. It prepares everybody for the unit's workload. It also acts as an interface between units.

Task 1 is one of the input materials in form of listening about the media discussed in the unit. It is primarily intended for learners to obtain information or advice by listening. The transcript is also provided for reading in print or on screen. The questions, answer activities etc. can be either completed over the Internet or in the printed book.

Task 2 is the process of collating, summarizing and commenting on the above information so far to prepare the necessary knowledge for the tasks ahead.

Tasks 3—6 center on reading tasks, covering the essential language training practice ranging from reading comprehension, vocabulary learning, translation to challenging discussions in a group. Some excerpts about Chinese Media refers to works written by native speakers of English. Some adaptation has been done in edition. Others are written, re-written, and revised by both Chinese and English native-speaker specialists. Most of the tasks are hands-on exercises involving exploring and reflecting to achieve progressive learning. In terms of the subject matter, these tasks are designed to promote deep learning about key concepts in Chinese media. In terms of language skills, they are intended for output training, that involves both oral and writing skills as well as thinking in English.

Task 7 is a public lecture delivered by a professor of media on a specific topic, which in general is also the theme of a given unit. In terms of content organization, the public lecture serves as a climax: The learners up to this point are guided and gently pushed by the speaker to reflect upon what they have learned, to do a bit of theorizing, as it were.

Task 8, the last one, is a follow-up forum. Learners are urged to organize an online debate discussing problems, issues and questions that have been raised in the public lecture. And finally, they should summarize what they have grasped.

How to use the package

The ***Package*** is by design self-contained. It is suitable for independent users for self-study. Self-study does not mean studying it in solitude or isolation. On the contrary, independent users are urged to join online study groups, and actively participate in online forums.

It is, of course, suitable for campus learning and credit-bearing programs. In this case, an integrated approach is recommended. Campus learners are encouraged to be first of all online learners, either independently or in groups. All the online learning activities are automatically guided, recorded, and assessed for later inspection. Moreover, teachers are also empowered to be able to check learning progress and homework, give and mark assignments — all online, both synchronously and asynchronously. If the timetable permits, teachers are advised to use face-to-face contact hours specifically for reading tasks and public lectures, since these two could be somewhat demanding to some students.

Pre-Course Activity

Task 1 Organizing the group

Introduction: This textbook is written from the students' perspective rather than from teachers'. A group of three students is assigned to probe the Chinese media from its history to its evolution or development assisted by two professors as their tutors or advisors. Such design aims at embodying two principles as mentioned in the above. One is the *Principle of 3-M Learning*, and the other is the *Principle of Learning by Doing*. This group will aim at exploring or discovering how Chinese media originated and progressed in content, evolution and convergence, meanwhile they are trained to learn English by integrating listening, speaking, reading, writing and translating together so that five language skills can facilitate their language acquisition.

This learning group was initiated by three students (Davis, Irene and Angela) assisted by two professors (Maynor and Edward).

Irene: Hello, I'm Irene, an undergraduate student majoring in journalism and publications here at BIGC (Beijing Institute of Graphic Communication). I specialize in New Media Technology. The feature of the major is that it is supported by digital compression and wireless network technology, and it uses its large capacity, real-time and interactivity to realize global media. However, I'm more interested in the journalism-related history and culture. Together with two other visiting students — Davis and Angela, we've formed a study group and aim rather ambitiously to share whatever we can obtain through our exploration with anyone else who shows interest.

It is well known that paper-making and printing technology were originated in China. This laid a solid foundation for dissemination of knowledge and news. Besides, China is a country of over 5,000 years of history. It is our duty or mission to introduce Chinese culture and civilization to the world. Ideologically, China is devoting itself to becoming not only culturally large, but also culturally powerful. Our group hopes to track Chinese media by telling

Chinese stories well. Our group will follow the principle of integrating the resources ranging from state-owned media to social media or We-media in an effort to demonstrate a panoramic view for our learners. So, a myriad tasks will await us.

Angela: I am an undergraduate student majoring in new media here at BIGC (Beijing Institute of Graphic Communication), which is unique in that it specializes in all forms of media. Being a representative, I'm happy to be one of the members doing this media-oriented program. I'm totally in agreement with Irene. I'm eager to witness both the splendor and the mystery of Chinese media history and its culture myself, especially the fantastic media origin and its dramatic development. Here we're learning new media technology by exploring or practicing it. Media is an indispensable channel for the dissemination of Chinese culture, news and everything. The world needs to understand China. Therefore, great significance should have been attached to the study of media. Hence, two classmates Irene, Davis and I have grouped ourselves, hoping to probe Chinese media source and sort out clearly its path of development.

Davis: Hello, I'm Davis. I'm from Salvador — a country located in the middle America. I am traveling thousands of miles across the Pacific Ocem to pursue my goal of new media interaction technology, virtual reality image editing, multimedia editing art and digital media. Besides, I hope to make friends with more students through the program, because this program can attract more learners to join us in studying how to transmit the ancient Chinese civilization to the world and how to peel away the mysterious oriental culture layer by layer chronologically. China's rapid development is increasingly attacting many foreigners. Media acts as a bridge to link China and the world. This is why I have joined membership. Moreover, I'll be able to take advantage of easy access to the Chinese Printing Museum to acquire first-hand information in person.

Irene: Apart from the above members, we have also invited two media specialists as our supervisors. Let's roll out the red

	carpet for them. One is the senior media professional Maynor, and the other is Professor Edward. Both of them will attend our discussion and guide us onto right track. Maynor will be responsible for offering us lecture on various media weekly, while Edward will act as a coordinator of all activities like designer, organizer, participant, promoter, evaluator etc.
Maynor:	Hello, it's my pleasure to introduce this series of lectures exploring Chinese media through which to diffuse Chinese culture and civilization. Professor Edward and I will deliver online lectures in addition to offering assistance to students face to face.
Edward:	Hi, I'm honored to be the supervisor for this study group. I'll be responsible for offering listening materials as supplement for the lecture, learning guidance and managing to help students to develop their autonomous studying ability.
Irene:	Okay, so much for our personal introductions. Now let's get down to business.

Task 2 Naming the group and setting up web connections

Edward:	Hi, everyone. What a nice day it is! The sunshine and blue sky must make us in good mood. Now that we have known each other. I recommend that we should figure out a resonant name for our group, don't you agree? Personally, I think the name should be meaningful. I suggest the name should contain the reference to people in our study group as well as our content. What do you name our learning group?
Irene:	Definitely agree. From today on, our group will start our journey with a better-sounding name to track the evolution process of Chinese media, reflect on media power on a country or even the world and discuss what actions our generation should take to keep Chinese media at the cutting edge internationally.
Davis:	Sure. I'm interested in exploring from the root of Chinese media. So, how can our group name be better-sounding as

well as meaningful? How about announcing the name of our group first?

Angela: You're absolutely right, Davis. A really catchy name will attract more students to join. Actually, our task is exploring Chinese culture through the use of media, and our group name should be an echo of what we do, right?

Davis: I think Professor Maynor and Edward must have been illuminated by the lovely weather, the warm sunshine and the blue sky.

Maynor: Aha, Thanks for encouragement. Edward's remark at the onset implied the name. Normally names of groups or associations are based on combinations of family names, or group functions, or popular themes of the times. What do you hope to highlight with your group name?

Edward: Repeat again: Our group name should be closely associated with our goal, our mission and our members attending this task.

Maynor: I approve entirely of your idea, Edward. Accordingly, that's MEDIA. Do you like it?

Davis: But why MEDIA? Just because we are doing media practice?

Irene: I see. It means we are media people, doesn't it?

Maynor: Partially right. Actually, this name has expression with double meaning. Why not explain it to our students, Professor Edward?

Edward: Well, I think you've all probably been clear about the explanation. I already pointed out that a group name can include the individual names plus your mission.

Irene: Oh, I am crystal clear now. I'm sorry to jump in.

Edward: Not at all, you're welcome to air your point of view.

Irene: MEDIA is a pun. It refers to both our key topic "media" and every one of the group.

Davis: Oh, I got it! Our group name is made up of the first letter of our names. M refers to Professor Maynor, E stands for Professor Edward, D is me, I for Irene, and A of course for Angela.

Angela: Figuratively, you are right. The name itself explains our mission. Amazing name!

Maynor:	Oh, you all have indeed got it.
Edward:	Absolutely correct. But I suggest you need to set up your own website. App is better, but it may beyond our affordability.
Angela:	Davis is good with the Internet. Why don't you display your wonderful cyber talents?
Davis:	Ha-ha. As a matter of fact, I've already had a good idea.
Irene & Angela:	Killing it! What is it?
Davis:	Here is our URL: www.bigc.edu.en/media.
Irene & Angela:	Yeah, "Davis the Great"!
Davis:	Now that I'm your webmaster, you all need to follow my advice to register first so that you can become a privileged user. There are a lot of extra benefits for privileged users. Please visit this website: www.bigc.edu.en/media for further information.
ALL:	MEDIA await you. Come on!

1

Unit

Media, Cultural and Soft Power in China

TABLE OF CONTENTS

1 Unit Media, Cultural and Soft Power in China

Warm-up: Be proactive

Direction: *MEDIA team are going to do warm-up activities by discussing, airing their views on the topic and discovering problems.*

Objectives: *To arouse students' interest, get a preliminary understanding of relevant knowledge and prepare for the following study.*

Edward: Hi, MEDIA group. We begin to embark on a new journey from today on. I am sure that your participation in the previous tasks in *Chinese Printing*, *Chinese Publishing* and *Chinese Painting* etc. must have accumulated a lot of experience for this mission. You will have a good job.

Maynor: Sure. You are definitely a well-organized group. But the mission may be full of landmines and will be quite challenging. You need to be well prepared. So, I'd like to remind you of why we want to inquire and clarify problems concerning Chinese media.

Irene: That's exactly what I hope to make clear. One problem I have been obsessed with is why media in many countries are state-owned. Once war happened, the side who occupied the media would be in an advantage...

Angela: That's because media can spread what had happened to the society and to the world.

Davis: In my viewpoint, dissemination of war information is just one aspect. The more crucial function of media is defeating the enemy from public opinion.

Irene: And inspiring their people to stand on their side. Take the current Russia-Ukraine conflict as example, Ukraine can take more advantage of media publicity than Russia.

Angela: The same as news broadcasting in the Iraq War in 2003. Iraq Minister of Publicity, Mohammed Said Sahaf, impressed almost everyone in this world. He held on broadcasting how Iraq army bravely resisted the attack from American army until the TV station was totally occupied.

Davis: So, it is never too enough to stress the power of media. The image, culture, politics and entertainment etc. all release to the world through diversity of media including newspaper, TV, radio, and particularly internet-based new media.

Maynor: What if media didn't exist, what would the world look? So, let's start with a listening passage to get preliminary concept of Media Power.

All: Welcome. (Applause)

Task 1 ▶ Listening activity

Direction: *MEDIA team are going to listen to an introduction of key concepts so as to lay the foundation for later learning.*

Objectives: *To understand the main conception, practice and strengthen the ability of listening comprehension.*

Media Power

When discussing media power, we refer to the interconnections between social actors, institutional structures, and the larger contexts of society, which are all involved in the allocation of symbolic resources to format specific influence. According to Des Freedman Goldsmiths (Professor of media and communication studies in the University of London), the relational conception of media power is constituted by four dimensions of related media scholarship: consensus, chaos, control, and contradiction.

Figure 1.1 Media power. Source: 《新媒体 —— 媒体形态的一种》, 科普中国, Baidu Baike.

The consensus paradigm reflects liberal pluralism in advancing democracy. In this case, a free and open market is required for competition between different outlets and exchanges of various content to limit the administration power. The market-driven media weaken the dominant political voice and concentrated authoritative power, while the non-profit media serves the common interests of the general public, consisting of individuals from diverse backgrounds.

The chaos paradigm refers to the cultural chaos of ideological dissemination and fundamental indetermination, especially in the digital empowerment of decentralized power models. With the rise of digital media, traditional order structures, from ideological control to production monopoly to consumer consumption attitude and behavior, have been tremendously dislocated and relocated. As the progressing technologies favour the audience with more choices and controls among what and when to access news and information, as well as chances to generate and publish content, the power in the digital age is operated in far less hierarchical ways. What is more, the popularization of social media and its significant promotion of online activism resulting in offline social-political actions around the world has proved the concept of media counterpower.

The control paradigm stems from the ruling authority's power of directing and determining symbolic resources to introduce hegemonic viewpoints and values. In other words, the privileged or powerful group regards the media as a cultural apparatus to exercise publicity and public relations, aiming for predictable outcomes. Consequently, mainstream media has then become an essential tool for state power to guide public opinions and actions.

Lastly, the contradiction paradigm refers to the contradictory relationships with the reproduction of existing relations of media power. Typical internal contradictions, based on Freedman, include structure and agency, contradiction and action, consensus and conflict, and producers and audiences. To provide a comprehensive approach to study the media, highlights of such contradictions from a wider social, political, economic, and cultural context are required.

With the emergence of computer-mediated-communication and the rapid growth of the Internet since the millennium, many media scholars have highlighted that the decentralized communications of the Internet have the potential to enhance the public sphere and democratic deliberation. The interactivity notion of the Internet is not only social interaction, person-to-person conversation, or face-to-face communication, but also a special case of mediated social interactions where impersonal interactions with media content also occur. Further, the Internet offers a relatively positive and critical approach for individuals to find new ways to develop their freedom through participation and engagements. That is, online interactive practices enable users in controlling their information consumption through personalized functions and offer them opportunities to express ideas or experiences as well as to participate in public debates. At the same time, the Internet transforms people from information receivers into information providers, while anybody with minimal skills and access to a computer network can post information online without a license or government permission. Although it becomes possible for citizens to get their voice heard through online political participation, they must still comply with the content guidelines set by either corporations or state authorities. As a result, new patterns of information flow have emerged where the power appears to be in the hands of the public, rather than the media corporations or state authorities.

Figure 1.2 Network-based media. Source: "Salt and Paper, Media and Its Power", July 3, 2018, https:// medium.com.

The Internet offers new modes of communication for people, as its global nature crosses national boundaries with affordable technologies, and increases potential access to a vast and diverse quantity of information. The many-to-many mode of communicative interaction online and the increasing interactivity of digital media both indicate the rise of a new form of public sphere regardless of linguistic, cultural and spatial differences. In the online sphere, unofficial and potentially unauthorized information can be quickly disseminated, and discussions of news events can take place in virtual-real-time. This leads to the return of social participation in which large groups of people are reading and commenting upon supposedly stable but questionable texts.

Task 2 ▶ Listening comprehension

Direction: *MEDIA team are going to have a topic-oriented discussion to exchange their views on the listening material and challenge each other with puzzling questions.*

Objectives: *To broaden students' horizon, develop their ability to sum up the skills of answering questions and strengthen language output ability.*

Davis: Hi, guys. How do you understand the notion concerning media power mentioned above? I feel totally confused. I am anxious to get your help.

Irene: Dear Davis, don't so worry about that. I assure you that I can offer you a hand even though it seems all tangled up. But I can first disentangle some of my thoughts to make an explicit explanation.

Angela: I think the notion about media power is well elaborated in a clear logical way. It told us from whom the definition of media power was originated, and listed what were the four elements consisting of media power. And...

Davis: Oh, wait, wait. What you said just enlightens me. The notion of media power was from Freedman. In his opinion, media power covered four dimensions of factors: consensus, chaos, control, and contradiction. Am I right?

Irene: Perfectly right. It is a consensus that only a free and open market for various outlets and contents can make the public voice heard.

Angela: And chaos appears because the market-driven media may break the original order and reorganize the discourse order. You know new technologies favour the audience with more choices and controls among how to access the useful content. Various voices can get involved in the making of the content.

Davis: Media is a sort of power because government can use media to direct and influence people's opinions and actions. But market-driven media can provide alternatives to the public.

Irene: From my perspective, market-driven media may spread some fake news though people can access diverse information. For those who are in short of judgement may be lost and completely carried away.

Angela: Exactly. But market-driven media is extremely popular with those who are knowledgeable and quick thinking with excellent judgement. As the saying goes: "Every coin has two sides."

Davis: No matter what kinds of media, market-driven media or state-owned media, we can safely conclude that media is powerful. Its impact on society, individuals, organizations, or even politics is dramatic.

Irene: This is why we need to spend so much time exploring media history and evolution, discussing the relationship between media and society.

Angela: Three of us are not enough. We should design more questions and invite more students to join us.

Davis: So, let's make a list of problems we encounter to share with our peers or counterparts.

Irene: I'm always ready to do what you want, Davis. Well then, let me raise my questions first and then we'll go on to yours. To start with, what is media? My explanation is that media is the main source of information. It creates awareness among the common people and makes them enlightened. It also creates public opinion about the burning issues of the country or even the world, exposes scandals and builds the confidence of people.

Angela: Wow, profound interpretation! I've got a question: Is there any relationship between media and government? I hold that the main duty of media is to disseminate news, knowledge, and information.

Davis: Just as we talked above, media is a powerful tool. It acts as a link between government and people because the different policies of the government are forwarded through the media.

Irene: I cannot agree more. Media is vast and we get all the pieces of information in a single touch either in any electronic gadgets or in newspapers. It is media that helps bringing the true facts in front of us. Just imagine if without media, what would the world be?

Angela: Without media, the world would have remained ignorant with no accurate knowledge to guide ahead. However, one of the limitations of media is that it will elaborate everything in such a way that even the false accusation may be believed.

Davis: And nobody tries to find out the truth since everything is discussed in media itself.

Irene: You did great in clearing up some questions. But I still hope to add that it would be unfair if I did not include the media as a critical thinking source either. The media plays a vital role in education because it helps adolescents and youth like us improve critical thinking skills. So, let's open up our discussion and welcome more contribution to the notion of media power.

All: Okay, Welcome and let's move ahead together.

Task 3 ▶ Pre-reading activity

Direction: *This part serves as connecting link between the preceding task and the following task. MEDIA team are required to ponder over some questions concerning the whole unit, reflect on them and then find solutions. The answers are open-ended.*

Objectives: *To cultivate students' capability of exploring questions, develop critical thinking ability and improve expression ability.*

1. How do you understand soft power?
2. What is the core of China's soft power?
3. How many kinds of thoughts on China's soft power are there? And what are they?
4. How do you understand the characteristics of China's soft power?
5. How important is soft power? Please exemplify it.
6. What do you know about media? How much do you understand Chinese media?
7. Please explain the role of media in enhancing national and international influence.
8. Please compare soft power with media power. Try to explain them.
9. Why is it important for China to carry out media construction?
10. Please explain the relationship among media, culture and soft power.

Task 4 ▶ Reading activity

Direction: *MEDIA team are required to read the following excerpt to obtain information, expand vocabulary volume, increase knowledge reserve, comprehend between lines, appreciate the writing style and evaluate the article.*

Objectives: *To cultivate students' capability of reading and absorbing information in a way that "eyes see quickly and brain processes quickly" to enhance reading comprehension, build up logic thinking, learn writing through reading and improve students' comprehensive quality.*

The Interpretation of China's Soft Power

The awareness of soft power in China

In the 1990s, Harvard professor Joseph Nye first coined the term "soft power" in his book. Nye's basic hypothesis regarding a state's capacity to exercise both hard and soft power found a receptive audience in China. Publications in this field began to emerge in large numbers. Some evaluated Nye's theory regarding the resources of soft power: culture, political values and ideas, and foreign policies. It is noteworthy that, given the central role subsequently accorded to culture in the exercise of China's soft power, back in 1993, many scholars focused on culture as the main source of a state's soft power. An admirable culture and ideological system should be as important as the expensive and less efficient hard power.

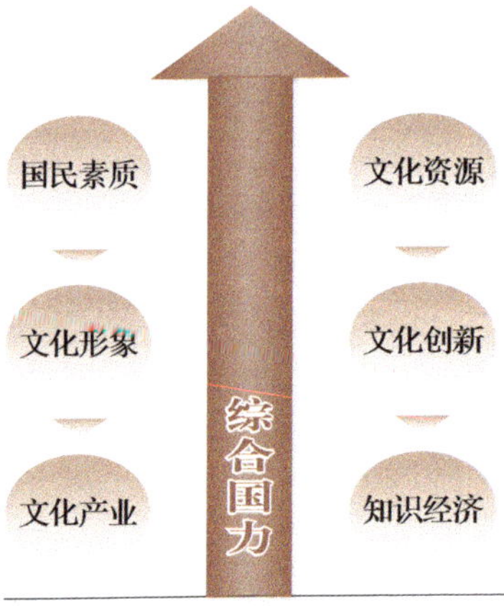

Figure 1.3 China's soft power.

Discussions about soft power really took off in China in the mid-2000s. As the issue moved beyond academic explorations of Nye's theory, Chinese theorists expanded upon Nye's original conceptual framework to formulate soft power with Chinese characteristics, which captured the attention of China's leadership as well as the general public. Soft power is currently a hot topic in China, a search of both academic databases and popular websites yields a plethora of articles, leadership speeches, polls, and blog entries on the subject. In the lively debates, soft power has featured prominently in building China's comprehensive national power, referring to the combined weight of economic, diplomatic, and military power necessary to guarantee China with appropriate influence on the world stage. Soft power has been a range of common threads from the reevaluation of Chinese traditional culture and socialist core value system to following the scientific development concept and establishing a harmonious society, and from the debate over keeping a low profile versus getting something accomplished to combating the Western "China threat" theory and establishing a harmonious world. Then the question arises as to why it achieved such popularity in China. One possible explanation is that the theory resonates with traditional Chinese concepts. For example, Confucianism extols a king who relies on moral force not physical force, believing that the kingly way will triumph over the hegemon's way. Another explanation is propitious timing. Nye's theory was introduced into China as people were reflecting on the rise and fall of great nations. Chinese intellectuals and the Party leadership believe that China need to build both hard and soft power in order to achieve or indeed recover great-power status and transform China into a great power. As one expert of think-tank explains: The consensus now is that soft power is critical for China, which has made strides in enhancing its hard power, while it is lagging behind soft power. China's soft

Figure 1.4 The core of Confucianism.

power should become proactive and aim largely at improving the country's image. Discussion on what is the main source of China's soft power is still going on.

Main thought on China's soft power

Two main schools of thought have emerged, around which the discourse on China's soft power is centered. The mainstream view, held by China's leading sociologists and philosophers, is that the core of soft power is culture, echoing the opinion first domestically advocated in the 1990s. The minority view, held by some experts on international relations, does not deny the importance of culture, but focuses instead on how soft power resources are applied, concluding that political power is the core of soft power. The culture school has had the greatest impact on policymaking: The central role of culture in the exercise of soft power has been embraced by China's leadership as well as the public. The detailed analysis will be as follows.

For the leading proponent of the culture school, soft power includes thoughts, ideas, and principles as well as institutions and policies, all of which operate within the context of, and cannot be separated from, a nation's culture. Some scholars believe that the more fashionable the ideology is, the more people will accept it and the greater the possibility to build the country's soft power is. China's ancient history and traditional culture are viewed by most scholars as a valuable source of soft power for attracting not only East Asian neighbours with whom China shares a Confucian heritage but also the wider international community. One leading analyst believes that China's modern-day emphasis on development, stability, and harmony has common appeal. Other scholars go even further and hold that traditional Chinese values, such as giving priority to harmony between humankind and nature, and harmony but difference, should be all revalued as the concepts of harmonious society and harmonious world.

With this in mind, some scholars warn of the deficit in China's "cultural trade" with the West, and others emphasize the importance of using cultural media to promote China's image and raise its profile on the international stage. In so doing, China can resist the image and values imposed on it by the West and assert its own discourse rights. The view that "the competition of cultural power is the core of soft power contention" remains dominant among many Chinese.

Soft power with Chinese characteristics

As elaborated above, many Chinese scholars have developed the conceptual framework of soft power forward. They believe that the theory needs to be enriched with Chinese practice. In contrast with Nye, who viewed soft power primarily as a means of improving the international standing of the United States, the Chinese approach to soft power is holistic: The domestic and foreign policy aspects of soft-power development are conceived as an organic whole. For example, the idea of establishing a harmonious society domestically and establishing a harmonious world internationally is seen as providing a comprehensive framework for the ongoing development of China's soft power. Most Chinese scholars agree that soft power must be developed not only internationally through the promotion of Chinese culture overseas, public diplomacy, and pursuit of peaceful development, but also at home through making China's culture, as well as economic and political values, attractive to both Chinese and international audiences.

The ultimate goal of the concept of scientific development is to establish a harmonious society. That is seeking to balance China's quest of economic growth with paying equal attention to resolving social welfare issues and putting the people's needs first. Hu Angang, a professor at Tsinghua University and an adviser to the Chinese government, opined that China's harmonious society undertaking is more influential and appealing. This begs the question, What is soft power? Indeed, This represents China's greatest instance of soft power.

In summary, it is imperative to build China's soft power, but this raises the question: To what ultimate goal? For those who believe that soft power is something that can be deliberately cultivated, its development is seen as necessary to build China's comprehensive national power, to rebalance China's growing hard power, and to refute the so-called "China threat" theory. They believe soft power can foster a stable and peaceful international environment and pave the way for the global acceptance of China's rise. To actively participate in the international competition and protect and promote Chinese interests, China needs to consistently and substantially augment its soft power.

Task 5 ▶ Reading comprehension

Direction: *MEDIA team are going to launch a discussion about the reading* *excerpt. They are required to summarize what they learned, share their puzzles as well as their comments on the article, and try to probe into more profound issues in this domain.*

Objectives: *Learning by doing. To cultivate students' capability of finding problems, reflecting on and solving problems independently so as to improve the comprehensive ability of using language.*

Irene:	Well, dear all. How do you perceive China's soft power after reading through this article? Honestly, I've heard about this term before, but I am not entirely clear about its implications. Here I appeal to you all to pose your own questions respectively, and then we air our views freely and have a heated discussion around the two schools of view until we understand the concept. Agree?
Davis:	I couldn't agree more. Let's pose questions in chronological order so that we will not miss anything.
Maynor:	Right. But I'd like to offer some advice. To fully understand a concept, we need to first clarify its background, including the context in which the term was introduced and how it has evolved up to now.
Edward:	Exactly. We should also look at this term in a comprehensive view. Besides cultural factors, political, economic and medium factors are also indispensable when talking about soft power.
Angela:	Dear me. It is so complicated that I am a little confused. May I ask a question: What is the relationship between soft power and media? It seems to me that soft power only has something to do with culture, economy and politics etc.
Edward:	Fantastic! Now, let's start with Angela's question and proceed in a straightforward sequence.
Irene:	Why did the term "soft power", coined by an American scholar, spark such immense interest both in academic and political circles in China? In my opinion, the international scenario plays a major role in this. And...
Davis:	Sorry to cut in. I am eager to answer this question. Academically, Nye's definition means that soft power is the ability to affect

others through the cooperative means of framing the agenda, persuading, and eliciting positive attraction in order to obtain preferred outcomes.

Angela: How did you become so familiar with the concept? I am waiting for the answer to Irene's question. And I've also got some information regarding why soft power became such a hot topic among Chinese scholars.

Irene: So, let me explain why we should take international situation into account. When the term was put forward, it was during an early phase of US and Chinese policy that sought to build a common approach to contentious issues. This expression in a degree of scholarly cooperation, involving Joseph Nye himself, could be dedicated to exploring areas of possible collaboration. However, the current situation is changing. Some US journalists and scholars are quite vocal in expressing concern about the "rise of China".

Angela: Thank you, Irene. To my knowledge, the proposal of this term was also related with Nye's opinion about American diplomatic policy then. Nye's most influential articulation was in the course of a critique of the foreign policy of the H. W. Bush administration, particularly its invasion of Iraq in 2003. He stressed the reciprocal links between hard power and soft power, and was particularly concerned with the way in which, in his opinion, the Bush administration's extravagant use of hard power was damaging US soft power, leading to an decline in its international influence.

Maynor: Fabulous! But be kindly noted that our focal points or key words are China's soft power and media, not America's.

Davis: Indeed, Let's not deviate from our topic. I am sure that every Chinese remember the notion of "the Chinese Dream" as a way of increasing China's international influence. Considerable efforts are being devoted to developing this both domesticaliy and internationally. The realization of the Chinese Dream calls for both hard power like economic forces and soft power like culture and amiable image.

Edward: So, Davis has brought us a good answer. But I still hope to add that China's glorious culture and civilization need to spread more widely so that the world can identify with us. This speaks for why media has close linkage with China's soft power and amiable image.

Irene: I am crystal clear now. The successfully televised Olympic Games by CCTV well exemplified the importance of media. It greatly boosted China's reputation internationally.

Angela: Apart from TV broadcasting, films, radios, newspapers and periodicals, art, and literature are all facets reflecting Chinese culture. The image of a country usually rises above short-term political preconceptions and engages audiences at an emotional level.

Davis: Definitely. Media can help build China's reputation, which is more rational representation and is about what China does, says and what others say about China. Meanwhile, this involves how China promotes, explains, justifies its political and economic actions and advances, and enriches its traditional culture.

Edward: Wow, it is really a rich and enlightening discussion. How about we continue it online so that more learners and students can participate? Our discussion is open to anyone who is interested in this topic.

All: Welcome to our discussion. Let's meet online.

Task 6 ▶ Translation practice

Direction: *MEDIA team are going to do Chinese-English translation, from which they can learn and compare how to express in cross-cultural way and convey the following paragraph in English accurately.*

Objectives: *To understand and master English morphology, syntax and idiomatic expressions, develop basic professional translation ability and promote English competence.*

构成媒体实力的两个方面："硬实力"与"软实力"，两者相互依存相互作用，要提升“软实力”，必须首先建设“硬实力”，“硬实力”是建设“软实力”的条件和基础。但是，光有“硬实力”是远远不够的，媒体要在日趋激烈的市场竞争中站稳脚跟、扩大影响，最终依靠的还是“软实力”。媒体“软实力”在很大程度上体现为媒体的自身文化建设，主要包括媒体文化、媒体精神和媒体责任。媒体“软实力”一旦确立并被人们感知之后，就具有稳定性和持久性，能够通过其价值取向及其在受众中的威望获得更多的社会资源，并且不会轻易被其他媒体复制和取代，对媒体发展具有决定性和长远性意义。总之，媒体“软实力”更强调媒体关系中的文化较量，是媒体内在文化建设的外在表现和社会效果。

Task 7 ▶ Attending a public lecture

Direction: *MEDIA team are going to attend a public lecture delivered by Professor Maynor. Students are required to thoroughly understand the lecture, broaden the vision, elaborate on the theme, get inspiration from the lecture and do some speech activities to extend their knowledge.*

Objectives: *To train students' capability of description, expression, discussion, refutation, humor and humanistic accomplishment required by making a speech, thus, improving students' English language competence and proficiency.*

Lecture 1

Media, Cultural Image and Soft Power in China

Professor Maynor

Hello everyone. It is my privilege to introduce a fascinating subject — “Symbol, Media and Soft Power in China”. The Beijing Institute of Graphic Communication, in conjunction with various noted scholars and historians, has developed this lecture series concerning Chinese civilization and culture, among which is Chinese media. Today, I'm going to present you the first lecture in this series of eight.

This lecture aims to guide you and all the other learners to look at Chinese media in broader perspectives, including cultural, social and communicative dimensions, so that you are aware of the value of Chinese media in developing

China's soft power.

Soft power is a relatively new concept in Chinese discourse. Primarily drawn from Joseph Nye's works, it has quickly caught on among China's policy and academic circles. Perhaps nowhere else has the idea of soft power been as widely discussed, embraced and appropriated as in China. Chinese scholars find soft power appealing because it is compatible with ancient Chinese traditions influenced by Confucius and Mencius, emphasizing the psychological and moral aspects of power. China has paid particular attention to these influences domestically and internationally. A key part of China's foreign policy has been projecting a favorable image of China to the world.

National image

This endeavor involved looking back to what China once was and the creation of a somewhat idealized historical Golden Age, most visibly associated with Confucius. Confucius Institutes and Classrooms were established overseas, and a nearly 10-meter-high statue of the Great Teacher was unveiled in Beijing in January 2011. In reality, the virtues and values that are at the heart of this Golden Age have a much wider base, incorporating elements of Daoism and Sun Zi's *The Art of War*. But as Confucianism itself owes at least as much to the later interpretations of Confucius by Mencius and other scholars as it does to the verifiable writings of Confucius himself, it is appropriate that he has become a symbol for a diverse body of thought.

So, the past is being constructed to serve the present. This seems to be partly because it builds on existing interests in Chinese history and traditions in many parts of the world, and it bespeaks the attraction of China as what it was. It is also because it can be used to build a basis for understanding China as it is today and how it will act in the future.

Meanwhile four decades of reform and opening up have enabled China to become the second-largest economic power, leaving imagination of what China will become in the future. The word "will" is deliberately used instead of "might", as China's future rise has been taken for granted by many. As a result, there has long been a tendency to develop policies towards China today based on its expected future power. Thus, China has been empowered by the way in which others think about it. Perceptions have altered realities. China's imagined power is typically built on assessments of its future economic power and traditional culture, playing a crucial role in shaping global responses to China.

China's cultural image

When assessing China's current cultural influence, China's international cultural impact cannot be ignored. Its Long history has resulted in well-developed philosophical systems, strong literary traditions, robust linguistic resources, distinctive musical forms and vibrant popular cultures that owe little or nothing to Western models. No one would ever imagine that Chinese culture might be in danger of being "swamped" by any other culture, although Chinese culture is likely to welcome and absorb some idea and artefacts from out of China. Across the full spectrum of cultural production and particularly in the audiovisual field, China has laid the material and symbolic foundation for much of the attraction globally. These abundant cultural resources have in fact proved themselves historically to be extremely influential, certainly in the immediate "Sino-sphere", and much more widely, for example, in important aspects of European poetry and visual culture. "Chinoiserie" was certainly never an accurate copy of its original inspiration, but the different imaginary renderings embodied are a recurrent theme in many aspects of European culture over the last 500 years. Such cultural influence has operated over relatively long timescales and will be still possible to purchase contemporary Chinoiserie everywhere.

Figure 1.5 Chinese artefacts / Chinoiserie.

The undoubted historical influence of Chinese culture in general exists alongside the immediate impact on all the aspects of the contemporary society. Any rounded assessment of China's potential cultural influence must analyze the interaction of these disparate elements. We can explore this dynamic interaction if we consider political philosophy, which is one of the aspects of Chinese culture that proved attractive to particular foreign social groups. Historically, a worldwide view that stressed continuity, embedded in a culture that displayed remarkable stability in the face of severe historical shocks like invasion and conquest, and embodied in what was then the most advanced extant civilization, had an understandable attraction to the ruling elites of some other societies. What does remain is the persistence of a cultural framework that provides an alternative to the dominant Western models, which can have a very real, if diffusing, international influence. While Chinese authentic Confucian philosophy may give much purchase on the contemporary world, the core idea of a society in which the common lot can be best advanced through the recognition of mutual interdependence and collective responsibility is far from alien even in the West.

The report of the 20th National Congress of the Communist Party of China states that nearly 100 million people have achieved poverty alleviation. No country in this world apart from China can lift such a huge population out of abject poverty, making tremendous contributions to the global poverty reduction cause. The number of Chinese middle class is on the rise. China has opened itself economically to the world. Chinese political philosophy embedded in the culture that is undergoing transformation to some extent and embodied in the most dynamic economy on earth, has an understandable attraction worldwide. After all, China provides a triumphantly successful developmental alternative to the countries that are in need of reform.

The tremendous economic success of China over the last four decades, and the ideological and political models that have accompanied it can be and are interpreted in the following ways. The gleaming and modern infrastructure that China is constructing so expeditiously without doubt holds a powerful appeal for other national elites seeking to improve their competitive position in the world market. It took China seven years to build the 2,200-kilometre high-speed rail line from Beijing to Shenzhen. It took more than eight years (from Jan. 1st, 2010 to Sept. 27th, 2018 according to Baidu Wikipedia) to build the last 26 kilometers to the West Kowloon terminal in the Hong Kong Special Administrative Region.

China has always had a unique traditional culture, but now it is entering the realm of global popular culture as well. Just because of these abundant cultural resources, we can expect to find that contemporary China exerts the multiple cultural influences around the world. We can see that the longer-term influence of Chinese culture, in both its elite and popular forms, is already a reality: As of July 23, 2020, 162 countries (regions) around the world have established 541 Confucius Institutes and 1,170 Confucius Classrooms. The Confucius Institute and Classroom programs, has undoubtedly increased the number of people who are learning Chinese language as well as Chinese culture. The contemporary Chinese visual art enjoys a high reputation and high prices in art centers throughout the developed world. In 2021, the number of international students exceeded 440,000, an increase of 35% compared to 2021. China has become the largest destination country for studying in Asia, and the attractiveness of studying in China is further matched with the country's economic and comprehensive strength. What's more, at a more popular level, various elements of martial arts have influenced the film industry and potentially provide an alternative mythological resource for computer gaming etc. Yao Ming, the Chinese basketball star, is rapidly becoming a household name, and China hosted the 2008 Summer Olympics successfully. Gu Ailing Eileen, an American born Chinese girl captured everyone's attention in this newly closed Winter Olympics held in Beijing — the first city to host both summer and winter Olympics. China loves to share its enormous achievement with the world. So, media construction and development become essential.

The drive to build up China's mass media

China is striving to extend the influence of its mass media, both domestically and internationally. So, it is essential for the mass media of China to provide alternatives to conventional narratives to reach larger audiences. TV and radio broadcasting in foreign languages has expanded substantially, in over 100 countries around the world plus Chinese local-language newspapers and magazines. China Radio International has increased its broadcasts in English to 24 hours. However, CCTV News or Xinhua's CNC World are still behind CNN as the dominant global news channel. Similarly, few of the cinematic or broadcast organizations in China are likely, in the short term at least, to replace Hollywood as the capital of the world's imagination. It is certainly feasible to move from being an importer of foreign films, programs and formats to developing markets for products that originate in China and are produced by Chinese organizations.

To identify such relatively modest, but more realistic objectives, however, is to confront directly the issue of the articulation of cultural, political and economic power. In China, the construction of soft power is mainly under government leadership, the advantage of which is that Chinese government can centrally coordinate Chinese TV stations at all levels to work together and expand public diplomacy activities. China can regulate the activities of diverse TV stations to follow the cultural policies so that they can develop and mature healthily. For example, in autumn 2011, the State Administration of Radio, Film and Television (SARFT) required Wuhan TV station to shift their programming of entertainment towards more serious material. This decision was to meet the need for television to avoid misguiding teenagers and do more to build a harmonious society.

How to strategically deal with the relationship between political, economic and cultural power matters greatly for China's international effort in achieving success in broadcasting. Chinese media undertake dual responsibilities. On the one hand, the media should make sure of the international cultural influence, on the other hand, they should facilitate the operation in terms of commercial interests. A large and increasingly wealthy industry contains enough diverse talents, both journalistic and creative, to ensure that new and attractive ideas and methods of working will be developed. Therefore, to protect these innovations is also extremely urgent.

To conclude, in the longer term, it is probable that in the cultural realm, or "soft power" as Nye put it, China's international influence will be on the rise substantially, and the core will involve the attractive power of Chinese culture. In 2010, China's GDP surpassed Japan and became the world's second largest economy. Its advanced civilization and culture was correspondingly influential internationally. The spread of culture benefits from social media. Whether in the history of China or in the contemporary world, soft power does not exist in isolation. Chinese culture's increasingly spreading cannot be separated with either the contribution of mass media or the strength of Chinese state and all Chinese people as well.

Task 8 ▶ Online forum and summary writing

Direction: *MEDIA team are going to launch an instant online post-talk about the lecture to appeal to more of other students who are interested in the topic to join them. This is an integrated practice of listening, speaking, reading and writing. They are particularly expected to write a summary of the entire unit.*

Objectives: *To provide a platform for MEDIA team to fully display their talents. To comb language learning with professional knowledge so as to cultivate students' professional learning, academic literacy and language competence. To realize the teaching objectives of acquiring professional knowledge through learning English language.*

Edward: Hi, everybody. What do you think of Maynor's lecture? Did you totally get it?

Irene: Yeah, it's really fabulous! I am sure all of us have learned much from it. But there does exist some questions. Am I right, Davis and Angela?

Angela: As for me, I think I've got most of the idea and really benefited from Maynor's lecture. And I've also prepared some questions that will be fairly challenging and await us to discuss.

Davis: Me too. And I really want to make the most of our supervisors' valuable time. I am eager to verify that my understanding is accurate. Now what I most like to say is "Thank you, dear Maynor." Just as the Chinese saying goes: "An accomplished disciple owes his accomplishment to his great teacher."

Maynor: You're very welcome, but perhaps your thanks are a little premature, since I have some tasks for you to carry out, and I believe Professor Edward also has some recommendation for you to consider.

Edward: Indeed, I have. As I'm sure you know, Professor Maynor's lecture will be a series, and they will define the focus for each unit. My suggestion is that you organize an online forum to discuss and elaborate further on the specific topic. It will be appealing to many other students. A good start is very crucial. So, wish you a smooth beginning.

Irene: Yes, we'll welcome all the others to reap the benefit of Maynor's lectures. Now, let's get down to business. I start with a pretty easy question: What do you think is the symbolic national image of China?

Davis: Wow, as a matter of fact, this a large issue. It's complicated to explain clearly, but generally speaking, Confucianism can be the symbol of Chinese nation.

Angela: I quite approve of the point. Chinese historical Golden Age is closely associated with Confucius especially when Confucius Institutes and Classroom programs become increasingly popular.

Irene: Exactly. People all over the world recognize the virtue of Chinese benevolence which is the core of Confucianism. And besides, Chinoiserie across the world markets also account for the amiable image of China because that means people identify with Chinese civilization.

Davis: And my question is how Chinese culture can be so influential? Is it just because of the identification of its traditional civilization or what else?

Angela: Oh, it's really a challenging question. I think China's glorious traditional culture plus its enormous economic volume should be responsible for its worldwide influence.

Irene: Apart from the traditional culture and contemporary economic development, China's contribution to the world is that no country except China can lift more than one billion out of poverty and enter a well-off society dependent on limited resources. In addition to culture and economy, China's political philosophy is embedded in the culture that is undergoing transformation to some extent and embodied in the most dynamic economy on earth. These all form an understandable attraction worldwide.

Davis: Wow, I must give you a "like", Irene. Your understanding of this issue is so profound and comprehensive.

Angela: I'd like to add one more question: Just imagine how could the world understand China if without media?

Edward: Just to the point. This is why Professor Maynor chose "Media, Cultural Image and Soft Power in China" as the topic of this lecture.

Davis: Your brilliant instruction has suddenly enlightened me. I'll volunteer to help organize the later-on discussion online.

Irene: Thank you Davis. Your contribution is always appreciated.

Angela: And will our dear Professors be able to continue with us on the forum online?

Maynor & Edward: Certainly, we're always ready to help.

All: See you on the online forum!

Appendix: Vocabulary for Unit 1

Listening Activity

allocation /ˌæləˈkeɪʃən/ *n.* 配给量，划拨款，份额；分配，分派

consensus /kənˈsensəs/ *n.* 一致看法，共识

paradigm /ˈpærədaɪm/ *n.* 典范，范例；样板，范式

authoritative /əˈθɔːrəteɪtɪv/ *adj.* 专断的，命令式的；可靠的，可信的，权威的

chaos /ˈkeɪɒs/ *n.* 混乱，无秩序状态；混沌

empowerment /ɪmˈpaʊərmənt/ *n.* 许可，授权

hierarchical /haɪəˈrɑːkɪkl/ *adj.* 分等级的，等级制度的

hegemonic /ˌhedʒɪˈmɒnɪk/ *adj.* 霸权的；支配的

apparatus /ˌæpəˈrætəs/ *n.* 设备，器具；机构，组织；器官；评论性注释

decentralized /ˌdiːˈsentrəlaɪzd/ *adj.* 分散管理的
vt. 使分散；使分权（decentralize 的过去式）

comply /kəmˈplaɪ/ *v.* 遵从，服从；（商品）符合特定标准

Reading Activity

subsequently /ˈsʌbsɪkwəntli/ *adv.* 后来，随后

plethora /ˈpleθərə/ *n.* 过多；过剩；［医］多血症

resonate /ˈrezəneɪt/ *v.* 发出回响，回荡；充满，弥漫（某种特质）；引起共鸣；产生（电或机械）共振

Confucianism /kənˈfjuːʃənɪzəm/ *n.* 孔子学说；儒家思想

extol /ɪkˈstəʊl/ *vt.* 颂扬；赞美；赞颂

hegemon /ˈhedʒəmɒn/ *n.* 霸王；霸权国

propitious /prəˈpɪʃəs/ *adj.* 适合的；吉利的；顺利的

embrace /ɪmˈbreɪs/ *v.* 拥抱；欣然接受，乐意采纳；包括，涉及；围绕，环绕
n. 拥抱；接受，信奉

deficit /ˈdefɪsɪt/ *n.* 亏损，赤字，不足额；缺乏，缺陷；（体育用语）失分数

assert /əˈsɜːt/ *v.* 坚称，断言；维护；坚持自己的主张，表现坚定；生效，起作用

holistic /həˈlɪstɪk/ *adj.* 整体的，全面的；功能整体性的

opine /əʊˈpaɪn/ *v.* 以为，表示意见，说明

appealing /əˈpiːlɪŋ/ *adj.* 有吸引力的，有趣的；求助的目光/语气等

imperative /ɪmˈperətɪv/ *adj.* 极重要的，必要的；命令的，强制的；祈使的
n. 重要紧急的事，必要的事；祈使语气，祈使语气动词；命令

Lecture

compatible /kəmˈpætəbl/ *adj.* 兼容的；可共存的；可和睦相处的；与……一致的
n. 兼容性计算机
unveil /ʌnˈveɪl/ *v.* 透露；展示；使公诸于众；（在揭幕仪式上）为……揭幕
virtue /ˈvɜːtʃuː/ *n.* 高尚的道德，德行；美德，优秀品质；优点，长处
Daoism /ˈdaʊizəm/ *n.* 道教
empower /ɪmˈpaʊə(r)/ *v.* 授权；给予（某人）权力，使自主
swamp /swɒmp/ *n.* 湿地，沼泽地
v. 浸没，吞没；（喻）压倒，淹没；使疲于应对，使应接不暇；（大批人等）涌入（某处），包围（某人）
artefact /ˈɑːtɪfækt/ *n.* 手工制品，人造物；［医］假象，人为现象
spectrum /ˈspektrəm/ *n.* 范围，幅度；光谱；波谱，频谱；余象
audiovisual /ˌɔːdiəʊˈvɪʒuəl/ *adj.* 视听的；视听教学的
n. 视听教材
Chinoiserie /ʃɪnˈwɑːzəri/ *n.* 具有中国艺术风格的物品；中国艺术风格
embody /ɪmˈbɒdi/ *v.* 具体表现，体现；收录，包括
disparate /ˈdɪspərət/ *adj.* 迥然不同的，无法比较的；多元的
n. 全异的东西，无法相比较的东西
embed /ɪmˈbed/ *v.*（使）嵌入，把……插入；深信，使深留脑中；（计算机中）内置；栽种；派遣
n. 随军记者
extant /ekˈstænt/ *adj.* 现存的；显著的
gleaming /ˈɡliːmɪŋ/ *n.* 微弱的闪光，瞬息的一现
adj. 闪闪发光的
expeditiously /ˌekspəˈdɪʃəsli/ *adv.* 迅速地；敏捷地
sterile /ˈsteraɪl/ *adj.* 无生殖能力的，不育的；无菌的，消过毒的；（争论或讨论）毫无新意的，无结果的；（建筑、房间等）呆板的，乏味的；（土地）贫瘠的，不长作物的
confront /kənˈfrʌnt/ *v.* 面对，面临；正视，处理；对峙，对抗；当面对证
articulation /ɑːˌtɪkjʊˈleɪʃn/ *n.*（想法、思想等的）语言表达；清楚的咬字（或发音），说话；关节连接，铰接式接头
dual /ˈdjuːəl/ *adj.* 双的，双重的；双数的；（飞机）双重控制的，复式操纵的；（定理、表达式等）对偶的
n. 双数词；对偶定理（或表达式等）
v.〈英〉把（道路）改为复式车行道

2 Unit

Print Media in Ancient China

TABLE OF CONTENTS

Unit 2 Print Media in Ancient China

Warm-up: Be proactive

Direction: *MEDIA team are going to do warm-up activities by discussing, airing their views on the topic and discovering problems.*

Objectives: *To arouse students' interest, get a preliminary understanding of relevant knowledge and prepare for the following study.*

Irene: Hi, MEDIA teammates. I am happy that we've smoothly completed the first unit learning. Now I am getting to have a preliminary understanding of the media. What do you think?

Angela: I totally agree with you. I am sure we can continue smoothly with the subsequent units. Now, I am still immersed in joy with the forum organized by Davis. Where is Davis? I am eager to thank him for his contribution to the first online forum.

Davis: Here I am, Angela. But you don't need to thank me. Every one of us was involved. We all should give our thanks to our professors' guidance so that we can get a much clearer picture of the topic.

Irene: I am getting even more confident in this unit. As you know, we've learned a lot about Chinese printing that has laid a solid foundation for print media in ancient China. The invention of Bi Sheng's movable type resulted in printing press that helped disseminate Chinese traditional culture and civilization wider and faster than ever before. So, the fact turns out to be true that science and technology are the primary productive forces.

Angela: Brilliant idea. In my perspective, the impact of printing press on human beings was due to its advantages over hand-copying. A printing press could create many more copies at a faster rate than even the best scribe, which greatly benefits the common people to acquire knowledge.

Davis: Yes. The impact of printing press on education became especially apparent right away. Handwritten books were slow and expensive to make. Only the wealthy could afford them, so there was no incentive for most people to learn to read. Printing made it possible to mass-produce books that the public could afford.

Irene: The impact of the printing press on education was also that it gave people reasons and ways of literacy. It's said that while textbooks were originally printed in Latin in the West, most people spoke in their country's native tongue. This led to printers translating Latin texts into other languages. In this sense, printing press promotes language communication.

Angela: Among other things, the most important is that print media plays an important role in articulating and disseminating information.

Davis: The more we talk about the influence of printing press, the more clearly we are aware of Chinese contribution to the world civilization. To my knowledge, far before the invention of movable type, Chinese had employed block-printing press to spread news and information.

Irene: Maybe we can say the invention of the printing technology was a game-changer. The printing press altered the way people learned, shared knowledge, spread opinions and amused themselves etc.

Angela: Ancient cultures employed a variety of systems and symbols in writing. They also used surfaces of papyrus, clay, stone, paper and sheepskin. Without printing, everything had to be handwritten and, if duplicates were needed, hand-copied.

Davis: Oh dear. I can't even imagine what the world would be like without the technology of printing and paper-making.

Irene: So today, Professor Edward will take us to go through Chinese contribution to global print media, and then Professor Maynor will give us a lecture on the earliest Chinese newspaper. Let's get ready for the new exploration of Chinese ancient culture.

Angela: That's terrific. Then our bits and pieces of knowledge will be brought together into a complete picture.

Davis: Then, it's turn for us to listen to some basic information on print media in ancient China provided by Professor Edward.

All: Okay. Let's go all the way.

Task 1 ▶ Listening activity

Direction: *MEDIA team are going to listen to an introduction of key concepts so as to lay the foundation for later learning.*

Objectives: *To understand the main conception, practice and strengthen the ability of listening comprehension.*

China's Contribution to Global Print Media

Modern media are mainly electronic or digital. It's hard for us to imagine how people had conveyed news and exchanged ideas before the invention of print media. The earliest civilization relied solely on oral communication. When they had news to tell, they would spread the word to the nearest person, who would then do the same until everyone had heard the news. Gradually, people began to write down their news in pictorial form and later in early forms of languages such as oracle bone inscriptions, papyrus characters, seal characters, wedge characters, etc., where symbols stood for words and letters. The invention of paper and printing press marked a significant leap in media development. Once they came into regular use, there was no turning back.

What is print media?

In simple terms, print media refers to the printed versions of news, primarily delivered through newspapers and magazines. Before the invention and widespread use of printing presses, printed materials had to be written by hand. Lenthy processes such as seal enlargement, stone tablet rubbing, engraving printing which were both time-consuming and expensive limited mass distribution. For example, news was once chiseled in stone. Later, it was handwritten and posted in public areas, much like today's posters, or read aloud from a scroll by a town crier. As early as 131 B.C.E, the ancient Roman government produced daily news sheets and informed the public in this way, a practice depicted in TV series like *Roman Imperial*. Over the years, print media has evolved to include entertainment and educational topics, expanding its purview keyond merely conveying news.

Figure 2.1 Ancient Chinese block printing template and its workshop. Source: China Printing Museum.

Figure 2.2 Ancient Chinese movable type printing template and its workshop. Source: China Printing Museum.

China's history of print media

Around the year 932, Chinese printers started to adapt wood blocks, typically used for printing illustrations and texts. This made the production of popular books more accessible. Each page of text was carved onto a separate block, making it possible to reproduce the same content repeatedly. About 100 years later, in the Song Dynasty, Bi Sheng invented movable type by carving individual characters onto small blocks of clay. Each small block was hardened by fire to become a porcelain piece that could be used again and again. The pieces were fixed to iron plates to make a page, allowing for multiple reproduction. Once the printing was done, the pieces were removed from the plates for reuse. More importantly, his idea spread all over the world. Others adapted the technology to using other materials such as wood, tin and copper.

Figure 2.3 Bi Sheng's statue in front of the library of Beijing Institute of Graphic Communication.

Still, the process was too cumbersome to mass-produce newspapers for the public.

The development process of printing press

It is widely acknowledged that the earliest printed book was the *Vajra Sutra* printed in China in 868. With the spread of movable type printing, in 1440, Johannes Gutenberg utilized movable type invention for his printing press, making it easier to change components, thereby enabling the mass production of news pages possible. The invention swiftly spread throughout Europe, and the printing and distributing news sheets became popular.

Figure 2.4 *Vajra Sutra* printed in ancient China. Source: China Printing Museum.

The World Association of Newspapers considers *The Relation*, published in Germany in 1604, as the first newspaper. It was published regularly (weekly), disseminating to the public and covering a range of news from politics to entertainment. *The Oxford Gazette* was the first English paper to be published in the world. It moved to London the next year and was renamed *The London Gazette*. It is still published today as the official publication of government news.

The London Gazette.

Figure 2.5 One of the earliest newspapers in the world: *The London Gazette*. Source: *The London Gazette*, the Diary of Samuel Pepys from Wikipedia on 20 June 2023.

Ironically, the early mass-produced newspapers were considered a luxury, as they cost nearly what most workers earned in a week; thus, only the wealthy could afford them. By the 1830s, newspapers became more accessible with copies printed at about one cent each, making them truly available to the masses. By 1900, newspapers became very popular, featuring attention-grabbing headlines, varied news, society pages, sports, comics and occasional use of spot colour.

China, the homeland of papermaking and printing, possessed its versions of newspapers several centuries before other country. Those early newspapers, serving exclusively for the royal court to transmit imperial edicts and memorials, may be regarded as the earliest newspaper in China. The most ancient Chinese newspaper was *Di Bao*, i.e. *Court Gazette*, which could be traced back as early as the Han Dynasty (206 B.C.E.-220 B.C.E). Early *Di Bao*, compiled by imperial scholars, was distributed within the feudal court as an official medium. The early *Di Bao* was handwritten on non-paper materials. Paper was used in the Tang Dynasty (618-907). Censorship appeared in the Song Dynasty (960-1279) when unofficial newspaper, called *Xiao Bao*, became popular among civil society. Printing was put into application in the Southern Song Dynasty (1127-1279). It was not widely used, however, until the mid-16th century when the official *Jing Bao* and folk newspapers formed a recognizable enterprise.

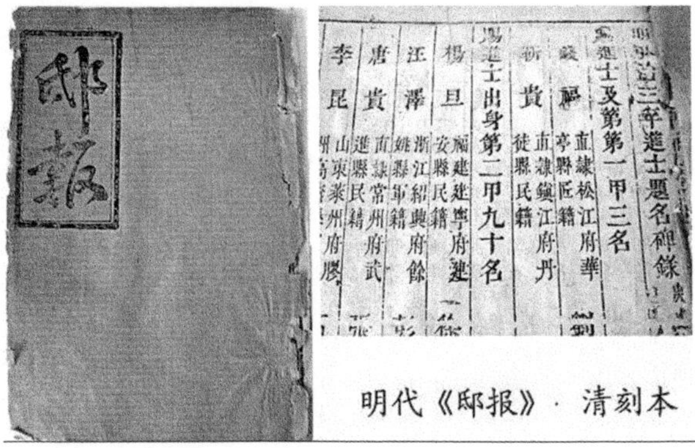

Figure 2.6 *Di Bao* of the Ming Dynasty.

Task 2 ▶ Listening comprehension

Direction: *MEDIA team are going to have a topic-oriented discussion to exchange their views on the listening material and challenge each other with puzzling questions.*

Objectives: *To broaden students' horizon, develop their ability to sum up the skills of answering questions and strengthen language output ability.*

Davis:	Hi, my teammates, what do you learn from the above listening excerpt? I am full of appreciation, for it helped to clear up my puzzle about print media and printing technology.
Irene:	I value the comparison between the origin of Chinese print media and that of the other countries, don't you think so, Angela?
Angela:	Of course. Otherwise, news circulation was still through word of mouth. The officials worldwide would have acted as criers like the ancient Roman, reading daily news sheets and informing the public orally.
Davis:	Sure. I am clear now that printing technology and print media are inter-permeated and inter-embraced each other. Both are inseparable from writing.
Irene:	We all have visited China Printing Museum several times. We know such early writing and materials as stone, wood, bamboo, clay, silk and the like, on which Chinese characters were chiseled, engraved or written. That was really painstaking and time-consuming.
Angela:	Despite the difficulties, writing on these materials was a great leap in human development. Before this, ancient people had to run a long distance so as to spread word or news to each other. And thus, the messages couldn't be exactly conveyed or kept.
Irene:	Yeah. And most people might have remained illiterate and common people like us might have had no chance to access written news pages. This is why China is famous for its four

great inventions, especially printing and paper-making. Bi Sheng's movable type laid the foundation for mass production of print media.

Davis: Yes. Gutenberg adapted the movable type to his printing press, starting the first step of the mass production of news pages.

Angela: The mass production of print media led to wide dissemination of everything including religion, technology, exchanges of knowledge, entertainment, life style and the like.

Davis: Oh wait. Let me ask a question. Do you know what the forerunner of Chinese print media or newspaper were? I mean in what form did the early Chinese newspaper appear?

Irene: It's said that the forerunner of newspapers in China took the form of government bulletins such as the *Peking Gazette*. And Chinese periodicals can date back to the *Spring and Autumn Annals*, spanning over a thousand years.

Angela: Irene always has a profound knowledge of Chinese history. But according to Edward, *Di Bao* was the earliest Chinese newspaper, wasn't it?

Irene: Yes, it was. I meant the forerunner of newspapers was bulletins. Am I clear now?

Angela: Crystal clear. Chinese newspapers evolved from bulletins, annals, and so on.

Davis: You've talked enough. Here is a challenge for you: Have you ever thought about what print media meant for governors in ancient times?

Irene: For emperors across various dynasties, print media could server as "beautifier" to eulogize their rule, while the public could employ print media to criticize the rulers and voice public opinion.

Angela: Then who was in charge of compiling the news?

Davis: Obviously imperial scholars. Common people couldn't do that because they were illiterates.

Irene: You know early *Di Bao* were handwritten on non-paper materials before paper appeared and was used in the Tang

	Dynasty. That means newspaper calls for not only authorities and scholars, but also craftsmen. As we learned in the first unit, media is power.
All:	So, let's go on with further exploration about media.

Task 3 ▶ Pre-reading activity

Direction: *This part serves as connecting link between the preceding and the following. MEDIA team are required to ponder over some questions concerning the whole unit, reflect on them and then find solutions. The answers are open-ended.*

Objectives: *To cultivate students' capability of exploring problems, develop critical thinking ability synchronously and improve their expression ability.*

1. Try to elaborate on the connection between printing technology and print media.
2. When and how did Chinese print media arise?
3. Please describe how ancient people both at home and abroad spread news.
4. In what forms did China's journalism originate and evolve?
5. Who did ancient print media serve? Is it completely negative? Why or why not?
6. Do you know anything about *Spring and Autumn Annals*? Did it have anything to do with print media?
7. How did *Di Bao* come into being?
8. How did *Xiao Bao* start to exist?
9. Compare *Di Bao* and *Xiao Bao*. Please exemplify it.
10. How do you think of the correlation among *Di Bao*, *Xiao Bao* and bureaucrats?

Task 4 ▶ Reading activity

Direction: *MEDIA team are required to read the following excerpt to obtain information, expand vocabulary volume, increase knowledge reserve, comprehend between lines, appreciate the writing style and evaluate the article.*

Objectives: *To cultivate students' capability of reading and absorbing information in a way that "eyes see quickly and brain processes quickly" to enhance reading comprehension, build up logic thinking, learn writing through reading and improve students' comprehensive quality.*

The Origins of Chinese Newspapers: Poetry, Annals or Bureaucracy

It is well known that the Chinese mastered paper-making and printing technologies ahead of the rest of the world. Without doubt, ancient China had a rich history in written communication, not to mention its versatile traditions of oral communication. However, within this scope, we will focus on print media that regularly disseminated journalistic content, such as newspapers, magazines and periodicals.

So, when did the practice of journalism originate in China? It is a controversial subject. While a majority of academics agree that the official gazette, either initiated in the Han or Tang Dynasty, constituted the earliest imperial newspaper. Others argue that the origins of print journalism traced back to the earlier poetic and historical writings. For instance, in 1896, in the inaugural issue of *Shiwu Bao (The Chinese Progress)*, Liang Qichao wrote an article entitled "Newspapers are beneficial to the state", in which he traced the earliest newspaper back to ancient Chinese ballads that were collected and presented to the "Son of the Heaven" to keep him updated on current affairs. Liang Qichao called the ballads the "People's Newspaper". In the 1930s, another Chinese writer, Lin Yutang, echoed this view. Lin believed that folk song rather than prose was the very origin of Chinese journalism. In his account, the ancient "epigrammatic verses and ballads" recording opinions on current affairs "were very effective as weapons of public criticism", which made them very similar to modern newspapers in terms of their function. He cites, for example, the great number of satirical poems contained in *Shijing (Classic of Poetry)* collected by Confucius.

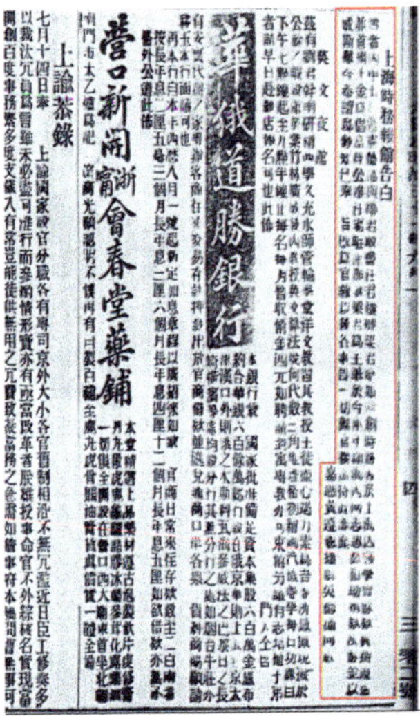

Figure 2.7 *Shiwu Bao*. Source: The library of Beijing Institute of Graphic Communication.

Other scholars held that journalism and poetry have been linked in detailed historical research and that ancient ballads played a very similar role to modern journalism in communicating public information. Despite such formal similarities between ancient ballads and modern journalism, the *Classic of Poetry* has more value as a literary and historical record of oral communication than as a link with printing journalism.

Apart from poetry, early historical works have been considered as another source of journalism. "Following the decline of the *Classic of Poetry* arose the *Spring and Autumn Annals*." This saying of Mencius was known to all the Chinese. The famous *Spring and Autumn Annals* were recognized by Lin as the beginning of the written press in China. He argued that the custom of news collection every spring and autumn from the 8th century was identified as "the earliest official gathering of news". In fact, many modern Chinese agreen that the *Spring and Autumn Annals* gave rise to Chinese journalism. The description "the King without a crown", which was given to Confucius for his compiling of the *Spring and Autumn Annals*, is often used as a phase describing modern journalists. The records contained in the *Spring and Autumn Annals* shared an enormous amount of common ground, in terms of their news-gathering value, with modern newspapers. Like present-day journalism, they recorded a wide range of current affairs and, moreover, these were, during the feudal period, remarkably open in terms of access to a wide readership, including scholars from different states.

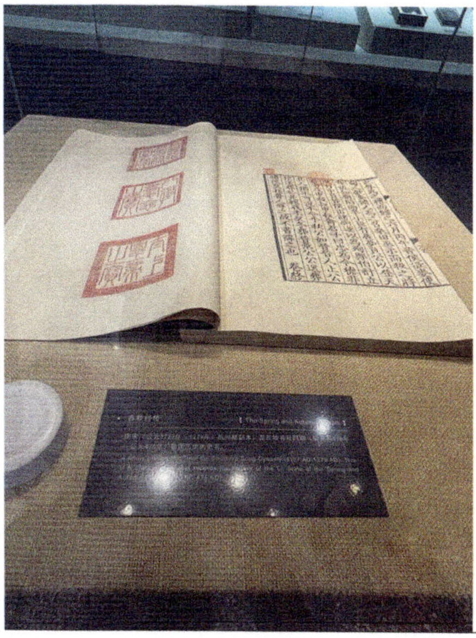

Figure 2.8 *Spring and Autumn Classic Biography* — one of the six classics of Confucianism. Source: China Printing Museum.

In these ways, a scholar concludes that these court historians can be compared to modern journalists. However, although the *Spring and Autumn Annals* may be narrowly regarded as the results of "the earliest official gathering of news", it seems more convincing to consider these court-historical records, in an era before paper and printing technology, as the earliest forms of Chinese historical work, rather than as a prototype for press in China.

The more widely accepted view that the Chinese newspaper was born of *Di Bao* — the official gazette — owes a debt to the scholar and journalist Ge Gongzhen. In his seminal book, *The History of Chinese Journalism*, Ge claimed that the Chinese newspaper developed from *Di Bao*, initially in its written form in the Han Dynasty, gradually to a printed form during the Tang Dynasty. Despite the various names it bore, such as *Zhao Bao, Tiao Bao,* and *Jing Bao* in the Qing Dynasty, the contents and general practice of the official gazette remained largely unchanged across the dynasties. Following Ge, the mainstream Chinese journalism studies endorse the view that Chinese journalism originated from *Di Bao*. It is still debatable when the term "Di Bao" was first used, different scholars held different views. Some suggested the Tang Dynasty but others insisted on the Song Dynasty. But certainly, the word "Di" occurs as early as in the statutes of the early Han Dynasty and was then defined as "the residence of provincial prefects for the purpose of communicating official reports".

And still others believed that the rise of military power, culture and trade in the Han Dynasty, particularly during Emperor Wu's reign, provided the impetus for an official gazette's production. The vast geographical area and centralized political structure in the Han Dynasty produced the requirement to circulate political information within the bureaucratic hierarchy.

However, it was in the Tang Dynasty that a specific bureau — the Bureau of Official Reports — was created to accommodate local representatives. During this time, there were many rising powerful dukes, princes or governors-general in charge of large territories, equal in size to a modern province in China. These landed aristocrats would naturally provide for their own news service in the capital Chang'an, which handled all official documents submitted by these representatives and transmitted imperial edicts in return. Recent archaeological research has uncovered such official reports since the Tang Dynasty. Two archive documents of that period originally found in Dunhuang have been regarded by Chinese scholars as the earliest form of newspaper in the world.

Whether or not one accepts this claim depends to some extent on whether written documents can be considered as printing journalism. The surviving archive documents were composed by handwriting and despite earlier suppositions that woodblock printing may have been utilized in the Tang official gazette, recent research suggests there is insufficient evidence for this.

It is probably wisest to discount handwritten documents. As Raymond Williams, a Welsh socialist and forerunner of contemporary culture studies in Britain, observes that, although writing had made possible the recording of communication, printing made possible its rapid distribution, and it was in this form that the press, literally defined as printing, is "the great means of modern communication". Viewed thus, we should regard the printing of *Di Bao* in the Song Dynasty as the first manifestation of the Chinese press, and it was *Di Bao* that dominated right up to the Qing Dynasty.

Since the liberation, right after liberating cities, the Communist Party of China established main national and city newspapers. *Xinshimen Daily* was published as its first large-city newspaper. Afterward, *Xinhua Daily* in Nanjing, *Liberation Daily* in Shanghai, *Yangtze Daily* in Wuhan, *Mass Daily* in Xi'an, *Tianjin Daily* in Tianjin, and *Public Daily* in Jinan acclaimed their establishment one after another. *Xinmin News* and *Wenhui News* were reinstated in Shanghai. In 1949 *Guangming Daily* and *Workers' Daily* were published and *People's Daily* in north China was proclaimed the official newspaper.

The economic reforms and opening-up brought about a newspaper boom. From then on, China's journalism industry has embarked on the track of rapid development.

Task 5 ▶ Reading comprehension

Direction: *MEDIA team are going to launch a discussion about the reading excerpt. They are required to summarize what they learned, share their puzzles as well as their comments on the article, and try to probe into more profound issues in this domain.*

Objectives: *Learning by doing. To cultivate students' capability of finding problems, reflecting on and solving problems independently so as to improve the comprehensive ability of using language.*

Maynor: Hello, everyone. I bet the reading excerpt above surprised and convinced you that media was originated from writing system, which was a reflection of not just culture, politics and literature, but also presented the culture image of a nation. Ancient China boasted glorious culture and civilization. That partially benefited from its invention of paper and printing, and its writing system. This can fully illustrate the importance of media construction and the soft power shown by the media.

Edward: I can't agree more with Maynor's remark. My suggestion is that you should keep your eyes open for the diverse forms of print media in ancient China. Different forms of print media disseminated different aspects of content and reached varied of audiences.

Irene: Thank you for your kind reminder. I am thinking why the early print media started with poetic writing rather than narration? How challenging writing poems is.

Davis: I think the ancient people were better at writing poems than we are today. Moreover, in ancient times, the elites were mainly the rich and they could afford home school with a private tutor while the poor have to remain illiterate.

Angela: In my submission, the reason why the ancient Chinese were so skilled with poetic writing was that they usually learned nothing else but writing and history in their home schools.

Irene: Oh, I think you are partially right. As far as I can see, poetic writing was the style or the feature of writing in ancient times.

Edward: Insightful reflections! The rich or the elites could express their views in poetic writing about history, scenery, and heroes, but the common people could also air their point of view in other forms. Am I correct?

Davis: I am in favour of your argument. I think the common or lower class possibly contributed to ancient ballads.

Irene: Maybe. But the mainstream of ancient print media belonged to bureaucrats and the elites. For example, *Spring and Autumn Annals* were identified by Lin Yutang as the beginning of the written press in China. And the earliest official news collection was compiled by imperial officials or intellectuals.

Angela: In this respect, we can say that the imperial officials or intellectuals belonged to the same class in ancient China.

Davis: Of course. Without knowledge, how could the ruling class maintain their power? And without media, how could the emperor publicize the fruits of his rule?

Maynor: By now, I think you are thoroughly aware of the significance of media and the evolution of print media. But what was the symbol of the ancient Chinese newspaper? Was it poetry anthology, *Spring and Autumn Annals*, or ballads?

Irene, Davis & Angela: It was *Di Bao*.

Irene: Let me continue with Davis's opinion. We can deduce that the emergence of *Di Bao* was due to the needs of the imperial court. The royal court demanded that the aristocracy should naturally provide for their own news service in the capital Chang'an, which handled all official documents submitted by these representatives and transmitted imperial edicts in return.

Angela: So, anyway, it was the court or ruling class that gave impetus to the development of *Di Bao* — the earliest newspaper in China.

Davis: But it was the working people, like Bi Sheng, who invented the movable type, that was the key.

Edward: Haha. Obviously, you are all crystal clear. Terrific!

Maynor: Perfectly indeed. So, why don't we move on to next part? I am excited to prepare the second lecture and hope you all like it.

Irene, Davis & Angela: We are looking forward to the lecture. See you.

Task 6 ▶ Translation practice

Direction: *MEDIA team are going to do Chinese-English translation, from which they can learn and compare how to express in cross-cultural way and convey the following paragraph in English accurately.*

Objectives: *To understand and master English morphology, syntax and idiomatic expressions, develop basic professional translation ability and promote English competence.*

纸质媒体发展历史悠久，其权威性和可信度是被公众高度认可的。纸质媒体作为第一媒体，受众覆盖面广，拥有庞大的受众群体，很容易满足各个阶层人士的需求。纸质媒体拥有很强的文字优势和极强的深度挖掘性。读者在阅读信息时不需要在第一时间做出反应，读者可以反复阅读思考，所以其挖掘的深度会更具客观性。纸质媒体阅读便利性很强，能使读者利用空余时间阅读。在当代社会，人们很少会专门花时间来获取各种新闻信息，大多数人习惯利用空余时间阅读，比如上下班等车、坐车的时间等，这使得报纸成为一种久盛不衰的媒介。

Task 7 ▶ Attending a public lecture

Direction: *MEDIA team are going to attend a public lecture delivered by Professor Maynor. Students are required to thoroughly understand the lecture, broaden the vision, elaborate on the theme, get inspiration from the lecture and do some speech activities to extend their knowledge.*

Objectives: *To train students' capability of description, expression, discussion, refutation, humor and humanistic accomplishment required by making a speech, thus improving students' English language competence and proficiency.*

Lecture 2

The Symbol of Ancient Chinese Newspapers: *Di Bao* vs *Xiao Bao*

Professor Maynor

Hello again. Today I'm going to present to you the second lecture in our lecture series on Chinese media. In my first lecture, I reviewed with you the media power. We have expounded the correlation between media, culture image and soft power. We have known how important media is for a country. Therefore, today it should come as no surprise that our lecture deals with the birth of the original media — print media in China.

The ancient official newspaper: *Di Bao*

To understand the advent of *Di* and *Di Bao*, we need to grasp the political institutional context of its emergence. In 221 B.C.E., the twenty-year war among the feudalistic states ended with the victory of Qin, who proclaimed himself Emperor of all China, leading to national unification. Emperor Qin introduced bureaucratic political institutions which shaped Chinese politics for the next two thousand years till the late Qing Dynasty. In order to replace the pre-Qin feudalistic power structure dominated by the aristocrats, Emperor Qin created a bureaucratic centralized government — dividing his kingdom into thirty-six "commanderies" (i.e. provinces). He sent officers chosen on their "proven ability", regardless of their family background, to manage these localities. In each commandery, there were three officers. Two of them were responsible, respectively, for defense, civil administration, economics and industry. The third one — directly responsible to the emperor — is the emperor's special envoy to oversee the two other officers.

As the Han Dynasty expanded its territory, the political structure remained but required a larger bureaucracy. In particular, more communication between the central authorities and the local level was required. In these circumstances, representatives began to be sent by the local authorities to the capital, and it was because of this that the *Di* appeared. Qin had in fact already laid some of the grounds for this mobile bureaucracy in the construction of military roads.

Under the Emperor Qin, military necessity had caused him to build an elaborate system of military roads and post-relays, with regular stations ten *li* apart, and his system of roads and relays was elaborated upon during the Han Dynasty, with regular post stations at regular intervals of thirty *li*. Both post-houses and post-chaises, with one to seven horses, were in use, as well as couriers on foot.

Thus, a material communicational infrastructure — the beginning of a postal system — can be attributed to Emperor Qin. But to understand how the *Di* became such effective form of political-bureaucratic communication, we should mention one further achievement of the emperor: his establishing of a standardized corpus of written characters, from which modern Chinese derived, making communication among different areas of the empire possible. This considerably contributed to the end of the political fragmentation of pre-Qin China and the rise of a centralized powerful state. It is instructive to notice the early and deeply embedded bond between language and written communication, on the one hand, and the bureaucratic political system, on the other. And this state control over the written medium was even further enhanced and sustained when Confucian ideology became authorized.

By the Tang Dynasty, the *Di* system had further developed due to territorial expansion and economic prosperity. During the reign of Emperor Taizong, archive records suggest plans to build over three hundred new *Di*s in the capital city Chang'an. In AD 777, the Bureau of Official Reports was set up to deal with correspondence sent to provincial authorities. The well-developed postal service of that time — some 1,643 postal stops, of which 1,293 operated by land, 260 by water and 86 by both — also greatly contributed to the circulation of *Di Bao*. With the government postal service, the capital of the

Figure 2.9 Prosperity of Chang'an in the Tang Dynasty. Source: The Library of Beijing Institute of Graphic Communication.

Chinese Empire, in Tang times, was only eight to fourteen days away from the most distant city of any importance.

Nevertheless, it is essential to remember that *Di Bao* in the Tang Dynasty were published only at irregular intervals. It was not until printing technology was adopted in the Song Dynasty that *Di Bao* grew into a standard official periodical gazette of ancient China.

Following the elaboration of the bureaucratic political institutions in the early Song Dynasty, the imperial authority terminated the *Di* set up by the local officers and instead established the "Central Petition Court" to regulate and control official news distribution. News gathering, editing and distributing then were divided among several departments of the central bureaucracy. In contrast with the random semiofficial handwritten newsletters in the Tang Dynasty, *Di Bao* in the Song Dynasty developed into an important system of daily printed official news with an increasing amount of information. What *Di Bao* carried were mostly details of imperial court affairs, such as the official edicts and orders for promotion and dismissals, memorandums by the ministers and provincial authorities, selected edicts of the emperor and other official documents.

More importantly, during the Song Dynasty, *Di Bao* started to enjoy a larger circulation among a wider range of officials and gentry-scholars all over the country. Extensive references to *Di Bao* are found in the notes, letters, poems and biographies of the scholars of that period. Su Shi, a well-known poet in the Song Dynasty, wrote that his source of information on officialdom was through reading *Di Bao*.

While *Di Bao* was reaching a wider readership from the Tang Dynasty to the Song Dynasty, it was also becoming more manipulated by the central authorities. It was moving from being the channel for mass communication to becoming the mouthpiece of the government. Through the Yuan, Ming and most of the Qing Dynasty, *Di Bao* continued to develop without significant changes and interruptions. Its dominance was not challenged until the arrival of the modern press in the 19th century.

Figure 2.10 Dissemination of *Di Bao* in the Qing Dynasty. Source: Baidu Picture Library.

The "unofficial press" in ancient China

Having sketched the emergence and development of the official ancient gazette *Di Bao*, we can now turn to the relationship between this and the emergence of an unofficial press.

During the Song Dynasty, while reading *Di Bao* became a general habit for many scholars, there emerged a kind of unofficial newspaper, the *Xiao Bao*. *Xiao Bao* were the "tabloid" newspapers of the Song Dynasty, originally established by the local representatives in the capital, the *Di* officials. They emerged as a result of a demand for up-to-date news among scholars. They were also considered to be potentially subversive because they often contained inaccurate or groundless statements damaging to imperial authority and were involved in leaking information from the Bureau of Official Reports.

Some scholars regard *Xiao Bao* as an attempt by the *Di* officials to confront imperial censorship and to break the control of the Bureau of Official Reports. And for this reason, *Xiao Bao* grew into the first important growth of journalism in China. The rise of *Xiao Bao* can be dated back to the early days of *Di Bao*, and the establishment of the Bureau of Official Reports was in part an attempt to thwart the development of *Xiao Bao*. Political messages became imperative in the Song Dynasty as political turmoil intensified. With its limited and often outdated official news, *Di Bao* became an insufficient and frustrating monopoly of intelligence for the rising political factions and the gentry officials in and out of the imperial court. *Xiao Bao*, therefore, provided for the growing appetite for more and more timely political information. In one sense, *Xiao Bao* emerged in direct reaction to the censorship and the restricted circulation of *Di Bao*. *Xiao Bao* were often handwritten by the *Di* officials and reached a very limited readership. But there was a more vigorous form in which information was collected by reporters rather than *Di* officials.

The "court reporters", "provincial reporters" and "yamen reporters" could be compared to present-day political correspondents who report in the national, provincial and local newspapers. They were professional reporters. The wide variety of sources of their reports may have contained court news, some of it censored, along with social and political gossip and rumors on the street. *Xiao Bao* contained some form of commentary on current affairs, though this must have been indirect so as to avoid official intolerance of the free expression of opinion. Because of the breath and diversity of their contents and their wide circulation, *Xiao Bao* could only have been produced by printing rather than handwriting. But since they were partially based on social and political rumors, they were lacking in journalistic credibility and, in fact, began to decline significantly by the early 19th century.

Task 8 ▶ Online forum and summary writing

Direction: *MEDIA team are going to launch an instant online post-talk about the lecture to appeal to more of other students who are interested in the topic to join them. This is an integrated practice of listening, speaking, reading and writing. They are particularly expected to write a summary of the entire unit.*

Objectives: *To provide a platform for MEDIA team to fully display their talents. To comb language learning with professional knowledge so as to cultivate students' professional learning, academic literacy and language competence. To realize the teaching objectives of acquiring professional knowledge through learning English language.*

Edward: What a fantastic lecture! I suggest that you start with the basic concept of *Di Bao* and explain it clearly to others to discuss or verify whether you understand it exactly, or misinterpret it or even lost it.

Maynor: I think so. It is also a sort of test.

Davis: I assure you that I can explain it clearly to all of you. *Di Bao* in Chinese is 《邸报》. It was a kind of palace reports, or imperial bulletins as we talked before, or gazettes published usually by central government and sometimes by local government in ancient China. And ...

Angela: Wait. Sorry to cut in. I know the content was around official announcements and news. It was intended to be seen only by bureaucrats.

Irene: Wow, both of you are almost experts now. How did average people gain access to the official information if it only circulated among bureaucrats?

Davis: Let me think for a second.

Angela: It is also a challenge for me.

Irene: I am not quite sure about it. But I think after *Di Bao* was published, some items selected from *Di Bao* might then be conveyed to local citizenry by word of mouth or posted announcements.

Maynor: You are quite right, Irene. A given *Di Bao* was truly intended for a certain subset of bureaucrats.

Davis: Oh, I see. How often was *Di Bao* published? Was it daily, weekly or irregularly?

Angela: I bet that it must be published monthly because *Di Bao* was emerging as early as in the Han Dynasty while Bi Sheng's movable type was invented in the Song Dynasty. It was hard for the government to publish it daily or weekly.

Irene: Wow, I got it. I am in favour of your opinion, Angela. According to the lecture, when *Di Bao* came into being remains controversy. But, anyway, it must have appeared in the Tang Dynasty at the latest. And at that time reports, news or early newspaper were hand-written or printed with wood block. This kind of technology could at least ensure regular publication.

Edward: Actually, the frequency of publication varied widely over time and place. So *Di Bao* in its early time was indeed published irregularly. And different sources place *Di Bao*'s first publication as early as the Han Dynasty, which would make *Di Bao* among the earliest newspapers in the world.

Davis: That's just what was in my mind.

Angela: Smart guy! I must try even harder or I might fall behind. So, would you mind if I ask one more question, Professor Maynor?

Maynor: Certainly not. You are always welcome and feel free to put forward your question, please.

Angela: What on earth were the content of *Di Bao*? I mean how many kinds of news *Di Bao* could convey to the officials?

Irene: May I try to explain to you first? It covered all kinds of important information, such as military events, political and administrative decrees etc.

Davis: How about the emperor's life and diplomacy?

Maynor:	Your questions tell me that you all have made great efforts. I am really proud of you. Generally, *Di Bao* covered four aspects that you have mentioned. First, the daily life of the emperor, second, the significant edicts, political decisions, and decrees, the third comes the dynamics of the imperial court, and the forth is the reports of miliary and diplomacy.
Irene:	I wonder why did *Di Bao* report the emperor's daily life.
Edward:	Under the influence of traditional Chinese ideology based on Confucianism, it was significant for both the publisher and readers to know the speech and behavior of the emperor, because the emperor in ancient China was regarded as the pivot of the whole empire.
Irene:	I got it. It seems that we had endless questions to discuss. How about attaching our questions to *Di Bao* discussing.com, where anyone interested in this topic can post profiles about his or her bright ideas?
Angela & Davis:	Great idea.
Maynor:	Then so much for today. But don't forget about *Xiao Bao*. It was a part of China's ancient newspapers.
Irene, Angela & Davis:	We will continue our online discussion about *Xiao Bao* together with other students.
All:	See you next time.

Appendix: Vocabulary for Unit 2

Listening Activity

inscriptions /ɪnˈskrɪpʃnz/ *n.* 铭文；碑文；题字（inscription的复数）

papyrus /pəˈpaɪrəs/ *n.* 纸莎草；纸莎草纸

wedge /wedʒ/ *n.* 楔子，三角木；楔形物，三角形物（尤指食物）；不和；（高尔夫）楔形铁头球棒；（高尔夫）楔形铁头球棒击出的球；有鞋跟的女鞋；坡跟鞋鞋跟；（人或动物组成的）楔形队形

v.（将……）楔入，插入，挤入；把……楔住，把……楔牢；

（制作陶瓷时）揉（陶土）

engraving /ɪnˈgreɪvɪŋ/ *n.* 雕刻；雕刻术；雕刻品
v. 在……上雕刻；给……深刻的印象（engrave的现在分词形式）

chisel /ˈtʃɪz(ə)l/ *n.* 凿子
v. 雕，刻，凿；（非正式）欺骗

illustration /ɪˌlʌsˈtreʃən/ *n.* ［印刷］插图；插画

porcelain /ˈpɔːsəlɪn/ *n.* 瓷；瓷器
adj. 瓷制的

cumbersome /ˈkʌmbəsəm/ *adj.* 笨重的；繁琐的，复杂的；（话语或措辞）冗长的

Vajra Sutra 金刚经

Gazette /gəˈzet/ *n.* 宪报；公报；报；报纸

exclusively /ɪkˈskluːsɪvli/ *adv.* 仅仅，单独地，专门地；作为唯一的（消息）来源

feudal /ˈfjuːd(ə)l/ *adj.* 封建（制度）的

Censorship /ˈsensəʃɪp/ *n.* 审查，检查，审查制度

Reading Activity

disseminate /dɪˈsemɪneɪt/ *v.* 散布，传播（信息、知识等）

periodical /ˌpɪəriˈɒdɪk(ə)l/ *n.* （尤指学术）期刊
adj. 间发性的，定期的，周期的；（杂志，报纸）定期出版的

controversial /ˌkɒntrəˈvɜːʃ(ə)l/ *adj.* 有争议的，引发争论的

ballad /ˈbæləd/ *n.* 歌谣，民谣；叙事歌谣；流行抒情歌曲

prose /prəʊz/ *n.* 散文，白话文；（尤指待翻译的）一段散文；平淡乏味的文章（或话语，表达法）
v. 冗长乏味地说；写散文
adj. 散文的，散文式的；平凡的，乏味的

epigrammatic /ˌepɪgrəˈmætɪk/ *adj.* 警句的；讽刺的

verse /vɜːs/ *n.* 诗，韵文；诗节，（歌曲的）节；（《圣经》或其他经文的）节；（赞美诗的）独唱部，小组唱部

satirical /səˈtɪrɪkl/ *adj.* 讽刺的，讥讽的；爱挖苦人的

annal /ˈæn(ə)l/ *n.* 记录；编年史

prototype /ˈprəʊtətaɪp/ *n.* （新型汽车、机器等的）原型，雏形；典型，范例；蓝本，最初形态；（电子）原型滤波网络；（生物、天体等的）原始型；（建筑、汽车等的）全真模型

v. 制作（产品的）原型
seminal /ˈsemɪn(ə)l/ *adj.* 有创造力的，对未来有影响的；重大的；种子的；精液的；生殖的
endorse /ɪnˈdɔːs/ *v.*（公开）赞同，认可；（在广告中对某种产品）宣传，吹捧；（尤指在支票背面）签名，背书；（在驾驶执照上）记录违章事项
prefect /ˈpriːfekt/ *n.* 长官，地方行政长官；级长
reign /reɪn/ *n.*（君主）在位时期，统治时期；领导期，任期；支配期，极盛期；（运动员或运动队）持有指明荣誉头衔的时期
v. 为王，统治；支配，盛行；成为最佳，成为最重要的
impetus /ˈɪmpɪtəs/ *n.* 动力，促进；动量，冲力
bureaucratic /ˌbjʊərəˈkrætɪk/ *adj.* 官僚的，官僚政治的
hierarchy /ˈhaɪərɑːki/ *n.* 等级制度；统治集团；等级体系
accommodate /əˈkɒmədeɪt/ *v.* 为……提供住宿；容纳，提供空间；考虑到，顾及；顺应，适应；帮助（某人），向……施以援手；迎合，迁就；调解
edict /ˈiːdɪkt/ *n.* 法令；布告
archaeological /ˌɑːkiəˈlɒdʒɪk(ə)l/ *adj.* 考古学的，考古的
supposition /ˌsʌpəˈzɪʃ(ə)n/ *n.* 推测，假定；毫无根据的想法，无稽之谈
discount /ˈdɪskaʊnt/ *n.* 减价，折扣；（汇票或期票到期前转手的）贴现率
adj. 打折的，减价出售的
v. 打折，减价；不重视，忽视；贴现
proclaim /prəˈkleɪm/ *v.*（正式）宣告，（公开）声明；强调，声称；（标志或通知）宣传，告知；清楚表明，显示
embark /ɪmˈbɑːk/ *v.* 上船，上飞机；着手，开始（新的或艰难的事情）

Lecture

aristocrat /ˈærɪstəkræt/ *n.* 贵族，贵族成员
commandery /kəˈmɑːndəri/ *n.* 骑士团管理地；会所
envoy /ˈenvɔɪ/ *n.* 使者，使节，（谈判等的）代表；公使（级别在大使之下）
relay /ˈriːleɪ/ *v.* 传递，传达（信息、新闻等）；中继转发，转播（广播或电视信号）；重铺，重新铺设（过去式和过去分词形式 relaid）
n. 接力赛；接班的人（或动物），轮换者；传递，传送；中继设备；继电器；中继转播的信息（或节目）；传输系统，传送系统
chaise /ʃeɪz/ *n.* 一种轻马车（通常有车篷，尤指单马双轮者）
infrastructure /ˈɪnfrəstrʌktʃə(r)/ *n.* 下面结构；永久性军事设施；基础设施，基础建设

corpus /ˈkɔːpəs/ *n.* 文集，全集；语料库；体，身体；胃体；本金

derive /dɪˈraɪv/ *v.* 获得，取得；起源于，来自；提取，衍生（化学物质）

sustain /səˈsteɪn/ *v.* 维持，保持；维持……的生命；遭受，经受

archive /ˈɑːkaɪv/ *n.* 存档材料，档案；档案室
v. 把……存档，把……归档

terminate /ˈtɜːmɪneɪt/ *v.*（使）结束，（使）终止；到达终点站；终止妊娠，人工流产；在……结尾，以……收尾

random /ˈrændəm/ *n.* 随意，随机；〈非正式〉不认识的人，陌生人
adj. 任意的，随机的，胡乱的
adv. 随机地，胡乱地

edict /ˈiːdɪkt/ *n.* 法令；布告

memorandum /ˌmeməˈrændəm/ *n.* 公务便条，备忘录；协议备忘录；建议书，报告；合同书，（法律文件细节的）摘要

gentry /ˈdʒentri/ *n.*〈英，旧〉上流人士，贵族；〈非正式，贬〉人们（尤指特定种类）

officialdom /əˈfɪʃldəm/ *n.* 官场；官员（总称）；官僚作风

sketch /sketʃ/ *n.* 素描，速写，草图；（任何作品的）粗样，初稿；简述，概述；幽默短剧，滑稽小品
v. 画速写，画素描；简述，概述；（用手或身体）做（姿势）

tabloid /ˈtæblɔɪd/ *n.* 小报，通俗小报，八卦小报
adj. 通俗小报的；耸人听闻的，引起轰动的

subversive /səbˈvɜːsɪv/ *adj.* 破坏性的；从事颠覆的
n. 危险分子；颠覆分子

censorship /ˈsensəʃɪp/ *n.* 审查，检查，审查制度

thwart /θwɔːt/ *v.* 反对，阻挠，挫败；横过
n.（划艇上的）横坐板
adj. 横放的；固执的

turmoil /ˈtɜːmɔɪl/ *n.* 混乱，骚动
v. 扰乱，使不安

faction /ˈfækʃ(ə)n/ *n.* 派系，宗派；派系之争，内讧；纪实与虚构相结合的电影（或书等）

vigorous /ˈvɪgərəs/ *adj.* 精力充沛的，充满活力的；强壮的，强健的

3

Unit

Broadcast Media: Radio, Film and TV

TABLE OF CONTENTS

Unit 3 Broadcast Media: Radio, Film and TV

Warm-up: Be proactive

Direction: *MEDIA team are going to do warm-up activities by discussing, airing their views on the topic and discovering problems.*

Objectives: *To arouse students' interest, get a preliminary understanding of relevant knowledge and prepare for the following study.*

Irene: Nice to see you again, my MEDIA partners! You got here so early that you must have been well prepared for the following topic. Didn't you?

Angela: Yeah bet. I just can't wait to get on with this unit. Through last unit, I have accessed to the door of ancient Chinese print media. For this unit I have equipped myself with knowledge in regard to the modern Chinese print media. I am sure that I can make it.

Davis: Hey, Angela. I hope you are right about what we are going to learn in this unit and what Professor Maynor will talk to us next. In my memory, our two supervisors announced to us last time that we would skip over modern paper media and enter electronic media learning directly.

Irene: Yes. I remember it clearly. You know young people prefer electronic media to paper newspaper though paper media do play a very important role in the development of Chinese media. Even today, a lot of elders choose to read paper newspaper or periodicals rather than read through iPad or mobile phones.

Angela: Oh, that's true. But old people are also fond of watching TV or listening to the radio. It seems that they love TV or radio much more than young people who obviously enjoy cell phones.

Davis: So, our professors hope to leave paper media part for self-study because our time is limited. Of course, we should choose the important parts to discuss together.

Irene: Exactly. But don't worry, Angela. You're an electronics fan while both of our supervisors are so considerate that they will take care of each of us carefully. They are always ready to offer help.

Angela: Thank you, both of you. I am so happy that our MEDIA team plus our supervisors are so friendly that we can always coordinate with each other, make up each other's shortcomings and share information and resources. Terrific team!

Davis: Now I think it's time for us to discuss something concerning electronic media like television, radio and film, so that we can get an overview.

Irene: Okay. To start with, I'd like to know how much we know about our Chinese electronic media. I am sure every one of us knows CCTV, but how about radio broadcasting?

Angela: Radio broadcasting is so popular in China. I bet every province or city has its own radio station. But I am afraid that only a few people listen to radio broadcasting now, or many people even put the radio aside.

Davis: It is the case. But in many other countries, radio broadcasting is still the mainstream of the access to news or other information domestically and globally.

Irene: Yes. China Radio International with its abbreviated name "CRI" provides quite well service to satisfy those who need radio broadcasting.

Angela: So, guys, are you ready for exploring CRI?

Davis & Irene: Yes. Let's go.

Task 1 ▶ Listening activity

Direction: *MEDIA team are going to listen to an introduction of key concepts so as to lay the foundation for later learning.*

Objectives: *To understand the main conception, practice and strengthen the ability of listening comprehension.*

Introduction of China Radio International (CRI)

Radio was first introduced to China in the 1920s and 1930s, when few households had radio receivers and only a few cities had commercial stations. Radio usage was primarily for political purpose, often at a local level.

The Communist Party of China first used radio in Yan'an, Shaanxi Province in March 1940, with a transmitter imported from Moscow. Xinhua News Chinese Radio (XNCR) went on the air from Yan'an on December 30, 1940. XNCR transmitted to a larger geographical area after 1945, and its programs became more regular and formalized, featuring broadcasts of news, official announcements, war bulletins, and art and literary programs.

Figure 3.1 Former site of Xinhua Radio Station. Source: 央广网.

The English service started on September 11, 1947, transmitting as XNCR from a cave located in the Taihang Mountains, during China's War of Liberation. XNCR reported on the war situation and broadcast Chinese political and cultural perspectives to the world at large. When the People's Republic of China was founded in 1949, its name was changed to Radio Peking on April 10, 1950, modified to Radio Beijing in 1983, and rebranded to China Radio International (CRI) on january 1, 1993, to avoid confusion with local Beijing radio broadcasting. Its online broadcasting platform China International Broadcasting Network (CIBN) was formally established in 2011, as a joint-venture of China Radio International.

As the state-owned international radio broadcaster of China, CRI endeavors to promote favourable relations between China and the world. It plays a significant role in China's soft power strategy and going out policy, aiming at expanding the influence of Chinese culture and media on the global stage.

CRI has 32 overseas correspondent bureaus, and broadcasts over 2,700 hours of programming each day (24 hours) in English, including news, current affairs, and features on politics, economy, culture, science, and technology. As a window of China to the world, its overseas reporting involves 65 languages. More than 50 shortwave transmitters are used to cover most of the world. Broadcasting via the Internet and numerous satellites, and its programs are rebroadcast by many local AM and FM radio stations worldwide.

With the advent of the Internet, CRI established its digital portal in December 1998. Together with other major Chinese state media outlets such as *People's Daily*, *XinhuaNet*, *China Daily* (the official English-language newspaper) and CCTV, CRI serves as news providers via the Internet. CRI integrated three Chinese websites: China news, Global Chinese Net and TV.com, giving birth to CRI Online.

Since then, CRI has been kept building up its modern international radio system and has become the pivot of the system in China. Its aim is to broaden the influence of China on the international public opinion. So, there is a strong need for CRI to strengthen the broadcasting activity of its radio system outside the country, as well as to raise the influence and the competitiveness of its radio in a global environment, with the purpose to build up a harmonious international public opinion environment and serve those who love radio broadcasting.

Despite progress, CRI's leaders acknowledged the gaps in scope and impact compared to Western counterparts like BBC and VOA, which have gained widespread credibility and recognition with the international audience, such as the international reach, the foreign partnerships and the services offered. It is imperative for CRI to fill the gap by integrating new technologies into its development path. Last but not least, market and users' reasons require the need to establish such a system.

Similar to the BBC and VOA, CRI has also established a number of tools to disseminate content globally by using the Internet and new technologies.

Besides, as a multilingual website, CRI Online is currently available in most languages and mainly delivers political, economic, sport and cultural information about China to an interational audience. Each website in the specific language offers services which are partially different from the others. For instance, the English version offers a page dedicated to online videos divided into seven categories: Traveler, Cultural Heritage, Beyond Stardom, Dynamic China, Life 360°, Panoramic Sports and Archives. Each category is continuously updated with new contents and can be shared with other online visitors.

Figure 3.2 Main building of China Radio International.

More services offered by CRI Online include e-Journals, Board Bulletin System (BBS), blogging and a multilingual podcasting. By allowing for richer contents and interactivity, all these services aim at stimulating interactive debates and opinion exchanges about China among users, CRI Online bloggers and visitors through an official media like CRI. This purpose is also achieved through a channel available on the website of each language called "Talk to CRI": Through the website itself and by sending SMSs, online users can express their opinions and preferences. A successful example of these web talks is provided by the Japanese version, launched in September 2005. All those should be a necessary and natural development of the international cooperation and relations of China with other countries in view of a deeper and more comprehensive understanding of China abroad.

Task 2 ▶ Listening comprehension

Direction: *MEDIA team are going to have a topic-oriented discussion to exchange their views on the listening material and challenge each other with puzzling questions.*

Objectives: *To broaden students' horizon, develop their ability to sum up the skills of answering questions and strengthen language output ability.*

Angela:	This listening material helps to dispel the doubt in my mind. As you know, I misunderstood the instruction given by our supervisors. Now the "weather" cleared up and the "fog" dispersed. I am greatly illuminated. How about you guys?
Irene:	As far as I'm concerned, I thought I had been clear about CRI because I am the beneficiary of CRI, because I have been listening to the news from CRI to strengthen my English listening capability. But I knew a little about its history before. What a shame!
Davis:	It seems to me that the report is only a start and just the first step, supposing that we hope to know more about CRI. I suddenly have a strong feeling to listen to CRI.
Irene:	You can listen to it at any time and choose your favourite FM or AM as you wish.
Angela:	Honestly, I do know something about CRI because I am crazy about sport events and I acquire a lot of information in this regard. CRI is absolutely rich in such information resources.
Irene:	Do you know anything about its history before the report provided by Edward, guys?
Davis:	I know CRI broadcast via shortwave radio, satellite and the Internet in English and other languages, and there are numerous AM and FM relays.
Angela:	CRI takes advantage of its journalists from all around the world. It reports international news, sports, entertainment and lifestyle programs for domestic listeners in Mandarin Chinese, aiming at making CRI a first-class news radio brand.

Irene: I believe CRI can definitely turn what they have been pursuing, namely, "First News, News First" and "On-the-Spot China, Live World" into reality.

Angela: I can share FM messages with you. CRI can be heard online as well as over the air in various locations across China: in Beijing on 90.5FM, in Tianjin on 90.6 FM, in Guangdong on 107.1FM etc.

Davis: A true electronic fan. I know several popular shows such as *Laowai's Viewpoint*, which is an international news program with three hosts from different countries, and *Bianzou Biankan*, a travel show dedicated to a new location every episode.

Irene: Fantastic! Do you know podcast programs? I'd love to share Chinese podcasts with you. News program comes from the *Xinhua News Agency*, and *Tangrenjie* is a program about overseas Chinese.

Davis: CRI also offers a list of podcast programs in English like *Hourly News*, *The Beijing Hour*, *Round Table* and *Chinese Studio* etc.

Angela: CRI once launched a *CRI Olympic Radio* program at 900 AM in Beijing in 2006. This special broadcast was done 24 hours a day in Chinese, Korean, English, Russian, French and Spanish, Arabic, Japanese and German. This service was terminated in late 2008 after conclusion of the Beijing Olympics; the frequency 900 AM is now under *CRI News Radio* which only covers Beijing.

Irene: But dear partners, I've realized that we are just talking about CRI programs rather than its history. so, I strongly suggest that we probe into its evolution progress to know more about CRI's contribution to the construction of China's soft power. Don't you agree?

Davis & Angela: Absolutely agree. Let's work hard together in this direction.

All: See you next time.

Task 3 ▶ Pre-reading activity

Direction: *This part serves as connecting link between the preceding and the following. MEDIA team are required to ponder over some problems concerning the whole unit, reflect on them and then find solutions. The answers are open-ended.*

Objectives: *To cultivate students' capability of exploring problems, develop critical thinking ability synchronously and improve expression ability.*

1. Please briefly introduce the evolution and development of CRI.
2. Do you know when and how radio was introduced into China?
3. What was the relationship between XNCR and CRI?
4. Have you ever heard of or seen the first Chinese-made film? Please try to comment on it.
5. Why and when were so many films imported into China in the early 19th century?
6. Please try to describe how Chinese film makers produced the domestic films.
7. How did "*Dianying*" in Chinese — the equivalent of "film" in English come into being?
8. What do you know about CCTV International? Please state it briefly.
9. Would you please introduce CCTV 4 or CCTV 9? What are their characteristics respectively?
10. Try to expound and verify how CCTV International contributes to building up China's soft power.

Task 4 ▶ Reading activity

Direction: *MEDIA team are required to read the following excerpt to obtain information, expand vocabulary volume, increase knowledge reserve, comprehend between lines, appreciate the writing style and evaluate the article.*

Objectives: *To cultivate students' capability of reading and absorbing information in a way that "eyes see quickly and brain processes quickly" to enhance reading* *comprehension, build up logic thinking, learn writing through reading and improve students' comprehensive quality.*

Early Film Activities in China

The first film was shown in China in 1896. Since then, this new medium has gradually sunk its roots in the country, becoming one of the most important forms of popular entertainment. Unlike artists working with other media and genres introduced into China from the West, such as oil painting, symphonic music and spoken drama, Chinese filmmakers had no indigenous traditions to draw on in their efforts to assimilate this foreign novelty. Despite this, over the past century they have completely mastered the art of filmmaking and their works have earned international recognition. To date, more than six hundred Chinese films have won film awards at various international film festivals, including Cannes, Berlin, Locarno, Nantes, New York, Toronto and Venice.

Many distinctive features developed by Chinese film over the last hundred years are the result and testimony of the particular kinds of interaction linking culture and politics in the 20th century in China. As a form of mass entertainment, Chinese film has been affected by historical forces in a unique way. To fully understand recurring motifs, narrative modes and thematic orientations in Chinese film, one must understand both the industry's internal development and broader societal and historical changes. In fact, one of the most striking attributes of Chinese film is the way it has responded and reacted to political events and history. Hence, any narrative history of Chinese film must be intimately informed by a broader understanding of China's general history.

The initiation of film activities

The first period of Chinese film begins with the introduction of film in 1896 and ends with the release of the first Chinese-made long feature *Yan Ruisheng* (dir. Ren Pengnian, 1921). During this period, China saw her final days of imperial rule under the Qing Dynasty, which was overthrown by the revolutionaries in 1911. However, the founding of the new republican government did not immediately bring wealth and power, goals cherished by the revolutionaries. On the contrary, the political disintegration that had already become evident in the late 19th century only accelerated during the early republican period. After the death of Yuan Shikai, the country descended into a warlord era. Meanwhile, Western and Japanese imperialists increased their political and economic exploitation of China. China's defeat in the Sino-Japanese war of 1894-1895 and the intervention of the Eight-Power Allied Forces following the Boxer Uprising of 1900 marked the high tide of imperialism in China. It was in this context of increasing foreign penetration and intensifying internal conflict that film was first imported.

A Spaniard named Galen Bocca exhibited the first motion picture to a Chinese audience at an entertainment center called Xu Garden (*Xuyuan*) in Shanghai where variety shows and acrobatic performances were given daily on 11 August, 1896. A year later, an American came to China and screened films at a number of teahouses in the city. These screenings lasted for more than ten days and created a sensation. At that time, as in most parts of the world, films were considered a novelty and were viewed as popular entertainment. Early films mostly took as their subject matter exotic places and peoples, thus reinforcing the view of film as exotica. Films shown in China during this period include *The Tsar's Visit to Paris*, *The Serpent Dance in Florida*, *The City of Madrid*, *The Spanish Dance*, *The Exhausted Mule* and *The Boxer*.

Figure 3.3 Shanghai Hongkou Grand Theatre.
Source:《中国最早的专业电影院——上海虹口影戏园》,《影博·影响》2015 年第 1 期（2015 年合订本上，总第 85 期），第 129 页.

These titles illustrate both the nature and the appeal of early film shows. According to one of the film audiences, some American electric shadow plays (*Yingxi*) contained wonderful scenes and were full of surprises. One scene showed two cute dancing blondes, who were then replaced by another scene of two Western wrestling men. In yet another scene, a man tried to sleep but was annoyed by insects. He got up, caught a few insects and put them into his mouth, which made the audience laugh. And still in one other scene, a magician covered a woman with a blanket. When he unfolded the blanket, the woman was gone. Minutes later the woman reappeared from behind the blanket. This early eyewitness's account suggests that the first films shown in China had not yet developed mature narrative techniques and were mostly one reeler. But works reminiscent of the two most important filmmakers of the day, the Lumière brothers and Mélies, were presented to Chinese audiences. The short film about a man trying to sleep arguably reminds one of the Lumières' own brands of cinematic realism, while the story of the magician seems to borrow heavily from Mélies' famous techniques. These two diametrically opposed orientations in filmmaking were to have tremendous impact on later developments, and they were to be echoed in China as well as throughout the rest of the world.

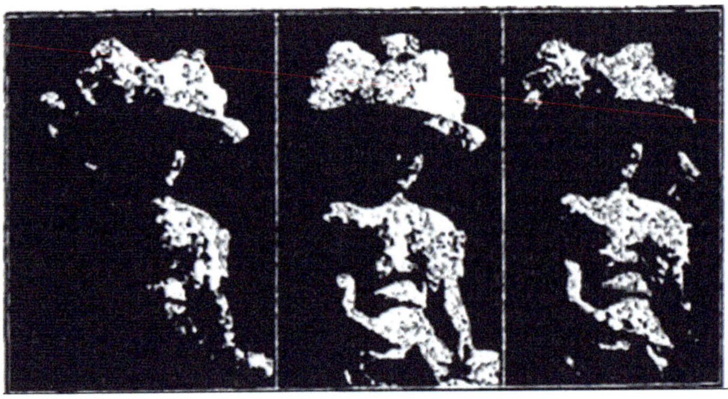

Figure 3.4 The earliest film. Source: 《东方杂志》所载电影胶片，郝秉键《电影在晚晴的传播》（"Development of the Cinema in the Late Qing Dynasty"），《寻根》，2022.7.

That the foreigners played such a prominent role in the early development of film in China should come as no surprise. China was not alone among non-Western nations in this regard. As an industrial enterprise, film first had to establish itself in the exhibition and distribution sectors in China, because there was hardly any native film production. As a result, the majority of early titles shown in China were Western imports, and all the first-run theatres were foreign-owned and located in foreign concessions.

The production of Chinese-made film

Chinese film production began in 1905. A photographer named Ren Fengtai (1850–1932), who owned a photographic studio in Beijing, built the city's first cinema at the turn of the century as a sideline business venture. By that time, filmgoing had become so fashionable that the supply of foreign films could meet the demand. So, Ren decided to make his own films. In spring 1905, with the help of his assistants, Ren filmed a segment of *Conquering Jun Mountain*, featuring Tan Xinpei (1847–1917), then the King of *Beijing Opera*, and he continued to film some more stage performances by Tan and other renowned Beijing opera singers later that year. The fact that the earliest films attempted to integrate the new Western medium with traditional Chinese theatre says much about the terms on which film was adopted by pioneering

Chinese filmmakers. In 1909, Ren's studio was mysteriously destroyed by fire, and his short adventure into film came to an end.

Besides Ren's filmed stage performances, a number of other experimental short features were also made during the 1910s, although without exception all these early productions involved foreigners who either worked as technicians or provided finance for pioneering Chinese filmmakers. Among many foreign filmmakers who came to China, the American Benjamin Brodsky was the first to set up a studio, Asia (*Yaxiya*) Film Company. Apart from a documentary entitled China, Brodsky also produced a couple of shorts before entrusting his business to another American named Yashell, who was interested in making films about Chinese life with Chinese casts, hired Zhang Shichuan to manage the new business. Within four years, Asia Film Company had produced about eighteen films, including the first Chinese short feature — *A Difficult Couple* (1913).

Figure 3.5 China's first feature film — *A difficult Couple*. Source: 谷茂金，《影史回忆录丨No.5. 早期中国电影历史》，https://www.sohu.com/a/412751118_120051945.

Although Asia Film Company was the first to start, the Commercial Press's Motion Picture Department actually became the industry leader. As a publishing house, the Commercial Press's involvement in filmmaking was initially only minor. In 1917, an American filmmaker arrived in China to launch a big film venture. However, in two years he had spent all his money and not produced anything particularly significant, with the result that he had to sell his film equipment for a return ticket to the USA. The Commercial Press seized the opportunity to purchase all of his equipment for only three thousand yuan. In 1920, the Board of Trustees of the Commercial Press officially approved the formation of the Motion Picture Department, and within a year the department had expanded its production base by purchasing more equipment from the USA. Besides producing films, the Motion Picture Department of the Commercial Press developed film stock for other studios.

When did the term "movie" appear in China?

The term "Dianying" is a translation of the Western word "film". At the beginning of its introduction to China, since no equivalent for the term "film or movie" was available in traditional Chinese vocabulary, there were mainly translations such as "live photo", "electric theater", "machine electric light theater", and "activity electric light theater" and the like.

Based on the newspapers and magazines in the late Qing Dynasty, *dianying* was reported no later than 1903. On May 20, 1903, the *Shuntian Times* reported "The Movie Arrives Again", in which it wrote "Yesterday, the American Huahui event movie opened in Weijia Hutong, Huangtu Keng, East Fourth Archway". On November 19 of the same year, the *Shuntian Times* published another news "Beijing News — Opening a Film" said: "In the north grape field of the small sand hat alley outside Qianmen, there was a Chinese who opened a movie at dusk ... many visitors."

Figure 3.6 刊载于《图画新报》的上海四马路观影景象 . Source: 郝秉键，《电影在晚晴的传播》（“Development of Cinema In the Late Qing Dynasty”），《寻根》，2022.7.

Based on Hao Bingjian, the above advertisements appeared in *Shuntian Times* were the earliest message about *dianying*. "Film or movie" should be abbreviated as "electro optic cinema" , "electro optic activity cinema", etc., and expressions such as "electrical shadow play" (*Dianguang Yingxi*) or simply "electric shadow" (*Dianying*). Since then, *dianying* were soon deployed. When searching *Ta Kung Pao* from 1905 to 1907, the word "film" has appeared in advertisements repeatedly. These terms are suggestive of how Chinese people understood what film was taken to be. While the "electric" component of this expression emphasized the technical aspects of this new medium, "shadow play" was simply an appropriation of an existing Chinese word referring to a traditional form of popular entertainment called leather shadow play (*Piying*

Xi). The techniques and operating principles of the Chinese shadow play is quite similar to that of the motion picture. In this form of Chinese folk art, human and animal figures are carved out of leather (mostly donkey skin, which is why in many parts of China this art is also called *Lü Piying* — donkey skin shadow play) and projected on to a screen. While the puppeteers and light sources are kept to one side of the screen, the audience watches the movements and shadowy images from the other side. An example of this practice can be found in *To Live* (dir. Zhang Yimou, 1994), where the protagonist was originally a shadowplay artist. Understandably, when the Chinese first saw motion pictures, they likened them to their traditional shadow play, and because of this similarity, some Chinese are still claiming to this day that the origins of motion pictures should be traced to the traditional shadow play in China.

Figure 3.7 Donkey skin shadow play. Source: Zhou YuNan (周昱楠), "Study on the Visual Form of Pingjiang Shadow Puppets" (湖南理工学院硕士论文, 2022.5).

While "electric shadow play" was the earliest Chinese expression for film, other terms such as "Western shadow play" were also used. In fact, from the 1910s and early 1920s, "shadow play" was the most frequently used word for films. It was not until the early 1920s that the Chinese began to use the current word *dianying* to refer to the motion pictures. This progression in terminology is indicative of the progression in the Chinese understanding of this foreign medium. Obviously, the Chinese were increasingly aware of the medium's technical aspects and so began to realize the incongruity of likening films to traditional Chinese shadow plays.

Outside of questions of naming the early Chinese response to films was nothing short of enthusiastic. While some commented on how the representation of the word in movies provides the supreme demonstration of the illusive nature of reality, others were more impressed by film realism. People were amused, amazed and ultimately entertained by this new technology and the various possibilities it presented. As more films were imported into China, film-watching also became more popular.

Task 5 ▶ Reading comprehension

Direction: *MEDIA team are going to launch a discussion about the reading excerpt. They are required to summarize what they learned, share their puzzles as well as their comments on the article, and try to probe into more profound issues in this domain.*

Objectives: *Learning by doing. To cultivate students' capability of finding problems, reflecting on and solving problems independently so as to improve the comprehensive ability of using language.*

Maynor: Hi, Media team. How do you feel after reading the material above? I hope you can reflect on the progress of the filmmaking in the early period in China. As we have known, China enjoyed a glorious ancient civilization and its print media contributed so much to the world that without it, we could hardly imagine how this world would have been. While entering the electronic era, China had fallen behind the West world, which took the lead in science and technology. Why was so?

Edward: Maynor's question is so thought provoking. I share the same with Maynor. I strongly recommend that MEDIA team should do some exploration on the root of China's backwardness in the early electronic times. What can we learn from that?

Irene: You know when China was experiencing the feudal system, the West was carrying out the industrial revolution. This may account for the backwardness in the modern time.

Angela: But China led the way in the technology of print media in the Tang and Song dynasties which were also feudalistic system. Was it right?

Davis: That's quite right. But China's Tang and Song dynasties corresponded to the Western feudal era. In other word, both the East and the West had undergone the feudal system.

Irene: The distinction lies in that the Western extricated themselves from the shackles of feudal society much earlier than China.

Angela: The advanced science and technology of the West benefited from the industrial revolution. Feudal society seems synonymous with ignorance and backwardness.

Davis: Exactly. Filmmaking calls for the electronic technology which can improve people's living standard and change people's life style.

Irene: From the naming of films in Chinese, we can see that people were amused, amazed and ultimately entertained by this new technology of film production as well as the various possibilities it presented.

Edward: You are indeed quick learners prodigies. The early imported films delighted people to such a degree that the early Chinese response to films was nothing short of enthusiastic. People expressed their opinions and suggestions on film naming in Chinese. Some commented on how films depicted the illusory nature of reality, and others were more impressed by film realism.

Maynor: So finally, *dianying* was determined as the Chinese equivalent for "film or movie" in English. And China's film industry would have developed much faster, if not for obstacles like Empress Dowager Cixi.

Angela: Was there anything to do with Empress Dowager Cixi? I thought she was merely symbolic of the feudal rulers who hindered social progress.

Maynor: Actually, Empress Dowager Cixi had a significant impact on the early Chinese film industry. During her seventieth birthday celebration in 1904 in the imperial palace, the British embassy in Beijing presented her with a film projector and several film reels. Unfortunately, though the generator exploded during the screening at the party, and Cixi, taking this as a bad omen, ordered the prohibition of any future film exhibitions in the Forbidden City.

Davis: Oh. That's why the Chinese film industry's early development was slow.

Edward: Yes, Cixi's decree to prohibit officials from watching films within the imperial palace dampened the pace of the Chinese film industry's development.

Irene:	But Cixi could not prevent the wheel of history rolling forward. Film must have attracted an ever-larger audience outside the palace walls.
Maynor:	It is documented in the historical archives that by 1926, the number of cinemas in China had mushroomed to 106, with a total seating capacity of 68,000. In some of these cinemas, films were shown regularly.
Angela:	So, despite many failures, the development of film eventually prepared Chinese filmmakers for the bigger strides in the next phase.
Davis:	To some extent, the prosperity of the film industry could mark China's realization of a great leap from centuries' old feudalistic autocratic politics to people's democratic politics.
Irene:	Not only film but also TV or other digitalized media in contemporary China are developing by leaps and bounds both in terms of technology and contents.
Angela:	Yes. The history of all these humiliations is gone forever. Then, let's enjoy the bright future of China's broadcast media.
All:	In full agreement. See you soon.

Task 6 ▶ Translation practice

Direction: *MEDIA team are going to do Chinese-English translation, from which they can learn and compare how to express in cross-cultural way and convey the following paragraph in English accurately.*

Objectives: *To understand and master English morphology, syntax and idiomatic expressions, develop basic professional translation ability and promote English competence.*

广播电视是通过无线电波或导线播送音像节目的大众传媒媒介。从物质技术基础而言，广播电视是电子媒介，其采录、制作、播出、传输、接收等都依靠电子设备。广播的信息形式是声音，电视的信息形式是声音和图像，因而一切可转化为声音或图像的符号系统都可以为广播或电视所采用。对于视听媒介而言，语言、音响、音乐是三个重要的组成部分，其中语言是广播电视所采用的重要传播手段。

电影行业是指围绕影视作品所进行的生产、营销、发行、后产品开发等一系列产业链环节、厂商及相关服务所构成的工业体系。电影工业指围绕影视作品生产所需要的所有产品及服务，包括前期制作、后期制作、成品制作等环节所需要的设备技术服务及厂商等所构成的影视生产工业体系。

Task 7 ▶ Attend a public lecture

Direction: *MEDIA team are going to attend a public lecture delivered by Professor Maynor. Students are required to thoroughly understand the lecture, broaden the vision, elaborate on the theme, get inspiration from the lecture and do some speech activities to extend their knowledge.*

Objectives: *To train students' capability of description, expression, discussion, refutation, humor and humanistic accomplishment required by making a speech, thus, improving students' English language competence and proficiency.*

Lecture 3

CCTV International/CGTN Broadcasting

Professor Maynor

Hello again. Welcome back to our third lecture on TV broadcasting in China. Last time I recommended you of many reference books and historical texts concerning China's TV broadcast like Digital TV and other electronic media. As you know, our lecture time is so limited that we cannot cover all about TV broadcast or not even all about CCTV. So, in this lecture, I will only address China Central Television, especially its international broadcasting, and you can utilise the reference materials for self-learning on the subject.

It's well known that CCTV is the largest TV media in China and among the biggest in the world. CCTV International — one of the subordinate units of CCTV, has consistantly adhered to the principle of "Let the world know China and let China go to the world" to air its views, enhance China's global influence, and showcase its rise in a nonthreatening and nonconfrontational manner. That has always been the foundation of the English Channel of CCTV International. Of course, CCTV International has developed into CGTN since

2016. I'd like to highlight the evolution of the channels in CCTV's international or CGTN, together with its programs and its future development. CCTV International, earlier known as CCTV-9 and later CCTV-4 in China and eventually renamed CCTV News in 2010, presents an interesting study in its ethos and how it projects China's cultural and political appeal. Finally, I will attempt to tentatively discuss a crucial question: How has China's state-centric model helped to advance China's soft power?

The evolution of CCTV International

CCTV's predecessor Beijing TV Station, was set up in 1958 as China's first TV station. In 1963 the Publicity Department of the CPC Central Committee held the first National TV Foreign Publicity Conference. Foreign publicity for TV stations in those days simply meant exchanging news documentaries with TV stations from other countries.

Figure 3.8 Former site of CCTV

With economic reforms from the late 1970s leading to a more open China, television just played an instrumental role in constructing political and cultural discourse that created and reproduced national identity, loyalty, and pride in Chinese society. During that period of time, rather than using satellite channels to reach out directly to foreign publics, China's strategy was to publicize itself through other countries' broadcasting networks, just as the old Chinese saying: "Borrow a boat to sail the sea." It began developing partnerships with overseas Chinese and foreign TV stations, and set up joint operations abroad so that overseas broadcasting networks could carry Chinese programs. In addition, CCTV actively sought to supply programs to overseas TV stations when they ran special feature programs on China. It provided transnational media groups with programs or related materials about Chinese economy and society when they came to China to make programs.

The early 1990s marked a new phase in China's outreach to foreign affairs with the launch of satellite TV channels for international broadcasting. In 1991, CCTV set up its "Overseas Broadcasting Center". On October 1, 1992, CCTV-4, China's first international channel in Mandarin, began its broadcasting service for overseas Chinese. In 2000, CCTV expanded further and launched the 24-hour satellite English Channel. The E&F Channel (Spanish and French) followed in 2004, and started to run separately in 2008, followed by CCTV-Arabic and CCTV-Russian in 2009. There are plans to launch a Portuguese channel in 2010, thus ensuring multilingual coverage through China's satellite TV channels.

With China's growing confidence, the target audiences also changed from the peripheral to the mainstream. Because overseas Chinese are minorities in Western societies, CCTV international believed that the focus for foreign publicity should shift to the mainstream society in the United States, Europe, and neighboring countries. Therefore, they chose to use English and other foreign languages in their promotion of soft power and publicity efforts.

CCTV International programming and China's image construction

The origin of CCTV International can be traced back to English educational programs such as *Follow Me* in the early 1980s. But English TV services did not really come into existence until English news was broadcast at the end of 1986. Together with an interview program called *Focus* and more entertaining programs such as *Cultural Lounge* and *Hello Beijing*, a network of English TV programs gradually formed at CCTV. This network was later converted into CCTV-4, which became an English satellite channel serving Chinese citizens living overseas, Chinese in other countries, and international viewers who were interested in China. In 2000, the 24-hour English Channel CCTV-9 was launched, and CCTV-4 became a Mandarin language channel maintaining its global coverage by targeting overseas Chinese.

Since its inception, CCTV International has been one of China's important platforms to improve the international opinion on the world stage. It has played a major role in defining, shaping, and projecting China's image and in promoting China's viewpoint concerning a variety of global issues. Over the years, it has revamped itself a few times in hopes of becoming more competitive globally, winning over viewers in the highly saturated international media marketplace. For example, CCTV International took on a whole new look in 2003 with dramatic changes in its programming. It even started to employ foreign news anchors, which was really a practice unprecedented in recent Chinese media history. Since then, CCTV has hired more international on-air personalities. Presently, dozens of international employees are working for the channel as newscasters and television hosts to greatly enhance both the professionalism and credibility of CCTV International as an international news provider. It also changed the name "News Hour" to "CCTV International" to assert its brand and increase its international competitiveness. The network changed its tagline from "CCTV International, your window on China" to "CCTV International, your window on China and the World" in 2004, to better reflect its refined mission of acting as "a window on China for the world" and "bringing to the world the Chinese and Asian perspective on Chinese, regional and international affairs." On April 26, 2010, CCTV International changed its name to "CCTV News", and the schedule was changed accordingly. Notably, the program *CCTV News* was changed back to *News Hour*, and the tagline to "CCTV News, Your Link to Asia."

CCTV International's programming consists of news, feature programs, and a language program. An examination of the news programs, e.g., *News Hour*, *News Update*, *Asia Today*, *Biz Asia*, *Biz Talk*, *New Money*, *Culture Express*, *Dialogue*, *Sports Scene*, *World Insight*, and *China 24*, shows that the channel not only provides extensive coverage on China, Asia, and other developing nations, but also aims to present its own version of issues and events happening in these countries, thereby providing a Chinese perspective in the global arena. In addition, the channel has increased coverage on other global affairs. It is also clear that the news reports on China are not limited to politics, but also highlight China's achievements, especially in cultural and economic developments. Economic success has given China the confidence to assert itself as a global player. It is also the country's economic development that projects an image of prosperity and societal accomplishment.

Although CCTV International aims to be a 24-hour news channel, its feature program consisting of a dozen or so shows, including *Story Board*, *Journeys in Times*, *Learning Chinese*, *Cross Over*, *Rediscovering China*, *Centre Stage*, *Nature and Science*, and *Travelogue*, not only takes up a significant number of the programs, but also covers largely on China itself. CCTV International's promotion of Chinese culture is of course part of an attempt to display China as an emerging power in a peaceful manner. The channel manages to tap into multiple cultural and ethnically symbolic resources — both traditional and contemporary — it becomes a showcase for the Chinese landscape, local customs, historical legacy, and cultural artifacts. For example, the regular magazine program *Around China* in the archived programs introduces people, culture, and economic development of various regions, offering a glimpse of the beautiful scenery and rich cultural heritage in China. Both officials and professionals alike clearly see these shows as important vehicles for promoting China's international image and reinforcing China's peaceful development and advocacy of a harmonious world.

Figure 3.9 Current site of CCTV (Guanghua Road).
Source: The Introduction of CCTV, Baidu Baike.

The global development of CCTV

The global advancement of satellite capacity and the widespread use of the Internet for content distribution are creating a significant change in the ecology of global news, leading to a widespread proliferation of news channels available in different regions and across the globe. Among the emerging players in this new environment is CCTV and its advent mirrors that is growing international status of China as an economic and political actor. The roles and missions of CCTV International are obvious: They are to tell China's story to foreign audiences.

With the significant improvement of China's international status, CCTV International took on the mission of promoting China's image and showcasing China's peaceful development by providing prompt, multi-angle and balanced information. Considering different audiences from different time zones may have different interests, CCTV-4, the 24-hour comprehensive Chinese international channel, which is mainly targeted at overseas Chinese, is divided into three editions — Asia edition, Europe edition and America edition since 2007. Thus, apparently, a basic potential audience exists in the approximately 50 million Chinese living outside China. Most of them are keen to hear about their homeland and many of them prefer programming in Chinese. There is a far greater number of foreigners who know little about China and might be willing to learn more. Most of them would never have been, and indeed are unlikely to go, to China, so they know very little about its people or culture. Thus, CCTV is targeting these viewers. According to data from the State Administration of Radio, Film and Television (SARFT), more than 100 million people have watched programs from four of the CCTV international channels like CCTV Chinese, English, French and Spanish by 2009. It sends signals to the world through six satellites and has landed well in Asia, Europe and the Americas with a total of 40 million users. It has a strong desire to promote foreign broadcasting as well to strengthen China's soft power and cultural development. CCTV International is expanding its global news by updating facilities and now has regional production centers in America and in Africa. CCTV broadcasts in 140 foreign countries and can be accessed by some 1.5 billion people. It has seven international channels that broadcast in English, French, Spanish, Arabic and Russian, as well as Chinese, and seven foreign channels which transmit by satellite as part of the CCTV-4 comprehensive channel. CCTV-News is its most important journalistic output. The CCTV-4 Chinese broadcast is specifically intended for Chinese speaking people abroad, as well as for people who want to learn the Chinese language.

In addition, two digital channels were launched in North America in 2004. The Traditional Opera Channel focuses on Chinese Opera, while the Entertainment Channel aims at building an entertainment site for Chinese people abroad. Most of the Chinese people in North America come from southern China and the output reflects this with programs from Fujian and Guangdong Opera. The entertainment programs cover opera, dancing, music, old Chinese folk art, acrobatics, varieties of shows and galas among other subjects. However, soft power should not be confused with resources. The rise of soft power is not only about the power of transmission, but also about the information transmitted and effective communication with the audience. The programs above are suitable for people of all ages and the two channels keep traditional Chinese art at the top of the agenda of being modern and humorous. Consequently, CCTV can promote and enhance a mutual understanding between China and the rest of the world.

On December 31, 2016, China International Television (China Global Television Network or CGTN) was officially launched. It is formed by integrating the core external communication resources of CCTV, including CCTV English News Channel, Spanish International Channel, French International Channel, Arabic International Channel, Russian International Channel, and English Record Channel. In addition to these TV channels, CGTN also includes the International Video Communication Company under CCTV International Television Corporation, which is mainly engaged in multilingual international video publishing business. CGTN also incorporate relevant administrative departments engaged in international communication and cooperation business, such as the overseas communication center engaged in overseas landing, liaison, and international communication coordination of international television channels. It can be seen that in the founding process of CGTN, CCTV has integrated its core external communication resources in order to form joint forces and improve its communication strength, ability and competitiveness in international communication.

Since its establishment, CGTN has placed the development of integrated media in an unprecedented position. CGTN put it to the top priority to tell a good story about China and spread a good voice of China with rich information, bright Chinese perspective and broad world vision. CGTN has also paid more attention to the principle of balance in its external dissemination. While allowing Chinese stories to "go global", it also attaches importance to "invite in" overseas stories, to continue to strengthen research on the audience and form discourse methods and expression techniques suitable for Western audiences in order to enhance international communication effectiveness and enhance discourse power. As the flagship media for publicity, CGTN keeps on treating the path innovation and content innovation of international communication as the core issue, and opens up the international communication road. With the theme of "Community of Shared Future", they aims to create a better tomorrow in the 21st century.

Figure 3.10 CGTN: China global television network. Source: Official website of CGTN.

That's all for what I want to talk today. I am sure that up to now you're convinced that the extensive global coverage of CCTV International or CGTV significantly improves the world's understanding of China and Chinese culture. It allows Chinese voice to be heared globally. With the goal of "Inherit civilization, explore and innovate", CCTV continues to modernize and move forward, striving to become a leading international TV station in the world.

Task 8 ▶ Online forum and summary writing

Direction: *MEDIA team are going to launch an instant online post-talk about the lecture to appeal to more of other students who are interested in the topic to join them. This is an integrated practice of listening, speaking, reading and writing. They are particularly expected to write a summary of the entire unit.*

Objectives: *To provide a platform for MEDIA team to fully display their talents. To comb language learning with professional knowledge so as to cultivate students' professional learning, academic literacy and language competence. To realize the teaching objectives of acquiring professional knowledge through learning English language.*

Irene: Oh, my partners. I finally recovered from my depression due to the early Chinese filmmaking period. Now I am cheerful about our contemporary TV services, especially CCTV International. People almost across the world can gain access to various information through CCTV International.

Davis: I want to share your joy. Since the establishment of CCTV International, it has adopted various strategies to drive it forward. I think it is inseparable from the support of the government.

Angela: I think so. It's widely known that China Central Television Station is a state-run television station and is the only station in China with a national network. CCTV International can be actually regarded as an example of how China keeps state-owned companies profitable while transitioning from government control toward a more market-orientated approach. It operates both as a mouthpiece for the government and a profitable commercial business, boasting an audience larger than any other major television network worldwide.

Irene: Yes. I couldn't agree more. This reflects the advantages of China's political system. From the lecture, we can safely conclude that CCTV International plays a variety of functions such as news dissemination, social education, cultural entertainment, information services and the like. It serves as the main channel for the national public to obtain information, an important window for China to understand the world and for the world to understand China, and a platform for CCTV to tell China's stories well.

Davis: Apart from your remark on its role of publicizing China and building its culture image and soft power, CCTV also earn revenue as well. For example, CCTV carries advertising and its rates have been rising at 20%–30% per year. The advertising slots are auctioned annually and, in November 2012, bids netted a record return of nearly $2.6 billion.

Angela: Absolutely. According to relevant research institutions, the broadcast revenue of the 2022 Beijing Winter Olympics alone exceeds $1.1 billion. The large sponsorship income and the high ratings have brought considerable profits to CCTV.

Edward: Your comments on CCTV are all reasonable. But I would like to remind everyone of the focus of Maynor's lecture and our discussion.

Irene: Yeah. We should turn back to CCTV International. Here I'd like to air my view about the nature of CCTV International, which is a multilingual, multi-faceted and multi-perspective broadcaster. It also undertakes to correct some misunderstanding by Western media that focus too extensively and exaggeratedly on negative issues when covering China.

Maynor: You make a very good point, Irene. CCTV International indeed faces significant competition from the famous media outlets such as BBC, CNN and VOA. Nevertheless, CCTV International ushers in a turnaround and is in the course of transformation.

Edward: By the way, what about Al Jazeera English Channel?

Maynor: Al Jazeera English Channel belongs to Qatar TV, which is owned by the state of Qatar. For some time, many foreign viewers viewed this broadcaster with suspicion, and some even labelled it as the "Negative Television" due to its coverage of non-state organizations challenging Western nations and culture.

Davis:	And what follows that?
Irene:	It was certainly regarded as a political tool of Qatar, right?
Angela:	From what I gathered, it is now one of the most powerful broadcasting media in the Middle East and the Islamic world, and there is no doubt that it has a significant influence on the wider international stage.
Maynor:	Exactly. No matter how the Western politicians and scholars defamed and slandered Al Jazeera, it has kept on marching forward bravely by sticking to what was thought right. And finally, its international reputation has improved over time and it is clear that Al Jazeera speaks with an independent voice and has its own viewpoint, except when matters concerning Qatari foreign policy arise.
Edward:	It's reported that the Al Jazeera English Channel successfully underwent a transformation since its caunch in 2006. It now reach a potential audience of some 206 million people in 130 countries worldwide.
Davis:	So, CCTV can learn from Al Jazeera's experience and has its own way ahead.
Irene:	I firmly belive that as the media transformation deepens, mutual learning among media outlets has become an essential aspact of their development.
Angela:	CCTV International will have higher ratings and loyal viewers.
All:	Let's go on with next topic.

Appendix: Vocabulary for Unit 3

Listening Activity

transmitter /træns'mɪtə(r)/ *n.*（尤指广播、电视信号）发射机，发射台；传播者，传递媒介

formalize /'fɔːməlaɪz/ *vt.* 使形式化；使正式；拘泥礼仪
vi. 拘泥于形式

bulletin /ˈbʊlətɪn/ *n.*（广播或电视中的）新闻简报；公告，布告；（机构或社团的）通讯，刊物

joint-venture /ˌdʒɔɪnt ˈventʃə(r)/ *n.* 合资企业；联合经营

endeavor /ɪnˈdevə(r)/ *n.* 努力；尽力

advent /ˈædvent/ *n.* 出现，到来，问世；基督降临节（Advent）

pivot /ˈpɪvət/ *n.* 支点，枢轴；最重要的人（或事物），核心；转动，旋转；
v.（使）在枢轴上旋转；（以脚为支点）转身；（为机械装置）提供枢轴

portal /ˈpɔːtl/ *n.*（建筑物的）壮观的大门，正门；门户网站，入口站点
adj.（剖）门静脉的，肝门的

counterpart /ˈkaʊntəpɑːt/ *n.* 对应的人（或事物）；（法律文件的）副本

panoramic /ˌpænəˈræmɪk/ *adj.* 全景的，远景的

Reading Activity

genre /ˈʒɒnrə/ *n.* 体裁，类型；风俗画
adj. 属于某类型的，按某种风格创作的

symphonic /sɪmˈfɒnɪk/ *adj.* 交响乐的；交响性的；和声的

indigenous /ɪnˈdɪdʒənəs/ *adj.* 本土的，固有的

assimilate /əˈsɪməleɪt/ *v.* 融入，（使）同化；吸收，理解；使相似，成为相似

novelty /ˈnɒv(ə)lti/ *n.* 新颖，新奇性；新奇的事物；廉价小饰物，小玩意儿
adj. 新奇的，风格独特的

testimony /ˈtestɪməni/ *n.*（尤指法庭上的）证词，证言；证据，证明

motif /məʊˈtiːf/ *n.* 主题；主旨；图形；意念；基序，模体

thematic /θɪˈmætɪk/ *adj.* 主题的，主旋律的；题目的；语干的

orientation /ˌɔːriənˈteɪʃ(ə)n/ *n.* 目标，定位；方向，朝向；（基本的）态度，倾向

overthrow /ˌəʊvəˈθrəʊ/ *v.* 推翻，打倒；背弃，摒弃；投（球）过猛，投球超过（接手或目标）
n. 推翻，打倒；投球过远，投球过猛

disintegration /dɪsˌɪntɪˈgreɪʃn/ *n.* 分裂，解体；蜕变，衰变

intervention /ˌɪntəˈvenʃ(ə)n/ *n.* 干预，介入；调停，斡旋

the Boxer Uprising 义和团；义和团运动

penetration /ˌpenəˈtreɪʃ(ə)n/ *n.* 穿透，渗透，进入；（产品对市场的）渗透度，占有率

Spaniard /ˈspænɪəd/ *n.* 西班牙人

acrobatic /ˌækrəˈbætɪk/ *adj.* 杂技的；特技的

exotica /ɪgˈzɒtɪkə/ *n.* 新奇事物，异族事物

blonde /blɒnd/ *adj.* 金黄色的，浅棕色的；金发的；浅色的
n. 长着金发的人
wrestle /ˈres(ə)l/ *v.* 摔跤，扭打；使劲搬动，用力操作；努力解决，艰难对付
n. 摔跤，角力；艰苦的斗争，搏斗
reminiscent /ˌremɪˈnɪs(ə)nt/ *adj.* 使人联想的；怀旧的，缅怀往事的；与……相像的
diametrically /ˌdaɪəˈmetrɪkli/ *adv.* 完全地；作为直径地；直接地；正好相反地
concession /kənˈseʃn/ *n.* 让步，妥协；特许权
renowned /rɪˈnaʊnd/ *adj.* 有名望的，著名的
v. 使有声誉（renown 的过去式和过去分词形式）
puppeteer /ˌpʌpɪˈtɪə(r)/ *n.* 操纵木偶的人；操纵傀儡
vt. 操纵
protagonist /prəˈtægənɪst/ *n.* （戏剧、电影、小说等的）主人公；（比赛、斗争中的）主要人物，主要参与者；（政策、运动的）倡导者，拥护者
liken /ˈlaɪkən/ *vt.* 比拟；把……比作
incongruity /ˌɪnkənˈgruːəti/ *n.* 不协调；不一致；不适宜

Lecture

ethos /ˈiːθɒs/ *n.* （某团体的）精神特质，道德意识
tentatively /ˈtentətɪvli/ *adv.* 暂时地；试验性地
predecessor /ˈpriːdəsesə(r)/ *n.* 前任，前辈；（被取代的）原有事物，前身
peripheral /pəˈrɪfərəl/ *adj.* 次要的，附带的；外围的，周边的；（计算机设备）外围的
n. （计算机的）外部设备
inception /ɪnˈsepʃn/ *n.* （机构、组织等的）开端，创始
revamp /ˈriːvæmp/ *v.* 修改，翻新，改进
n. 翻新，改建，改组
saturate /ˈsætʃəreɪt/ *v.* 使湿透，浸透；使充满，使饱和；充斥（市场），使（市场）供大于求；使（化学溶液）饱和；饱和磁化；饱和充电；饱和轰炸
adj. 湿透的；饱和的
n. 饱和脂肪
anchor /ˈæŋkə(r)/ *n.* 锚；支柱，靠山；商场；〈美〉新闻节目主持人
v. 抛锚，泊（船）；使稳固，使固定；成为支柱；主持（新闻节目）
adj. 末棒的，最后一棒的

tagline /ˈtæglaɪn/ *n.* 标语；品牌口号

assert /əˈsɜːt/ *v.* 坚称，断言；维护，坚持（权利或权威）；坚持自己的主张，表现坚定；生效，起作用

legacy /ˈlegəsi/ *n.* 遗产，遗赠物；遗留问题，后遗症
adj.（软件或硬件）已过时但因使用范围广而难以替代的

arena /əˈriːnə/ *n.* 竞技场，圆形剧场；斗争场所，活动舞台

artifact /ˈɑːtɪfækt/ *n.*（尤指有文化价值或历史价值的）人工制品，历史文物

proliferation /prəˌlɪfəˈreɪʃn/ *n.*（数量的）激增，剧增；（细胞、组织、有机体的）繁殖，增生

acrobatics /ˌækrəˈbætɪks/ *n.* 杂技；巧妙手法

gala /ˈgɑːlə/ *n.* 盛会，庆典；〈英〉体育运动会，体育竞赛（尤指游泳）
adj. 节日的，欢庆的，欢乐的

Unit 4

New Media and Its Impact on China

TABLE OF CONTENTS

Unit 4 New Media and Its Impact on China

Warm-up: Be proactive

Direction: *MEDIA team are going to do warm-up activities by discussing, airing their views on the topic and discovering problems.*

Objectives: *To arouse students' interest, get a preliminary understanding of relevant knowledge and prepare for the following study.*

Irene: Hello dear MEDIA partners. It's time for a new topic on new media. I think all of us will enjoy this because nobody could live without cellphone or internet. In short, new media become a must for almost everyone. Are you ready for that?

Angela: All set for me. I think I have equipped myself with a reservoir of knowledge in this domain. I am eager to accept challenges from either you or our supervisors.

Davis: Are you sure you're not bragging, Angela? I hope that I'm on a par with you.

Irene: Now that you've got over-ready, please share with us by initiating the relay-question and whoever can answer this question will continue put forward another question, and like this, round after round.

Davis: I wholeheartedly agree with you, Irene. Let's give Angela a round of warm applause.

Angela: As a Chinese saying goes: "Let me throw a cast to attract jade." Guys, have you thought about the new changes brought about by the emergence of any new technology? For instance, technological innovations such as the steam engine, electricity, wireless communication and the Internet all have had lasting and significant effects on our world.

Davis: That's right, Angela. You did think profoundly. Your questions are so philosophical. We can safely say that new media technologies both spring from and cause social changes alike. And the birth of one new technology usually depends on the other and brings out the best in each other.

Irene: Exactly. Everything in the world is interrelated. The contemporary media can trace its origin back to the electrical telegraph. Thanks to the telegraph, communication was no longer linked to the physical transportation of messages. It didn't matter whether a message needed to travel 5 or 500 miles.

Angela: Yes. Why information from distant places was nearly as accessible as local news was because telegraph lines began to stretch across the globe, making their own kind of World Wide Web.

Davis: In this way, we can say the telegraph acted as the precursor to much of the communication technology that followed, including the telephone, radio, television, and Internet.

Angela: That's only too true. To my knowledge, when the first transatlantic cable was laid in approximately 1858, allowing nearly instantaneous communication from the United States to Europe, the *London Times* described it as "the greatest discovery since that of Columbus, a vast enlargement... given to the sphere of human activity".

Irene: So transatlantic cable made wireless communication available, and eventually led to the development of radio, television, and other broadcast media which emerged as an extension of telegraph technology.

Davis: Therefore, what we've actually expounded is the transitional progress that new media have been experiencing constant changes from traditional face-to-face communication to print media, TV, radio and to internet-based media.

Angela: So, we can say that the history of media evolution represents the history of the development of human society.

Irene: So, it's necessary for us to go on comparing the differences between new media and traditional media. How does new media change this world?

Davis: Don't worry about that. In the following listening practice, Professor Edward will deliver us a wonderful report on new media and old media, which will greatly enrich our knowledge in this field.

Angela: Wow, I am really looking forward to obtain more information.

All: Let's go on with the listening activity.

Task 1 ▶ Listening activity

Direction: *MEDIA team are going to listen to an introduction of key concepts so as to lay the foundation for later learning.*

Objectives: *To understand the main conception, practice and strengthen the ability of listening comprehension.*

Contrastive Analysis: New Media vs Traditional Media

New media is a new tool of information dissemination with the Internet as its carrier. It is different from traditional media and was born out of the rapid development of internet technology. The disseminator of information has changed from some authoritative media organizations to every individual. Everyone can spread information through new media platforms without any identity restrictions. Relying on the Internet, communication costs are very low. Compared with old media, communication technology and costs are essentially different. This internet-based new media enjoys the feature of high interaction, something difficult in traditional media where fans rarely interact with the authors. New media prefers content plus social activity. It is the general name of internet-based communication. Therefore, one important question should be firstly clarified: What is new about new media represented by the Internet compared with old media?

New media have brought a plurality of news forms and participation models, subverting the traditional media's monopoly on news production. Despite this, new media still rely upon the reporting generated by traditional media to grow. Traditional media consumers have slowly evolved from passive, isolated individuals into creators as well as consumers of information. However, these untrained news information producers often rely on emotion or sensationalism to judge the validity and worth of their content, resulting in variable quality. The best part is that bloggers, Web-loggers, and other amateur journalists are scooping traditional news outlets as well as pointing out errors, while people who have been made subjects of news articles are responding online, posting supplementary information to provide context and counterpoints. Increasingly, the public is turning to online sources for news.

Figure 4.1 New media vs. traditional media. Source: Team Leverage Edu., "New Media Definition, Courses and Scope", updated in Apr. 2023.

As traditional media slowly become more integrated with new media, causing changes in content. While at first traditional media simply duplicated content and republished information online, their online presence has quickly evolved into a more hybridized system, closely mirroring the structure of portal websites. This evolution led to quicker information updates, more interactive news pages and more multimedia elements. For example, Caijing, Caixin Media, and other traditional media outlets have added blogs to their sites; both CCTV and People's Daily provide Weibo services to their readers; the Southern Metropolitan News website has a video section; and many others solicit and use reader-contributed content. Journalists are blogging live from the field; for breaking news, Weibo allows them to post frequent updates in near real-time.

Commercial portal websites mostly assimilate already existing information. As traditional media news websites implement faster updates and increased interactivity, portal websites have increasingly organized news stories and comments into different "special topics" like web pages and packages devoted to a special issue or niche interests to facilitate readers' access and to provide in-depth analysis.

The advent of new internet media technologies and applications, such as mobile internet and Web logging, has created a convenient and easy-to-use channel for ordinary people to quickly create and retrieve information. Social Networks (SNS) rely on interpersonal connections between users, increasing the speed at which news information travels across social groups, as well as the scope and depth that it permeates society. The expansion of these new communications channels has greatly promote the dissemination of knowledge and ideas through content producers, professional news producers and media organizations. New media supported by technology fostered the development of three important elements that changed the structure of traditional journalistic practices: configurative resources, production rules and authoritative resources, which enable us to see clearly the "change" and the "invariance" of traditional media in the changing times. The adoption of new media technologies forms the way that people engage in social interaction and meaning construction on the Internet.

New media thoroughly breaks the stereotypes and misconceptions on information reception and dissemination across various social strata. It not only deepens our understanding of the potential of media technology, but also provides a reference for future consideration on communication methodologies.

Task 2 ▶ Listening comprehension

Direction: *MEDIA team are going to have a topic-oriented discussion to exchange their views on the listening material and challenge each other with puzzling questions.*

Objectives: *To broaden students' horizon, develop their ability to sum up the skills of answering questions and strengthen language output ability.*

Maynor: Hello again, MEDIA team. Having heard the above analysis, you must have been quite inspired. Although I am sure you may be fairly aware of the distinction between old media and new media, I still can't help recommending you to take such points as the concepts of new media, its way of communication, its multiple functions and its impact etc. into consideration, because these issues are fundamental.

Irene: We certainly cherish your valuable recommendation. I propose that we start with the definition of new media. May I have your opinion, guys?

Davis: I give total consent to Professor Maynor and Irene. But I think the definition of new media is too easy to discuss.

I can explain it myself. New media is internet-based communication media, isn't it?

Angela: Davis, you are just partially right. Actually, it is so complicated that we can't summarize the definition in just one sentence.

Irene: I think so. New media cover so many aspects and hardware like internet, wireless radio signal, computer, and mobile phones, and so on.

Davis: I see now. Then we should try to simplify these complex problems. How about categorizing all contents contained in new media first?

Angela: Davis has a good head on his shoulders. Let me try to identify the roles that new media perform in our society.

Edward: Honestly, I acknowledge Angela's view. Media do fulfill several basic roles in our society. One obvious role is to provide information and education, and the next role is entertainment. Media can act as a springboard for our imaginations, a source of fantasy, and an outlet for escapism. And...

Irene: Excuse me. But I cann't wait to interpose a remark. Above all, the most useful aspect of media is its ability to act as a public forum for the discussion of important issues as we do online or through mobile devices. You guys agree with me?

Edward: You have fared particularly well, Irene. One more role of new media is used to monitor government, business, and other institutions.

Maynor: So, we can categorize new media into four domains: entertaining and providing an outlet for the imagination; educating and informing; serving as a public forum for the discussion of important issues; acting as a watchdog for government, business, and other institutions.

Irene, Angela & Davis: What a brilliant summary!

Irene: How about stepping into the next discussion about the communication way of new media?

Angela: I am eager to make clear about its multiple functions and its impact.

Davis: Let's express our opinions at will instead of according to the regulations, OK?

Maynor: No problem, as you wish. Only one requirement is that your standpoints of view should be internally connected and logically coherent.

Edward: And fundamental questions should have priority so that your comprehension is of integration rather than fragmentation.

Angela: We'll try to be on track. Different media possesses different function and impact. While some forms of new media are better suited to entertainment, others make more sense as a venue for spreading information.

Davis: Sure. Take television as an example. It provides vastly more visual information than radio and is more dynamic than a static printed page. It can also be used to broadcast live events to a nationwide audience or even worldwide.

Irene: Compared with internet media, TV is a one-way medium. I mean it allows for very little direct person-to-person communication. In contrast, the Internet encourages public discussion of issues and allows nearly everyone who wants a voice.

Angela: But the Internet is also largely unmoderated. Users may have to wade through thousands of inane comments or misinformed amateur opinions to find quality information.

Davis: This is confirmed by what the computer scientist Alan Kay said: "Each medium has a special way of representing ideas that emphasize particular ways of thinking and de-emphasize others."

Irene: Together with the Internet, the inventions of random-access memory (RAM) chips and microprocessors in the 1970s laid the foundation for the full internet age. The technological innovation gave birth to personal computers and the Internet which revolutionized the way people lived.

Angela: Web has become an important and indispensable global communication channel, which make it available for individuals to present themselves freely in virtual reality. Without Web, there would be no social media and social network sites (SNSs). However, it's just social media and social network sites that have tremendous impact on almost every aspect of the society including individual's social life.

Edward: Dear all, I think your discussion has covered almost all basic problems with regard to new media. How about marching on the further exploration?

All: Okay. So much for today. See you later.

Task 3 ▶ Pre-reading activity

Direction: *This part serves as connecting link between the preceding and the following. MEDIA team are required to ponder over some problems concerning the whole unit, reflect on them and then find solutions. The answers are open-ended.*

Objectives: *To cultivate students' capability of exploring problems, develop critical thinking ability synchronously and improve expression ability.*

1. How do you interpret the concept of "new media"?
2. Please try to explain the distinction between new media and old media.
3. How does new media affect both society and individuals?
4. How was new media related to many other key words concerning new communication technology at the onset?
5. What stages has new media gone through?
6. How did the emergence of new media reshape the value logic of many arenas on the macro level?
7. How did Douyin exemplify the impact of new media on individuals on the micro level?
8. Who are the leading practitioners of new media? And why?
9. Why were texting messages once ubiquitous?
10. Why are internet-based new media so influential or even powerful?

Task 4 ▶ Reading activity

Direction: *MEDIA team are required to read the following excerpt to obtain information, expand vocabulary volume, increase knowledge reserve, comprehend between lines, appreciate the writing style and evaluate the article.*

Objectives: *To cultivate students' capability of reading and absorbing information in a way that "eyes see quickly and brain processes quickly" to enhance reading comprehension, build up logic thinking, learn writing through reading and improve students' comprehensive quality.*

A Review of Internet-Based New Media in China

The origin of new media

China formally joined the Internet in 1994, marking the onset of a new era of communication. 28 years later, China's internet has flourished along with its economy. The number of Chinese internet users has reached 1.01 billion, accounting more than 70% of population of China and for one-fifth of the global internet population. The Internet penetration rate has reached 71.6%, exceeding the global average as of June 2021. Many activities in the traditional offline world have been made online. In this sense, China has basically entered the "network society". Internet-based communication technology has gradually replaced traditional media and underpinned the whole society. New media covered four main clusters, namely media convergence, internet-based communication, social media, and big data. The synonyms in the keywords were merged. For example, medium convergence was the merging of distinct technologies or devices into a unified whole, i.e., media convergence; socialized media was merged into social media; internet public opinion and microblog public opinion were merged into public opinion; and network governance was merged into Internet governance.

In terms of keyword frequency, new media, media convergence, internet, social media, microblog, public opinion and big data were among in the top seven. Among them, internet was the first to appear and reached its peak in 2001, and has remained stable since then. From 2002 to 2005, no new high-frequency keyword emerged. The period from 2006 to 2012 saw the emergence of a number of Web2.0-related concepts. These include Web2.0 and social network. And between 2013 and 2016, some new hot topics related to internet governance started to appear. Microblog, social media, public opinion and big data grew strongly in 2011, 2012, and 2013 respectively. Microblog, in particular, broke the monopoly of new media and media convergence in 2013 and became the most frequently used keyword that year. The academic began to be more concerned with terminals connected by the network — the computer — and preferred to define the future as the computer age. In other words, it was not the network but the computer that seemed powerful. The network was just an optical fiber medium to connect terminals for the purpose of communication, which did not look essentially different from the existing telephone and television networks. New hot topics after 2016 are mainly related to "intelligence", such as artificial intelligence and algorithms etc.

The progress of internet-based new media

The inception of the Internet coincided with the global popularity of the concept of "information highway". Western countries attached great importance to national information infrastructure, bringing the information network represented by computer networks to the forefront. In China, the information highway became a precursor of internet-based communication.

At the same time, commercialization of China's internet also took place. In 1998, with the establishment of websites such as Sina, Sohu and NetEase, the Chinese internet entered the portal era. The concept of the Internet as the "fourth media" after newspaper, radio and television has drawn people's attention. From the initial focus on how the network or information highway affected the mass media, to the later emphasis on how the Internet affected communication way, and then to the impact of the network on society, especially democratic politics, China's internet-based communication reached some preliminary results and were gaining momentum fast.

The term "network media" became increasingly popular. A large number of teaching materials and monographs were published, mainly focusing on the

Figure 4.2 Web-based media. Source: 《2017 世界移动互联网大会暨新媒体门户大会》, https://www.sohu.com/a/133212103_572633.

impact of the Internet on traditional media, with quite a number of practical studies on news-related topics such as online journalism. Universities and colleges also set up specialized institutions for internet-based communication to conduct related teaching and research. The conceptual thinking on the Internet was further deepened, and the multiple attributes of the network were observed in various dimensions. This was also the heyday of Bulletin Board Systems (BBS) represented by Mop, Tian, Xici and Strong Nation Forum under the *People's Daily*. The rise of e-commerce websites such as Taobao brought the internet economy into view. Generally, internet media covers three types: news media, social media and web media.

In 2005, the blog, born several years ago, finally reached an inflexion point. China's earliest blog site Blog China received around 70 million yuan in venture capital; Sina, Tencent, Sohu and other portals made every effort to build a blog business. Blogging became the third major form of Internet media after portals and BBS. A part of very active internet users spread from BBS to blogs, and became the first group of online opinion leaders (commonly known as "Big Vs"). A large number of mass incidents began to attract broad attention, and internet mobilization and activism emerged. This heralded the beginning of a new era for China's internet.

This exciting atmosphere began to spread to especially the academic world around 2006, leading to a new understanding of the Internet and the acceleration of Western concepts such as "new media" and Web2.0 to replace the old inventory of "fourth media" and information highway as the mainstream discourse. Public opinion, public sentiment and citizen journalism got the first taste of the spotlight.

After 2009, microblogging *Weibo* emerged as a new force and soon replaced blogs as the most powerful digital medium. Microblog sites, especially Sina Weibo, became the curator of a series of major public discussions. "New media" and "Weibo" emerged as keywords in the six major Chinese journalism

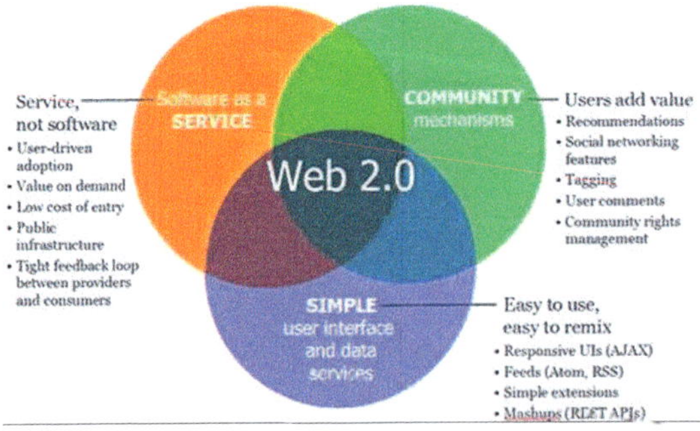

Figure 4.3 The features of Web 2.0-based media. Source: 《关于 Web 2.0》, www.iteye.com/blog/kay2008-166428.

and communication journals and related studies surged and peaked between 2009 and 2013.

2013 marked a turning point for the Internet in China. A large number of central-level media such as provincial and municipal newspapers opened official microblogs, joining hands with nearly 200,000 microblog accounts of government departments to create a "microblogging national team" to guide public opinions on unexpected events and sensitive issues. All these initiatives had effectively changed the ecology of public opinion on the Internet. By 2015, microblogs became one loud voice on China's internet as a tremendous source of public debates.

China's Internet is seeing a new spring in commercialization. In 2013, the Ministry of Industry and Information Technology (MIIT) officially issued 4G licenses to China's three major telecom operators, namely, China Mobile, China Unicom, and China Telecom. With the launch of a new generation of mobile internet, killer applications and business models kept emerging: 2014 saw the strong rise of WeChat. In 2016, live streaming and mobile games were in full swing, while in 2017, short videos were on fire across the country, and in 2019, live-streaming e-commerce became a new gold mine. During this period, as mobile internet users surpassed desktop internet users, China leapfrogged the West on consumer internet innovations: from scan to pay to dock-less bike sharing, from knowledge payment to short video social networking, China's internet became a force to be reckoned with in the global cyberspace. New trends in cloud computing, big data and artificial intelligence made internet-based communication thriving.

Around 2016, a mixture of digital populism and popular culture centered on the post-90s began to be in vogue. Influenced by fan culture, this group brought the "battle" experience formed in the process of commercial consumption in star worshipping into patriotic actions. New communication and the popular culture industry exerted a great influence, especially in ACG (Animation, Comic, Game) culture where national discourse has to be transformed into a coding system of cuteness that can project emotional identity. The new logic of collective actions of youth groups in the era of visual communication turned into a new type of political participation. Online mimics had strong communication effects and infectious power, providing a new mobilization model for cyber nationalist movements.

After 2019, China's commercial internet experienced yet another important turn. In business field, with a high internet penetration rate and the disappearance of the population dividend, internet companies are all looking for new development opportunities. Pony Ma, Chairman and CEO of Tencent, said in an exclusive interview that China's internet was facing "transformation from a consumer internet to an industrial internet", which means "it is gradually transforming from providing services such as information, searching, e-commerce, shopping and social networking to being deeply integrated with various industries". This view also triggered echoes across the country, forming a social media landscape.

Figure 4.4 A social media landscape.
Source: 漂石，《浅谈国内社会化媒体营销和营销案例分析》.

New media's impact on China

The communication characteristics of new media generates the impact on individuals and society as well, thus building a logic of "change of communication tools — change of communication models — change of living styles plus change of communication relationships and reconstruction of values".

At the macro level, the biggest impact is the reconfiguration of power relations. The development of the Internet in China over the past 20 years had been a process in which information technologies evolved from communication tools, channels, media and platforms to fundamental social elements, which had essentially changed the scenes and ways of human interactions, and promoted the transformation of social relation networks from a differential mode of association and an organizational mode of association to an open, interactive and complex distributed network, triggering a change in the rules of resource allocation and power distribution patterns. As a new source of power, the Internet activates individuals and self-organized groups to participate in the media publicity, facilitating the interaction between people.

The emergence of new media has also reshaped the value logic of many arenas. The social media agenda is influencing the professional media agenda. After interventions of multiple actors in the news field, the boundaries of news are increasingly blurred, bringing a series of outcomes: News becomes the product of collaboration and competition among multiple subjects; journalism is more opinion-based rather than news-based; and the traditional news matrix is overturned by a new narrative of social media. News values have also experienced great changes, from "being new" to "being live", from salience to usefulness, from geographical proximity to psychological intimacy, and from human interest to pleasing the crowd. The charm of news content itself has been replaced by the charm of news rhetoric. For example, regarding the impact of microblogging on the public sphere, microblogs serve as a distribution center of multivariate information, an amplifier of grassroots opinion and a test zone of communicative rationality. However, at the same time, they also find that the fragmentation of microblog content and communication modes make microbloggers akin to "a fleeting public" with "bad news syndrome" and "shock experience".

New media has largely changed the original social relations and the way Chinese people participate in the public life. It is "seeing" rather than "hiding" that forms the foundation of the public sphere. Only through "visibility", i.e., fully displaying differentiated discourses and legitimizing differences, can there be real dialogues and understanding.

On the micro level, the impact of new media on individuals is more diverse, involving many dimensions, such as individual perceptions, degree of rationality, self-awareness, and emotions. In terms of self-awareness, *Douyin* can be an example. It provides users with a highly selective self-reference system and promotes a unique value standard, while viewers realize their cognitive selves and accomplish value perception of their social class through aimless immersive viewing, imagination of co-viewers and a specific interactive mode. As for shedding new lights on online dialogue, the decentralization and individualization of new media have made the dissemination of subcultures more like a monologue. People are increasingly self-talking and immerse in a self-created online mini-world. In addition, *Jinri Toutiao* (literally "Today's Headlines"), a news aggregator, is effective in increasing users' awareness of current news and therefore enhancing their self-confidence, despite the fact that the application presents a mix of serious news, opinion, entertainment and practical information. The quality of news content it aggregates fluctuates greatly.

To conclude, the profound changes brought about by new media are far from stopping at the functional level of satisfying the various needs of internet users. They are and will continue to construct new ways of human existence and the meaning of that existence. Therefore, the internet-based new media will further propel human communication. So, it is important to deepen the exploration and discovery of the subjective and inner world of human beings by studying the core internet issues, the personal experiences and social practices of ordinary people. Hence, the Internet is not just a technology tool, but has created a whole set of systems and cultures that are closely intertwined with human daily life.

Task 5 ▶ Reading comprehension

Direction: *MEDIA team are going to launch a discussion about the reading excerpt. They are required to summarize what they learned, share their puzzles as well as their comments on the article, and try to probe into more profound issues in this domain.*

Objectives: *Learning by doing. To cultivate students' capability of finding problems, reflecting on and solving problems independently so as to improve the comprehensive ability of using language.*

Edward: Hi, dear all. What impress you most from this reading excerpt? Professor Maynor and I hold that through this reading you can draw a panoramic view. So this time both of us will act as your viewers instead of participants. Do you agree?

Maynor: But we will be very particular about your performance. Why we leave you doing discussion by yourselves is that this excerpt is written in chronological way and the language itself is simple and clear. You can make it definitely. Of course, the analysis and language output will still be very challenging. But we are confident in all of you.

Irene: Are you aware of what our supervisors mean, Angela and Davis? I think this discussion is actually a kind of test or at least a quiz.

Davis: Whatever it is, we'd better take it seriously. That is what we students should always adhere to. The first thing for us to do is to determine what we will focus on in our discussion. In my viewpoint, since the reading material has offered us an overall review, what we should do is to explore the deeper implication of both old and new media. Am I right?

Angela: Yes. In view of the present topic "A Review of Internet-Based New Media in China", why do new media are internet-based? What effect do internet-based new media have on both Chinese society and people?

Irene: Your question is really valuable. Let me try to explain your questions. Firstly, Internet and Web function mutually have become an important and indispensable global communication channel. It's said that more than four billion users, about 45% of the world population, have internet connection. China has the most users, accounting for nearly 30% of the total. Following that, Web presence is vital for business. Website manifests as the company image in new media to promote company brand, provide company information and services to customers or business partners. In a word, Internet is influencing all the aspects of the society.

Davis: Terrific, Irene. The interactivity of new media reshapes the way we interact and communicate with others from originally "one to one" and "one to many" to "many to many". Thus, new media can drive globalization on cross-cultural communication and facilitate democratization in a way to promote social change.

Angela: You guys are really quick-minded. I am pleased that I share the same view. Whether traditional or new media both act as the mass communication channel disseminating culture, entertainment, information, and edification in the old forms such as radio, television, and print media and more recently in the new digital forms through Internet with technology advancement. All in all, the key is how Chinese culture influences new media or specifically what Chinese cultural values are reflected through new media.

Irene: So, when examining the impact of new media in the context of China, we should take a cultural perspective. As can be seen, Chinese society has experienced changes in its social ecology with industrialization, advanced education, urbanization, and media development for the last several decades.

Davis: Obviously, culture values are reflected in the website contents and structures, and cultural adaption in the websites can enhance usability.

Angela: And new media can be especially sensitive to cultural differences due to its characteristics. Web is an open network and the global accessibility which makes the vast cultural variability of websites. The interactive nature of Web provides functions such as hyperlinks and search.

Irene: Internet technology promotes media convergence that supports creation of websites with audio, video, graphic, and text. According to some research findings, culturally congruent websites that closely match the social perceptions of users are more likely to engage the users.

Maynor: Wow, I think you have discussed deep-seated issues. You expounded the core problems or essence of the reading material.

Edward: I am truly proud of you — MEDIA team. Each of you has well devoted to your assignment and fulfilled a good job. I am sure that Maynor shares the same as I.

Maynor: Exactly. Let's pause here and save energy for the following courses.

All: Okay. Let's get going.

Task 6 ▶ Translation practice

Direction: *MEDIA team are going to do Chinese-English translation, from which they can learn and compare how to express in cross-cultural way and convey the following paragraph in English accurately.*

Objectives: *To understand and master English morphology, syntax and idiomatic expressions, develop basic professional translation ability and promote English competence.*

新媒体指数字化信息技术时代在新的技术主导下应运而生的一种全新的媒体形态。新媒体是一个动态的概念，其内涵本身在不断发展和变化。新媒体主要包括互联网新媒体、手机新媒体、户外新媒体和衍生新媒体四类，其中以手机和计算机作为信息载体的新媒体对社会的影响最为深刻，任何行为个体都可以应用它们达到获取信息、分享信息、生产信息、表达感情等目的。新媒体注重个性化服务，具有个性化与海量化的特点。互联网新媒体是以互联网为传播渠道的新媒体类型，存在于人们的日常生活中，比如互联网参政议政、电子商务、网上银行、网上缴纳生活费用等。手机新媒体是一种以随身携带的手机为载体的新兴媒体，它集互联网、电话、小说、报纸、银行卡、电影于一身，具有强大的功能，一经推广便迅速成为新媒体时代的宠物。户外媒体指人们能直接看到的数字电视、移动电视、LED彩色显示屏等，其主要内容是广告。衍生媒体是应用Web2.0技术的基础上衍生而来的维基、博客、播客、RSS等。衍生媒体的出现创新了新媒体的外延，推动了新媒体向更深层面的发展。

Task 7 ▶ Attending a public lecture

Direction: *MEDIA team are going to attend a public lecture delivered by Professor Maynor. Students are required to thoroughly understand the lecture, broaden the vision, elaborate on the theme, get inspiration from the lecture and do some speech activities to extend their knowledge.*

Objectives: *To train students' capability of description, expression, discussion, refutation, humor and humanistic accomplishment required by making a speech, thus, improving students' English language competence and proficiency.*

Lecture 4

New Media Practices in China

Professor Maynor

Hello, MEDIA members. You look so fine. I guess that you are all confident in and well ready for the coming lecture because you are the skilled users of new media, am I right? If so, our interaction will be quite smooth. But before I start, I hope you keep several questions in mind. First, you'd better clarify several forms of new media and its development process. Next, the correlation and distinction between old media and new media should be further elaborated. Finally, every one of you is required to give an account of new media practice in China and generalize and arrive at a conclusion about its implication. Now, I'm going to talk to you about the practice of new media in China.

To begin with, we have to commence on the background and put more emphasis on the different practices between internet media and mobile media conducted by young people, then we move on probing the practice from cultural perspective step-by-step.

Introduction

China has vigorously promoted the construction of a network power. The communication industry has advanced by leaps and bounds, and the number of mobile phone users has increased greatly. The diffusion of new media technologies such as the Internet and mobile phones has become an indispensable common phenomenon. Internet and mobile devices have become prevailing to circulate viewpoints. So different practices, discourses, and relationships are articulated or linked to new media technologies within China's contemporary sociocultural context. There exists the complex, contingent,

Figure 4.5 The power of new media.

and mutually constitutive relationship between culture and technology. It is essential to discuss new media practices including networked community and identity, gaming, networked public sphere and civic engagement etc. These themes provide an analytical framework for understanding new media use at the individual, peer group, and collective levels as these arise within cultural norms and institutional structures.

As elsewhere in the world, all people, whether young or older, male or female in China consist of the mainstream users of new media. The current generation, especially China's urban youth, have mostly grown up without siblings. They grew up accompanying by various electronic devices, making them the loyal lovers of modern new media. Meanwhile they face tremendous pressure, as huge expectations are often placed on their shoulders in terms of academic performance and future professional success. Nearly all youth graduate from high school and then go on to higher education. Chinese youth, both those known as the "post-nineties generation" and the "the post-00s generation", have enjoyed a higher standard of living than previous generations. However, they are perceived by older generations to be devoid of a clear moral compass, obsessed with the Internet and mobile phones, shallow, and over materialistic. Internet facilitates their access to the Western world. Affected by the Western culture, most of them enjoy Western entertainment and fashion, but they also have a strong mistrust of Western media. They are more individualistic than their collectivistic elders. In general, they manifest a need for self-expression far greater than their elders. This may partially lead to the dynamism of new media practices in China particularly among youngsters and young adults.

Mobile phone practice

The advancement of high technology directly corresponds to China's remarkably rapid expansion of mobile telephones. By early 2010, China had

Figure 4.6 Internet-based new media.

roughly 766 million mobile phone subscribers, the largest number in the world, representing a penetration rate of about 58%. Not only major cities are saturated with mobile phones but also the rural areas where the new mobile subscribers have been on the rise.

About 90% of mobile phone users in China rely on prepaid phone cards, which come in a range of plans, e.g., caller pays, bulk text messages. Out of courtesy, Chinese people rarely let their mobile phone go unanswered, and business people in China make voice calls frequently, the majority of other mobile phone users, including youth, communicate primarily via text message during the early time when cell phones came into use, especially when the mobile phone charged for answering and making calls. In most cases, text messaging is used for the reason of courtesy and being shy to expressing intimacy. Another reason for the prevalence of texting is that it is cheaper. Text messages in China are often self-written, but the use of prewritten messages is also common. These types of messages are widely available and can either be copied and forwarded. The message contents usually include jokes, sentimental poems, or holiday greetings etc. Texting may be ubiquitous. However, as early as in December 2009, millions of Chinese people had used their mobile phone to surf the Internet. As usage costs have fallen, a broad range of youth have started a shift from texting to internet chat via a social networking site as a primary means of media.

Primarily, the access to the Internet in China is via a desktop or laptop computer, which has been replaced by the mobile phone that has emerged in China as a key tool for identity and community building, albeit with distinct uses by diverse populations. In the early days, the mobile phone's diffusion in China was linked to an urban, sophisticated, fashionable lifestyle, as in other places around the world. Now, mobile phones have become a must for almost everyone in China. Everyone can express similar connections between owning a mobile phone and social status or maintenance of self-esteem. However, the differences of gender, age, and income lead to the differences in preferences of mobile phone types, usage patterns, and discourses. Mobile phones and text messaging in particular contribute to various expression including business message, advertisements as well as trivial and meaningless information. Apart from mobile phones, Chinese people have minimal access to landlines outside of public phones. Some people use mobile phones to maintain as well as to expand their social networks. Dating via the mobile phone, where a relationship is initiated and sustained through text messaging rather than voice calls or with a face-to-face meeting for several months, has also become common. In using mobile phones to autonomously establish intimate relationships, some youngsters challenge parental authority in such decisions, yet they also engage in practices that blend the traditional with the technological, for example, relying on intermediaries for introductions. Others, however, enjoy meeting strangers via mobile networks designed to help people find friends or lovers. Though people from all walks of life in China send prewritten messages, they can rely on such messages to compensate for low literacy levels, especially difficulty with inputting characters, and to communicate emotions they feel they cannot properly express in their own words.

Internet telecommunications practice

China's telecommunications landscape has developed rapidly over the last couple of decades. Through a series of reforms and restructuring three major telecom companies: China Telecom, China Mobile, and China Unicom. These have become world known multinational enterprises. They provide communication service including fixed telephone, mobile phone and internet access to serve users.

Internet growth in China has been rapid and unevenly distributed between the cities and the countryside at the beginning. As early as in December 2009, China enjoyed the largest number in the world, representing a 28.9% penetration rate, with roughly 72% concentrated in urban areas. Over 90% of China's internet users access the Internet via broadband. Many use desktop computers for such access, although the use of mobile phones has grown increasingly fast. Most urban families have a computer with a broadband internet connection in their homes. The majority of China's internet users are under 30 years old.

Generally, Internet activities in China mainly cover the following: listening to or downloading music, reading news including infotainment, using a search engine, instant messaging, playing games, watching videos, using a blog or personal space, emailing, using a social networking service, and reading net literature. Furthermore, some of China's internet users participate in a Bulletin Board System (BBS) or forum. Chinese cyberspace provides an arena where people are able not only to enjoy themselves, but also to express opinions, build community, engage in fantasy, and mobilize for collective action. In all, new media technologies have become key tools for expressing lifestyles and for processes of community building and identity formation in China, especially for youngsters and young adults. Such processes align with what appear to be universal tendencies, meanwhile, they also reveal particular characteristics that have emerged within the context of China's four decades of reform. Since opening its first public internet service in 1995, China's virtual realm has been featured by mutually competing and complementary, as well as by community formations whose networks merge online and offline.

BBS and blogs practice

BBSs are one of the oldest internet applications in China, having remained popular since the mid-to-late 1990s. They are operated by noncommercial and commercial internet service or content providers such as Sina, Sohu, and Tianya, as well as by government entities, e.g., the People's Net. These forums are a virtual space where people feel free to post news and opinions, largely because their free-for-all structure allows for more anonymity, though some are moderately regulated now. Most BBSs are devoted to myriad lifestyle topics, including art, culture, education, health, love, cars, and finance etc. Group identity and community are built on such interests, as well as through the use of playful language and homonyms that are only understood by participants. It is noteworthy that BBSs are also used frequently to merge online and offline activities, as many are aimed at regional, local, and ethnic affiliations. Moreover, although many websites and affiliated BBSs maintain a socially conservative stance regarding gender and family, others offer space for various subaltern groups to form community and have a voice that is often silenced in the real world.

Though fora are a major space for developing community online, blogs are another realm for individual expression and cultivating identities that both challenge and maintain the status quo. The first blog went online in China in 2002, and since then, the number of blogs has increased dramatically every year. By the end of 2009, there were 221 million bloggers, accounting for nearly 58% of all internet users. Not all of China's millions of blogs are active, nor are they all political. Like their Western counterparts, most are personal narratives written by young people, usually college students, about their daily lives. Though the Chinese blogosphere has become an important source of information outside official media channels for many, the most popular blogs in China are those written by celebrities, including film stars, authors, athletes, and successful entrepreneurs.

Gaming practice and traditional morality

Gaming in China has become a huge phenomenon in recent years, both in terms of China's own domestic gaming industry and through the sheer number of gamers. Digital gaming in China began in the 1980s with video arcades and home game consoles. Since then, China's online gaming industry has developed into a multibillion-dollar business. While PC-based games are still played, massively multiplayer online role-playing games (MMORPGs) such as World of Warcraft, as well as domestic titles, including NetEase's Fantasy Westward Journey, are becoming extremely popular, especially among young people. As early as in 2009, some 265 million internet users played online games, an approximately 42% increase from the previous year. Such growth was attributed to the enriched content and format of gaming products, as well as to various social networking sites adding gaming elements to their offerings.

Figure 4.7 World of Warcraft. Source: 朱勇，海云飞，《从魔兽事件看游戏行业发展》,《服务外包》2023 年第 3 期，第 66-72 页 .

However, the popularity of online games in China has brought a focus in both popular and official discourse on the negative effects of gaming. 55.5% of users and 49.5% of non-users of the Internet agreed that online gaming should be managed or controlled. The Chinese government has been a major proponent of controlling online gaming because of what it perceives as a direct connection between game-playing and internet addiction, and because of its desire to promote a civilized or healthy internet culture. The public media feature stories frequently on the perils of internet like addiction, exhaustion, failure in school, and even death. Murderous gamers have also been the source for sensational news. To deal with such issues, the government has taken a number of measures, including everything from setting up boot camps to cure internet-addicted youth, to electronically limiting the number of hours a day a minor can play an online game without experiencing a reduction in game points, and to forbidding the opening of new internet cafés. In general, the games should align with the public view that game contents could benefit the young to grow up healthy and sound not the other way around. It is better if games could bear the function of promoting traditional Chinese culture and values. In such social context, games that draw upon Chinese history, legends, and martial arts are getting more and more popular.

The tension between the perceived benefits and drawbacks of online gameplay is also reflected on gaming in China. Online gaming is often associated with internet addiction. Some "Chinese Internet Addiction Inventory" have been building for the assessment of the correlation between long hours online and mood changes and conflicts. The comparison between university students to those that have failed in their coursework shows that online game playing should be a factor in the latter's poor academic performance.

Conclusion

It can be seen that myriad practices, processes, and politics are articulated to new technologies in a dynamic, multi-faceted assemblage. In recent years, as more and more people have integrated these technologies into their lives, new identities, communities, and lifestyles have emerged, and have modes of civic engagement and new media production that challenge established rules and norms. New media technologies thus have been constitutive of individual, social, and political changes in China, some quite progressive, and some not.

Definitely, the most of China's digital youth will continue to use new media technologies the ways other youth around the world do, that is, to listen to music, chat with friends, express intimate feelings, play games, poke fun, and browse news. When they use it to debate issues and mobilize against corruption and injustice, they will continue building China's virtual public sphere. And in engaging in these forms of personal expression, they will feel that their lives are colorful. It's suggested that more research should focus on these sociocultural processes and reflect on how these emerge within particular circumstances and discourses. In this way, we will gain a deeper understanding of the larger societal transformations taking place in China, and about the role of new media in these.

The more important is that in 2021, "the 14th Five-Year Plan" for the Development of the Cultural Industry was released. It stated clearly that improving the quality and efficiency of the animation industry, building Chinese animation brands, and promoting the development of the "entire industry chain" and "all age groups" of animation have become policy priorities. That means that the animation industry will continue to receive policy support in areas such as industry integration, promotion, tax incentives, and financial support. China's animation and game industry has produced a lot of high-quality original animation and game works, such as *The Bright Moon in the Qin Dynasty, The Five Elements of Misty Mountain, The Battle Records of Luo Xiaohei, The Glory of the King* etc., not only earning a lot, but also displaying

Figure 4.8 Animation and game works. Source: 高磊，《动漫作品〈秦时明月〉之形象设计研究》，《丝路视野》2016 年第 23 期，第 72-74 页 .

and spreading Chinese culture through the window of national style.

The Chinese gaming industry is continuously undergoing transformation driven by technologies such as 5G, cloud computing, VR, and AR. With device scenario conversion, industry cap increases and user experience is optimized. Seizing the development opportunities of the times is the focus of the future of the gaming industry.

Before ending this lecture, I still hope that you can not only answer the questions in Task 3, but also to reflect on the following questions: Do you agree with the notion that older people are more or less one step slower than young people in accepting new things, often positioning themselves as critics or fault finders? Why (not)? Just as Elon Musk, the world's richest man, saids that old patients should not be prolonged so that the science and technology can proceed without hindrance. How do you think of that? And with that question I will say goodbye for this time, and see you next time.

Task 8 ▶ Online forum and summary writing

Direction: *MEDIA team are going to launch an instant online post-talk about the lecture to appeal to more of other students who are interested in the topic to join them. This is an integrated practice of listening, speaking, reading and writing. They are particularly expected to write a summary of the entire unit.*

Objectives: *To provide a platform for MEDIA team to fully display their talents. To comb language learning with professional knowledge so as to cultivate students' professional learning, academic literacy and language competence. To realize the teaching objectives of acquiring professional knowledge through learning English language.*

Edward: Well, MEDIA group, that was a pretty comprehensive lecture on new media practices in China, wasn't it? Professor Maynor's words were worthy of reflection. I was especially lost in thought on the last question. I am eager to share with you about how you feel.

Irene: I feel the same as you. I'd like to express my opinion on why youngsters became the leading group of new media practice. Firstly, the nature of youth is curiosity and they are very keen on pursuing new things. New technology leads the new era. The new era has created new youth. New youth integrate into the new era and create new technology! Do you think so?

Davis: Well done, Irene. In the context of family planning in China, our generation was raised like a little "emperor". We have been spoiled by the elders. When we were toddlers, we began to gain access to various electronic products including recreational machines. We grew up with electronic products, mobile phones, computers and the internet-based devices etc. How couldn't we possibly love such era or such sophisticated technology?

Angela: Sometimes, we were regarded as "flowers in the greenhouse" and mistaken as knowing nothing about how to "eat bitterness". But in essence, we are under great pressure from both schools, peers and parents. Our views on new technologies, fashion trend, continuous wireless communication and network terminologies etc. are not recognized by our elders, resulting in a huge generation gap. Parents hate their children's use of mobile phones and playing games, but we think these are the characteristics of our times. We are firmly resolved to keep pace with the times.

Maynor: How do you think about BBS and Blogs practice in China? Internet and Web came into practice as early as in 1994. So many years IT development must have changed people's standpoints and life style as well including parents. After all, social media and social network sites (SNSs) have tremendously irresistible influence on almost every aspect of the society like individual's social life. Don't you think your parents or grandparents are also willing to accept social media like WeChat, Weblog, and websites etc.?

Irene: As far as my parents concerned, they are using mobiles around ten more hours. But their usage is just limited in message greeting, watching short video, searching some health-related information, online shopping and so like. However, as long as they find we were playing games, they absolutely can't tolerate us.

Davis: Some parents can only accept opinions that align with theirs in BBS, others don't believe the news or advertisements online, and still others reject every kind of internet banking because they put an end to every internet banking. By contrast, many others are fond of social media and sending messages in WeChat circle of friends as their biggest entertainment. But in all, nobody is not sensitive to exposing personal information.

Edward: I fully agree with you. But I still strongly recommend you considering the following questions: Why do such phenomena exist? What do new media bring to people? Benefits, convenience, identity disclosure or harm? How and why?

Angela: To date, I am quite sure most people have accepted the internet-based new media. Different people choose different function to satisfy their specific purpose. Hence, there is no identical answer to the question about whether or not new technology brings people benefits or harms.

Irene: For many people, they enjoy the convenience and joy offered by new media while they hate identity disclosure when registering. They search various information through web while they feel hesitating to believe it because of too much false information and fake news.

Davis: But generally speaking, I think the advantages of new media outweigh the disadvantages. The progress of society is developing in constant error correction. China's online information department has strict control over bad online information and false advertising. Moreover, the management rules and regulations are also being improved. With the advancement of new media and media convergence, we are expecting more humanized service and bright future.

Edward: Hi, guys, we haven't touch the future development of anime online up to now. I think this question together with the last two will be left on online discussion, right?

Irene: Among other things, I am sure that with the stable launch of original high-quality games, more and more high-quality Chinese animations have repeatedly been exported to various countries. The trend of high-quality anime game products has become mainstream, and technological innovation has opened up a new experience for anime games in the 5G era. So, Chinese culture will go with these excellent games across the world.

Maynor: Perfect conclusion, Irene. Your reply is just to the point. It means games promote the development of technology, economy, and culture despite its possibility of young people's addictiveness. Besides, the consensus is that new media including social media like BBS, SNSs WeChat, and Weblog etc. have become most popular among younger users such as university students and those who pursue the freedom to express themselves on these online platforms. And cross-national differences in offline and online social ties on SNSs with universities students do exist worldwide. Based on the cultural differences in collectivism-individualism, traditional proposition of offline social ties suggests that in individualistic culture people have less strong ties, whereas in collectivistic culture the pattern is opposite. I hope you can broaden your horizons and diverge thinking to analyze problems from a multidimensional perspective.

Angela, Irene & Angela: Okay. Knowledge has no limit. We will redouble our efforts.

All: So much for today. See you next time.

Appendix: Vocabulary for Unit 4

Listening Activity

dissemination /dɪˌsemɪˈneɪʃn/ *n.* 宣传，散播；宣传，散播

plurality /plʊəˈrælәti/ *n.* 多数；复数；兼职；胜出票数

subvert /sәbˈvɜːt/ *v.* 颠覆，破坏；腐蚀，使道德败坏

scoop /skuːp/ *n.* 勺，球形勺；铲，铲斗；〈非正式〉（抢先报道的）独家新闻；〈美，非正式〉（尤指私人的）最新内幕（the scoop）
v. 用勺舀，用铲子铲；挖出，挖空；（急速地）捡起，抱起；〈非正式〉抢先报道（新闻）

hybridize /ˈhaɪbrɪdaɪz/ *vt.* 使杂交；混合生成
vi. 杂交；混合

solicit /sәˈlɪsɪt/ *v.* 请求，索求，征求（意见）；〈美〉兜售，推销；拉（客），卖淫

assimilate /әˈsɪmәleɪt/ *v.* 融入，（使）同化；吸收，理解；使相似，成为相似

niche /niːʃ; nɪtʃ/ *n.* 合适（称心）的工作（活动）（one's niche）；壁龛；（产品的）商机
v. 把……放在壁龛中
adj.（产品）针对特定小群体的

retrieve /rɪˈtriːv/ *v.* 找回，收回；检索（储存于计算机的信息）；（狗等）衔回（物品、猎物）；挽救，挽回；回忆，追忆；收绕钓鱼线
n.（尤指中枪猎物的）找回；收绕钓鱼线

permeate /ˈpɜːmieɪt/ *v.* 渗透，弥漫；（观点、信念、感情等）充满，充斥

configurative / kәnˈfɪgjʊrәtɪv/ *adj.* 结构的；构型的；组态的

invariance /ɪnˈveәrɪәns/ *n.* 不变性；不变式

stereotype /ˈsteriәtaɪp/ *n.* 模式化的思想，老一套；公式化人物；铅版，铅版浇铸，铅版印刷
v. 对……形成刻板的看法，（尤指）对……有成见；使用铅版

strata /ˈstrɑːtә/ *n.* 层；［地质］地层；阶层

Reading Activity

cluster /ˈklʌstә(r)/ *n.* 组，簇；星团；一连串同类事件；（聚集在同一地方的）一群人；（计算机磁盘上的）丛集，群集；辅音群，辅音连缀
v. 群聚，聚集；（数据点）具近似数值

convergence /kәnˈvɜːdʒәns/ *n.* 趋同；汇集，相交；会聚区；收敛（性）

monopoly /məˈnɒpəli/ *n.* 垄断，垄断权；垄断企业，专卖者；独占，专利品
optical /ˈɒptɪk(ə)l/ *adj.* 视力的，视觉的；有助于视力的，光学的；光读取的，光存贮的；（装置）光电的
n.〈印度〉（一副）眼镜（opticals）
fiber /ˈfaɪbə(r)/ *n.* 纤维（等于 fibre）
artificial /ˌɑːtɪˈfɪʃl/ *adj.* 人造的，人工的；人为的；不真挚的，矫揉造作的
algorithms /ˈælgərɪðəmz/ *n.* 算法；算法式（algorithm 的复数）
inception /ɪnˈsepʃn/ *n.*（机构、组织等的）开端，创始
coincide /ˌkəʊɪnˈsaɪd/ *v.* 巧合，同时发生；一致，相符；相交，重叠（过去式和过去分词 coincided）
precursor /priˈkɜːsə(r)/ *n.*（事物）先驱，先兆；（尤指经新陈代谢形成另一种物质的）前体，前质
initial /ɪˈnɪʃl/ *adj.* 开始的，最初的；（字母）位于词首的
n.（姓名的）首字母
v. 用姓名的首字母作标记（或签名）于
preliminary /prɪˈlɪmɪnəri/ *adj.* 初步的，预备的
n. 初步行动，准备工作；预赛，预试
momentum /məˈmentəm/ *n.* 冲力，推力；动力，势头；动量，冲量
monograph /ˈmɒnəgrɑːf/ *n.* 专题著作，专题论文
vt. 写关于……的专著
dimension /daɪˈmenʃn; dɪˈmenʃn/ *n.* 大小，尺寸；（空间的）维度；范围，规模；方面，部分
v. 切削（或制作）成特定尺寸；标出尺寸
inflexion /ɪnˈflekʃən/ *n.* 弯曲；转调；屈折；回折点
venture /ˈventʃə(r)/ *n.* 风险项目，冒险事业；冒险旅行，冒险行动
v. 冒险；小心地说，谨慎地做；敢说，大胆表示
herald /ˈherəld/ *v.* 预示……的来临；宣布，宣传；热烈欢迎；公开称赞（过去式和过去分词 heralded）
n. 预兆；使者，先驱；棘翅夜蛾；
acceleration /əkˌseləˈreɪʃ(ə)n/ *n.* 加速，加快；（车辆）加速能力，加速幅度；加速度
surge /sɜːdʒ/ *n.* 激增，猛增；（风、水等的）奔涌，汹涌；（情感的）涌起，翻涌；（人群的）蜂拥；电流急冲，电涌；增兵，增援
v. 急剧上升，激增；（人群，自然力）汹涌，奔腾；（感情）涌起，涌现；（电压，电流）猛增，浪涌（过去式 surged）
municipal /mjuːˈnɪsɪpl/ *adj.* 城市的，市政的；自治城市的，地方自治的；内政的

leapfrog /ˈliːpfrɒg/ *n.* 跳背游戏
v. 玩跳背游戏；越级提升；超过，超越（过去式和过去分词 leapfrogged）
vogue /vəʊg/ *n.* 流行，时髦
adj. 时髦的，流行的
v.（模仿模特在T形台上的姿态）随音乐跳舞
mimic /ˈmɪmɪk/ *vt.* 模仿，模拟
n. 善于模仿的人；会模拟的动物（或植物）（mimic的复数）
dividend /ˈdɪvɪdend/ *n.* 红利，股息；好处，回报；（足球彩票的）彩金；被除数
v. 回响，发出回声；重复，附和
allocation /ˌæləˈkeɪʃ(ə)n/ *n.* 配给量，划拨款，份额；分配，分派
blur /blɜː(r)/ *n.* 模糊不清的事物；模糊的记忆，记不清的事情；污迹
v.（使）看不清楚，记不清；（使）难以区分；玷污
matrix /ˈmeɪtrɪks/ *n.* 矩阵；模型；社会环境；矩阵转接电路；线路网，道路网；交叉结构
salience /ˈseɪljəns/ *n.* 显著（等于saliency）；突出；卓越
intimacy /ˈɪntɪməsi/ *n.* 亲密；性，性关系；熟知，精通
charm /tʃɑːm/ *n.* 魅力，魔力；护身符，咒语；小挂件，小饰物
v. 吸引，迷住；诱使，哄诱；向……施魔法，用魔法控制；有魔力
rhetoric /ˈretərɪk/ *n.* 花言巧语，浮夸之词；修辞，修辞学
proximity /prɒkˈsɪməti/ *n.*（时间、空间、关系的）靠近，亲近
immersive /ɪˈmɜːsɪv/ *adj.*（计算机系统或图像）沉浸式虚拟现实的
aggregator /ˈægrɪgeɪtə(r)/ *n.* 聚合器，整合者；汇集者，聚合
fluctuate /ˈflʌktʃueɪt/ *v.* 波动，起伏不定；使波动，使动摇（过去式和过去分词 fluctuated）
propel /prəˈpel/ *v.* 推进，驱动；推搡（某人走向特定方向）；驱使，促使

Lecture

vigorously /ˈvɪgərəsli/ *adv.* 精神旺盛地，有力地，活泼地；坚决地
contingent /kənˈtɪndʒənt/ *n.*（军队的）分遣队；代表团
adj. 附带的，依情况而定的；偶然（发生）的，可能的
norm /nɔːm/ *n.* [标准] 标准，规范；基准
sibling /ˈsɪblɪŋ/ *n.* 〈正式〉兄弟姐妹

devoid /dɪˈvɔɪd/ *adj.* 缺乏，完全没有

obsess /əbˈses/ *v.* 使着迷；使心神不宁；挂牵，念念不忘（过去式和过去分词 obsessed）

manifest /ˈmænɪfest/ *v.* 显示，表明；（病症）显现；把……列入货单
adj. 明显的，显而易见的
n. 旅客名单，载货清单；货运列车编组清单

subscriber /səbˈskraɪbə(r)/ *n.* 订购者，订阅人，订户；消费者，用户；

penetration /ˌpenəˈtreɪʃ(ə)n/ *n.* 穿透，渗透，进入；（产品对市场的）渗透度，占有率

courtesy /ˈkɜːtəsi/ *n.* 礼貌，彬彬有礼；礼貌的行为（言语）；〈古〉屈膝礼
adj. 免费提供的；礼节性的

ubiquitous /juːˈbɪkwɪtəs/ *adj.* 普遍存在的，无所不在的

albeit /ˌɔːlˈbiːɪt/ *conj.* 虽然，尽管

intermediary /ˌɪntəˈmiːdiəri/ *adj.* 中间的，过渡的
n. 调解人，中间人；媒介

fantasy /ˈfæntəsi/ *n.* 幻想，想象；想象产物，幻想作品；虚拟比赛（游戏）；幻想曲
v. 想象，幻想

align /əˈlaɪn/ *v.* 公开支持，与……结盟；（使）排成一条直线，使平行；调整，使一致

anonymity /ˌænəˈnɪməti/ *n.* 匿名；无特色，无个性；匿名者

myriad /ˈmɪriəd; ˈmɪriæd/ *n.* 〈文〉无数，大量；（多用于古典历史剧中）一万
adj. 无数的，大量的

ethnic /ˈeθnɪk/ *adj.*（有关）种族的，民族的；少数民族的；具有民族特色的，异国风味的
n. 少数民族成员，某民族群体的人

affiliate /əˈfɪlieɪt/ *v.* 使隶属，使紧密联系；〈正式〉加入；（组织）接纳……为成员（过去式和过去分词 affiliated）
n. 附属机构，分支机构

subaltern /ˈsʌbltən/ *n.* 中尉；副官；部下
adj. 次的；陆军中尉的

fora /ˈfɔːrə/ *n.* 论坛；讨论会；法庭；专题讲话节目（forum 的复数形式）

quo /kwəʊ/ *v.* 〈古〉说（用于第一和第三人称单数主语前）

arcade /ɑːˈkeɪd/ *n.* 拱廊；（上有顶盖的）拱廊式街道；电子游戏厅

console /kənˈsəʊl; ˈkɒnsəʊl/ *v.* 安慰，慰藉
n. 控制台，仪表盘；电视机（或收音机）柜；风琴的操作部分；（带装饰的）支架，支托

proponent /prəˈpəʊnənt/ *n.*〈正式〉支持者，建议者；提出认证遗嘱者

peril /ˈperəl/ *n.* 巨大的危险，危难；（某活动或行为的）危险，问题
v.〈古〉使有危险，使临险境，危及

drawback /ˈdrɔːbæk/ *n.* 缺点，不利条件；出口退税

assemblage /əˈsemblɪdʒ/ *n.* 装配；集合；聚集；集会；集合物；聚集的物或人

corruption /kəˈrʌpʃ(ə)n/ *n.* 贪污，腐败；堕落，腐蚀；（电脑上资讯的）破坏，损坏

5
Unit

Social Media in China

TABLE OF CONTENTS

5 Unit Social Media in China

Warm-up: Be proactive

Direction: *MEDIA team are going to do warm-up activities by discussing, airing their views on the topic and discovering problems.*

Objectives: *To arouse students' interest, get a preliminary understanding of relevant knowledge and prepare for the following study.*

Angela: Hi, there MEDIA partners. From today on, we'll commence on the topic about social media. In my life, social media means everything ranging from news source to learning resources, interactive platforms and online shopping. I could hardly imagine how our ancestors spent their poor and dull life in their era. Without social media, I just could not live even one day.

Irene: You are true fan of social media. Actually, I share the majority part of your view.

Davis: So do I. But as for news source, I usually prefer to believe the official press release on the basis of facts confirmation.

Angela: But you shouldn't deny all the social media. Some social media provide diverse messages for audiences to judge. More detailed news may be acquired through social media. I mean social media provide more alternatives.

Irene: And social media, especially social platforms, offer so much convenience that the official media can't. Online shopping is a very good example. And the fierce market competition has driven a variety of social platforms regulating themselves internally. In other word, the regulatory role of the market itself will take effect. Therefore, social platform can offer more and more considerate service and the higher quality so that they cannot be defeated.

Davis: Right. How to acquire more audiences from social platforms and mobile channels is the biggest challenge faced by the media groups, but it is also the greatest chance of survival for them in the future.

Angela: Social media have changed the way we all interact with each other online. It gives us the ability to discover what's happening in the world in real-time, to connect with each other, stay in touch with long-distance friends, and have access to endless amounts of information at our fingertips. In many senses, social media have helped many individuals find common ground with others online, making the world more approachable.

Irene: Exactly. Social media has become a major part of numerous lives through countless websites and apps, through which people have been able to connect with one another and share their thoughts, emotions, experiences, etc. As everyone must admit, human beings are emotional animals. When people's basic survival needs are met, spiritual life is people's greatest pursuit. From this perspective, social media brings pleasure to human beings.

Davis: You just partially convinced me. Even if social media has its positive side, many social platforms are increasingly blamed. People begin to call out negative features, likening its overuse to an addiction. Some people believe that social media contribute to inattentiveness, stress, and jealousy or even mental health, self-confidence, and personal security. All these are unavoidable.

Irene: Quite reasonable. Every coin has two sides. Social media have caused numerous teens to waste a lot of time doing things that aren't so important. The problem lies in that they get involved in very extensively and are eventually cut off from the society. It can also waste individual time that could have been utilized by productive tasks and activities.

Angela: Yes. In this way, another negative result is that how easy it is for people nowadays to use scams that allow access to others' private information. This could be very dangerous to one's identity and security.

Davis: All in all, social media has been growing into the cause of many advantages and disadvantages. Let's go on validating our predictions.

All: Okay, let's see what we can gain through the following listening. See you soon.

Task 1 ▶ Listening activity

Direction: *MEDIA team are going to listen to an introduction of key concepts so as to lay the foundation for later learning.*

Objectives: *To understand the main conception, practice and strengthen the ability of listening comprehension.*

Media Landscape in China

Social media is a form of electronic communication that enables users to create and share information, ideas, messages, and all sorts of contents via social networking websites and applications. However, the term "social media" is often used interchangeably with "social network". In fact, social network is a concept that was around long before the advent of the Internet. Social network refers to a group of people who know each other or connected in some way. Today, the terms "social networking site" or "social networking service" are a little outdated, but they essentially refer to the same services as "social media". Social media is now mainstream media, but it is difficult to define it accurately because there are exceptions to every definition. It differentiates itself by being interactive – a two-way communication. Social media includes websites that are available for social networking.

Traditional media refers to everything that runs via traditional media channels such as television, radio, newspaper, magazine etc. When you look at a TV commercial or listen to the radio or read a magazine or newspaper, you're experiencing marketing through traditional media channels. Traditional media are predominantly push media where the message is broadcast from company

Figure 5.1 Social media. 秦婧颖编译，《全球社交媒体使用洞察分析》, 2021-01-19, https://datareport.com/report.

to customer and other stakeholders. Traditional media has been a part of our culture for over half a century. It proved to be a powerful tool in the process of making learning and teaching more effective and interesting. In traditional media, the sender usually decides what to publish, broadcast or telecast, while the receiver always receives the information. In private organizations, the owners are usually responsible for the content or material published.

Figure 5.2 Traditional media. Source: "Why Traditional Media Advertising Is Still Important?" https://adwisemarketing.ca.

Whether the traditional or social media are the most important news sources plus communication tools for people in contemporary time. Although to date, there are over 1,900 kinds of newspapers in China, most of which are local, government-sponsored publications in China. Such traditional media as newspapers and magazines are rapidly declining due to the rapid development of the internet-based social media. Television and broadcasting still have a major influence in China, but people tend to only use them to watch entertainment programs, films and TV shows. The proliferation of digital and social media is changing the landscape of newsrooms day after day. In terms of economic income, the publishing channels and advertising revenue of print media are losing their market sharply, but the newspaper's newsrooms still maintain a strong competence in original content. As a matter of fact, the transformation of traditional media has been shifting to online and mobile channels, as well as social media platforms.

The most commonly used channels to access information are search engines, web portals, and social apps like WeChat, Weibo and mobile news applications. Baidu.com is a Chinese search engine that has the greatest market share where Google is absent. WeChat and QQ.COM are both developed by Tencent. Sina.com, Sina Weibo and Toutiao.com are the major web portals and social media platforms. The mobile internet is also well developed in China and widely used. In big cities like Beijing and Shanghai, you can hardly see any news stands in the streets and few read newspapers in the bus or subway anymore.

What you see everywhere is that people just keep checking their phones. The truth is, China has 1.12 billion mobile internet users, among whom 90% of Chinese people use their phones to surf the Internet, read news, have social activities, play games, do online shopping and practically pay for everything by their Alipay or WeChat Wallet. This is very cool and really convenient.

WeChat and Weibo are the two leading social media platforms in China. WeChat has 938 million monthly active users, far beyond any IM tool, and is also the most influential social network and news information portal of China. Sina Weibo has over 34 million users and its affiliation with the media is more obvious. In addition, there are also mobile news applications such as Top buzz, Zaker, Tencent, Sina, Sohu and NetEase serving as major sources for news and information. Beyond that, video and online entertainment applications in China are highly advanced, with most internet users spending their time with social exchanges, news consumption, online gaming and watching video content.

Of course, fake news is also a major concern in China. According to a survey conducted by the Media Research Institute of Chinese Academy of Social Sciences, 59% of fake news come from social media like Weibo. Sina Weibo has enforced its position against fake news and false information. When journalists are writing a news report or are confirming a news source, approximately 90 percent (87.1%) of them view press releases as an authoritative source to obtain and verify facts. This is followed by companies' senior executives and news spokesmen (51.7%), information released by official enterprises based on social media (41.6%) and companies' official websites (39.7%).

In stark contrast, the average credibility of information spreading on social media is only lower than 5%. Web portals in China like Sina.com require that editors cannot use anonymous information sources and most newspapers have an editor-in-chief review mechanism, so the possibility of fake news is weakened on traditional media. According to an iResearch.com survey, over 95% of users are more attentive to news sources, including media brands and information sources.

Task 2 ▶ Listening comprehension

Direction: *MEDIA team are going to have a topic-oriented discussion to exchange their views on the listening material and challenge each other with puzzling questions.*

Objectives: *To broaden students' horizon, develop their ability to sum up the skills of answering questions and strengthen language output ability.*

Irene: Hello again everyone. Professor Edward provided and drew a panorama view about Chinese social media, especially most popular ones: WeChat, Weblog and Web portal. I suggest that each of us focus on one aspect in the following discussion. Don't you agree?

Davis: No, we don't. Lady first. Irene, you can initiate the following discussion from what you hope to talk.

Irene: It's really appreciated. You are always so considerate. I gain more interest in WeChat, for it may be the most frequently used medium.

Angela: Hi, Davis. You can just talk your preference. As you know, I'm okay with any sort of media. No kidding.

Davis: Then thanks, Angela. Weblog may be within my knowledge. Actually, there is no absolute cut-off point. We can complement each other.

Irene: Sure. It is a must. When mentioning WeChat, I think the features are somewhat endless. Commonly, the following are the most popular with users including options to pay bills, phone credit, hail taxis, book cinema or train tickets, order food and share messages and photos to friends individually, in group messages or via your "Moments". Really a wonderful app.

Angela: I think most Chinese uses the search-engine Baidu, and over 90% of all searches online are done through it. But just a few may know Baidu Post Bar. So, I'd like to do some introduction of what I know about Baidu Post Bar or "Tiebas" in Chinese, which is a reddit-equivalent user-driven network site established in 2003.

Davis: Weblog, also known as microblog, or Weibo in Chinese is a microblogging site, which offers users various features for their posts. These range from the ability to load up to 9 pictures per post, to being able to use up to 2000 characters to release their thoughts across on Weibo or Weblog.

Irene: These forms of social media are all news sources. However, the way to release news may vary from one to another. WeChat users usually text greetings, job-related messages, or forward pictures or short videos. The long articles or excerpt are mainly transmitted from Weblog.

Davis: Weibo is also not just a microblogging site for sharing personal thoughts, memes and comment on current affairs, but also has stories and a reward system for users who have consistently popular posts.

Angela: Baidu Post Bar operates as a forum, allowing community discussions to build up around various keywords or topics, referred to as "Tieba". The slogan of Baidu Tieba is "Born for your interest", highlighting the purpose of the site, made for and by the people for their interests.

Irene: Actually, various news, information, audio, video, comments and articles are interwoven cross platforms and cross forwarded and disseminated from various media, forming a huge flow of information. One of the most important features of WeChat is that it allows users to register their bank details, in order to pay for things through the app. You can also send money to friends through "red packets" on festive holidays. I think this function is quite appealing.

Davis: Something similar to Weblog is its reward system for users who have consistently popular posts. Rewards can be used to buy items from the Sina-Weibo linked store. Vlogs have more recently launched too, encouraging users to livestream and make more video-based contents.

Angela: Baidu Post Bar or Tieba also has its incentive means. Users can score "experience points", gaining rank for presence on the site. By posting, responding to others etc., users can climb ranks. Each Tieba is independent, with a different focus. Almost any topic of interest will probably have an existing discussion live, ranging from chats about celebrities, travel, films etc. Every Tieba will have a host, selected from their experience points and community engagement.

Irene: No matter what social platform it is, the prominent feature is the Chinese social media site has one of the largest online

	Chinese communities and still continues to grow. So is definitely worth taking the time to familiarize yourself with them.
Angela & Davis:	Yes, let's go on tapping more underlying issues so as to realize the sustainable development of Chinese social media.
All:	Okay. See you.

Task 3 ▶ Pre-reading activity

Direction: *This part serves as connecting link between the preceding and the following. MEDIA team are required to ponder over some problems concerning the whole unit, reflect on them and then find solutions. The answers are open-ended.*

Objectives: *To cultivate students' capability of exploring problems, develop critical thinking ability synchronously and improve expression ability.*

1. How do social media influence Chinese people's life? Please exemplify it.
2. What can be regarded as the most popular symbolic social platform in China? And why?
3. What are the hidden problems when people take social media as news source?
4. What causes China's social media platforms and online behaviors to differ from their international equivalents?
5. According to Ogilvy, how different are social platforms in China from those in the United States?
6. How do social media relate to public discourse?
7. How do social media help to build up public engagement?
8. How do social media influence business practices?
9. How do you think of the conventional prediction that the Internet would disengage public participation?

Task 4 ▶ Reading activity

Direction: *MEDIA team are required to read the following excerpt to obtain information, expand vocabulary volume, increase knowledge reserve, comprehend between lines, appreciate the writing style and evaluate the article.*

Objectives: *To cultivate students' capability of reading and absorbing information in a way that "eyes see quickly and brain processes quickly" to enhance reading comprehension, build up logic thinking, learn writing through reading and improve students' comprehensive quality.*

The Main Social Media in China

Social apps in China are more integral to domestic life than they are elsewhere. As China's population moves online, consumer behavior shifts. Crucially, this makes it a haven for social media sites to thrive within. That means if companies can acknowledge the shifts in their marketing strategies, they can successfully reach consumers anywhere. Social media has grown to become the shared commons where Chinese consumers offer opinions, ask for advice, and discuss brands. Ignoring the Internet could be considered a lost opportunity or even a business risk.

The Internet has opened access to information for ordinary Chinese citizens in unimaginable ways. Despite of some information was pre-filtered by editors at state-run media, China's internet is freewheeling by comparison. Chinese state-approved ecosystem resulted in a flourishing home-grown social media with Chinese-owned properties thriving. By some measures, usage of Chinese social media is some of the most intense in the world. A survey data shows that Chinese internet users are online for an average of 2.7 hours per day, considerably more than other developing countries and more on par with usage patterns in Japan and the United States.

Numerous factors help drive Chinese, more than other populations, to engage in social media. These include rural-to-urban migration that has separated families for some time, the loneliness of the one-child generation and the like. A 2008 MTV Music Matters survey found that young people across Asia have made a similar number of friends online and offline. Only in China, however, did young people actually have more friends online than offline. This points to a convergence of the offline and online worlds, where it is less important to distinguish between what happens online from the "real world".

In China, more than in many countries, social media has become deeply integrated into people's lives.

Chinese netizens actively engage in discussions that could directly affect companies. A recent study by Ogilvy One in China found that 55 percent of China's netizens had initiated or participated in online discussions about companies. Understanding social media is no longer a luxury for companies operating in China — it is an imperative. Formerly, a lack of engagement with netizens could be considered a lost opportunity. Now, the penetration and impact of social media is such that failing to understand what consumers are saying about a company online has become a business risk.

Figure 5.3 Social platform in China. Source:《社交媒体对集客营销至关重要的 5 大理由》, https://zhuanlan.zhihu.com.

Social media platforms

To explain the development of social media in Asia, Ogilvy's 360 Digital influence team has developed a series of social media "bulls-eyes" that place international platforms on the outside ring and their local equivalents on an inner ring. With China, as with other countries, this bulls-eye system has strengths and weaknesses. For example, the bulls-eye shows that the most influential social platforms cover Sina Weibo, Tudou and Youku and the like. China's social media platforms and online behaviors vary in important ways from those that may be considered their international equivalents. In China, as elsewhere in Asia, local variations of internet usage are driven by language, culture, levels of economic development, and the underlying digital ecosystem. Digital ecosystems — the platforms around which populations focus online communications — can vary wildly between countries and within a single country. Substantial differences can exist even in countries at similar levels of economic development. Even without government blocks, internet users in Japan and South Korea, for example, flock to domestically developed social media platforms such as GREE and Cyworld, respectively, rather than internationally known sites.

Youku and Tudou

Youku, as the first video website in China, was officially launched on December 21, 2006. With the product concept of "the fastest is the king" and the product characteristics of "fast playback, fast release, and fast search", it fully meets the growing interactive needs of users and diversified video experiences. It has now become one of the most influential and popular video media in Chinese internet field.

Youku has continuously implemented its mission of "integrating the three networks into one", covering three major terminals: PC, TV, and mobile. It combines the three major content forms of film and television, variety shows, and information, and connects the three major links of video content production, broadcasting, and distribution. It has become a truly meaningful internet television media, leading the video industry and the overall pattern of the all media era.

While Tudou, as one of the earliest and most influential online video platforms in China, is a leading brand in Chinese online video industry. Tudou.com was officially launched on April 15, 2005 and is one of the earliest video websites in the world.

On April 6, 2016, Youku and Tudou completed privatization, collectively known as Youku Tudou Co., Ltd., and officially became wholly-owned subsidiaries of Alibaba. The group is a leading enterprise in the Chinese online video industry, focusing on the video field. It owns Youku, which ranks first on Chinese video websites, and Tudou, which ranks second.

Youku Tudou has a huge user base, diverse content resources, and strong technological platform advantages. Besides a huge user base, it also enjoys diverse content resources, and strong technological platform advantages. The monthly user base of Youku Tudou has exceeded 400 million, indicating that one-third of Chinese people have become users of Youku Tudou. Youku Tudou provides users with the most comprehensive and diverse content, helping them watch high-quality videos more conveniently on multiple terminals, fully meeting their growing interactive needs and diverse video experiences. Youku and Tudou have now covered the three major terminals of PC, TV, and mobile, combining the three major content forms of film and television, variety shows, and information, connecting the three major links of video content production, broadcasting, and distribution, becoming truly meaningful internet media platforms.

Youku Tudou is often compared with American YouTube. Different social media usage patterns tell a great deal about the Internet and the country involved. For example, Chinese netizens use Youku Tudou quite differently from how Americans use YouTube. Rather than short videos of cute animals or silly domestic mishaps that may be popular among YouTube watchers, Youku and Tudou are filled with longer form content, up to 70 percent of which is professionally produced. Users in China spend up to an hour per day on the sites, compared with less than 15 minutes spent by Americans on YouTube. In the way they present programs, the Chinese sites seem more like online television stations or a replacement for digital video recorders. What's more, individuals in China produce and post videos a lot, a large portion of online video content is longer-format professional videos, because China is increasingly focusing on protecting intellectual property rights to effectively mobilize the enthusiasm of knowledge innovators and promote the development and prosperity of socialist culture and scientific undertakings. The demand for original content on Youku and Tudou has resulted in a boom of companies that focus purely on online video. Youku Tudou has carried out a series of cooperation in the fields of basic technology, big data and video marketing. Youku Tudou has connected with Big data in the background, cooperated with Alibaba Cloud in the field of CDN, accessed Alipay, developed a series of products such as "buy while watching" relying on Alimama, which is affiliated to Alibaba. It is the leading big data marketing platform in China and has the core business data of Alibaba Group, and jointly built a marketing laboratory to help businesses carry out video marketing.

The television-like feel of Youku and Tudou reflects the usage pattern of young Chinese. University students in China often express skepticism when told that the United States has one of the highest levels of social media engagement in the world, because they expect that their country would rank first. Youngsters in China as well as in elsewhere, spend more time on social media like Youku and Tudou rather than on official media. This switchover to social media does more than demonstrate the popularity of new media — it affects the whole advertising industry. In China's case, certain demographics can no longer be reached effectively via traditional media channels.

Sina Weibo

Some differences between Chinese and foreign social media are rooted in culture and language. At first glance, Sina Weibo is a latecomer to the microblog phenomenon. However, since it was launched in 2009, it has become an information sharing and exchange platform that provides entertainment and leisure life services for the public. Sina Weibo is by far the most popular microblogging platform in China. Weibo is a social media platform based on user relationships. Users can access it through various mobile terminals such as PCs and mobile phones, and achieve instant sharing, dissemination, and interaction of information through multimedia forms such as text, images, and videos. Weibo is based on an open platform architecture, providing a simple and unprecedented way for users to publicly publish content in real-time. Through fission propagation, users interact with others and are closely connected to the world. As a new entry point to the internet after portals and searches, Weibo has changed the way information is disseminated and achieved instant sharing of information. On September 25, 2009, Sina Weibo officially added @ and private message functions, as well as "comment" and "forward" functions for users to communicate. Sina Weibo adopts the same promotion strategy as Sina Blog, which invites celebrities and celebrities to join and establish micro blogs, and authenticates them with their real names. After authentication, users will add a letter V to their username (the authentication personal letter V is golden, and the authentication enterprise letter V is dark blue) to distinguish them from ordinary users, while also avoiding the behavior of impersonating celebrity Weibo, but the Weibo function is the same as that of regular users. On November 3, 2009, the Sina App Engine Alpha version was launched, and information can be published using third-party software or plugins through APIs. As of March 2014, Weibo had a monthly active user base of 143.8 million and a daily active user base of 66.6 million, including a large number of government agencies, officials, enterprises, and individual authenticated accounts. The open communication mechanism has made Sina Weibo the "public conference hall"of China. On December 29, 2021, Weibo announced that it would become the "media partner for the promotion of Chinese ice and snow culture" of the Winter sports management center of the General Administration of Sport of China. From now on, all the Chinese ice and snow national teams will enter the Weibo platform. Meanwhile, Weibo has reached strategic cooperation with the China Ice and Snow Conference.

2022 witnessed the great changes concerning Weibo. As of March 15,

2022, Weibo has launched an algorithm shutdown button that allows users to turn off "personalized recommendations" with just one click in the background. On August 22, 2022, after the personal homepage display comment function was launched, the public comments posted by users on media accounts and government accounts under Weibo will be considered as public comment content in the public space and displayed on the user's personal homepage. On December 11, 2022, it was reported that the Weibo web version was restructured using the Vue framework in 2020, with significant UI changes. Weibo officials have previously indicated that the original version of Weibo will be taken offline in the near future.

The term "Weibo" lists the top ten "new words of the times" with the highest life vitality index in China over the past 20 years in the "Dictionary of Chinese New Words (2000-2020) "released by the Commercial Press.

Social networks

What are social platforms or social networks? In a broad sense, such as Weibo, Xiaohongshu, Tiktok and Kaishou are social platforms; from the subconscious perspective of the public, social media platforms, such as WeChat, QQ, and Momo, are also social media platforms. Those social networks are so popular with almost all Chinese people that they heavily influence people's life, work, and study. The most representative social network platforms are as follows.

WeChat definitely ranks the top followed by QQ, Tiktok, Kaishou, Momo, Douban and so many other platforms. WeChat and QQ are used by almost everyone. These two platforms, developed by Tencent and focused on socializing with acquaintances, become the leading social media platforms today. They both have multiple functions and displays, and as long as it is Tencent software, it can be logged in and used by these two softwares. The most important thing is that the WeChat Pay function has also been widely popularized and has become an indispensable part of life.

QQ covers various operating platforms such as Windows, macOS, iPadOS, Android, iOS, Windows Phone, Linux, etc. Its logo is a small penguin wearing a red scarf. Tencent QQ supports various functions such as online chat, video call, peer-to-peer breakpoint file renewal, shared files, network hard drive, custom panel, QQ email, and can be connected to various communication terminals. Qzone is a personalized space developed by Tencent in 2005. It has the function of blog and has been loved by many people since its inception. QQ email is an email product launched by Tencent in 2002, providing users with secure, stable, fast, and convenient email services. QQ Music is the largest online music platform in China and a leading provider of legitimate digital music services in the internet industry. It has always been at the forefront of the music trend, providing convenient and smooth online music and rich and colorful music community services to users. QQ Image is Tencent's latest desktop image processing software. With its refreshing interface and simple and lightweight operation, we provide you with a one-stop experience in processing images. In short, there are too many functions in QQ to be able to mention here.

Tiktok is a music creative short video social software incubated by ByteDance.This software was launched on September 20, 2016 and is a short video community platform for all ages. Users can choose songs and shoot music works to form their own works through this software. In December 2019, Tiktok was selected as one of the 100 brands in the "2019 China Brand Power Ceremony". As of January 2020, the number of daily active users has exceeded 400 million and continues to maintain rapid growth. In August 2020, Volcano Video and Tiktok officially announced the brand integration and upgrading. Volcano Video was then renamed Tiktok Volcano Edition, and new icons were used. In addition, Tiktok continues to develop new businesses. In August 2022, Ele.me and Tiktok reached a cooperation agreement. Based on Tiktok's Open platform, Ele.me helped millions of businesses to provide local life services of "seeing, clicking, and arriving" for 600 million Tiktok's daily active users with small programs as the carrier. In December of the same year, Tiktok and Dada Express reached a strategic cooperation. It is reported that Tiktok will launch the national take away service on March 1, 2023. In short, Tiktok has gradually become a social platform integrating entertainment, life and express delivery.

Douban, a more specialized social networking site, is also worth mentioning. It attracts art students and those passionate about books, film, culture, and music. Users connect according to their interests and often hold offline activities, such as trips to local art exhibitions

Lastly, Momo, established in 2011, is an open social platform in China and one of the most commonly used stranger making apps. Through this platform, users can use videos, text, voice, and pictures to showcase themselves, discover nearby people based on geographical location, and establish real, effective, and healthy social relationships. However, with the development of the platform and market demand, Momo has also added functions such as groups, forums, and live streaming. Currently, it is a communication platform that goes beyond social interaction.

Generally speaking, social media has become an indispensable part of people's daily lives. Social media can not only help people stay in touch with friends and family, but also help them obtain information, share experiences, and establish social networks. The positive role of social media is not only reflected at the individual level, but can also have a positive impact on society. On social media, people can express their opinions, attracting public attention and discussion. This kind of discussion can promote social progress and promote the resolution of social problems. In addition, social media can also help people understand social welfare undertakings, participate in various public welfare activities, and make contributions to society.

Figure 5.4 Social networks. Source:《知识图谱 | 一文读懂社交网络分析》, https://www.zhihu.com.

Bulletin Board Systems

Beyond these sites that have more modern internet functionality, some original forms of social media still flourish in China. Bulletin Board Systems (BBSs) generally refer to online forums, an online communication venue related to network technology. The full English name of BBS is Bulletin Board System, which translates to electronic bulletin board in Chinese. By running service software on a computer, users are allowed to connect through the Internet using terminal programs, perform functions such as downloading data or programs, and exchanging messages with users. Many BBSs are maintained by webmasters on an amateur basis, while others offer paid services. BBSs, which were a primal form of the early Internet, allow people to post basic messages online through Blogs, Bulletin Boards, and Business. In contrast to many countries, a wide range of BBSs still flourish in China today, with users relying on them for critical consumer comments about products and services from clothes and cosmetics to restaurants and cars. Postings are anonymous, which encourages users to give unvarnished views. Writing under pseudonyms, many users that frequently post on BBS build reputations and sizable followings. Anonymity does, of course, also open the system to abuse by competitors writing negative comments.

Conclusion

A broader impact of China's deep involvement in social media is that some netizens only experience the Internet through social media platforms. This is partly because of the large population of new netizens coming online at any given time. The China Internet Network Information Center (CNNIC) released the 49th Statistical Report on the Development of Internet in China in Beijing. The report showed that by December 2023, the number of Internet users in China had reached 1.032 billion, an increase of 42.96 million over December 2023, and the Internet penetration rate had reached 73.0%. This means that China's internet user base is larger than the total US and European online population combined. Crucially, this makes it a haven for social media sites to thrive within. Tencent communication and social services connect over 1 billion people worldwide, helping them connect with family and friends and enjoy convenient travel, payment, and entertainment life. Despite the terrible pandemic, Tencent made 5545.52 billion RMB in 2022. The majority of its social media services are, almost entirely, based in China.

When new users join the Internet, a friend will often introduce them to one particularly relevant service, such as how to communicate with friends for free via Sina Weibo or buy goods via China's e-Bay equivalent — Taobao, so that service becomes their concept of the Internet. These examples show how many Chinese netizens would not distinguish between social media and the Internet itself. To them, the Internet is social media and vice versa.

Task 5 ▶ Reading comprehension

Direction: *MEDIA team are going to launch a discussion about the reading excerpt. They are required to summarize what they learned, share their puzzles as well as their comments on the article, and try to probe into more profound issues in this domain.*

Objectives: *Learning by doing. To cultivate students' capability of finding problems, reflecting on and solving problems independently so as to improve the comprehensive ability of using language.*

Edward: Well, MEDIA team, how do you understand the reading passage?

Angela: That's easy — it's about the development of Chinese social media.

Irene: Yes, it does make some comparisons in the form of apps, platforms and users. All these are easier to understand. I wonder what is the hidden reasons for the distinctions.

Davis: Yeah, I got that. I think multidimensional factors contribute to the existing differences such as language, culture and geographical factors.

Maynor: You're all amazing! You did ponder over the comparisons instead of just scratching the surface. It implies the unification between social benefits and economic profits etc.

Angela: Oh, my goodness. Dear Maynor, your comment seems beyond my comprehension. But you really provide us opportunities to engage in cognitive thinking and learn to make connections between appearance and essence.

Davis: My comprehension is that different national conditions in various countries lead to different social ways which disseminate different social platforms.

Irene: Exactly. As you know China is making effort to develop culture industries, rebalancing domestic media control and international cultural transmission and influence. So, to some extent, social media in China will possess its own characteristics.

Angela: But social media is actually We-Media. It has little to do with the state.

Irene: I don't think so. Socialism with Chinese characteristics determines that the development of media industry is inseparable from the support of the government. There must exist the intersection among culture, media policies and market.

Edward: I agree with Irene. From the rapid advancement of social media in China, we can summarize the six areas: (1) management mechanisms; (2) the prescribed nature of a media organization; (3) media censorship; (4) media consolidation and economies of scale; (5) the entry of private capital into the Chinese media industries; and (6) China's soft power and public diplomacy.

Maynor: Yes, yes. These stress the government's role as administrator rather than player in managing cultural agencies. This is framed as a measure to further cultural reforms that aim to coordinate operations of the government from those of the enterprise. Specifically, the proposes to establish unified management organizations linking party and state to administer cultural staff, affairs, capital, and orientation.

Davis: Sure. Thanks to this sort of leadership model, most of the videos from China's social media, such as Youku and Tudou, will be pre edited to filter out bad elements, so as to ensure that the social platform is rich in information and reduce the spread of wrong information.

Angela: I got it. China has the largest netizens in the world. The Chinese organization of social media or social platform should serve as the dual roles. They are both an instrument of cultural publicity and an operating entity.

Irene: In the era of reform, media organizations have been advocated to simultaneously serve as an official organ of the state and at the same time operating business according to market forces.

Edward: China has been pursuing media consolidation and economies of scale. It also endeavors to push consolidation and acquisitions of cultural enterprises across geography, industry, and different kinds of ownership and improve the scale, concentration, and professionalism of the cultural industries.

Maynor: So, it's pleasant to see that Tencent became the first Chinese tech giant to be valued at over US$500 billion. This ranked the company, which owns the popular messaging service WeChat, ahead of other internation social platform. Tencent's now world's fifth most valuable tech company based on market value, behind Apple, Google, Microsoft and Amazon.

Davis: China is home to some of the world's largest social and messaging networks.

Angela:	Chinese social networks and messaging apps are hubs for innovation, featuring a range of video, news, e-commerce and other services.
Irene:	Right. In terms of service apps, we all love Dianping and Ctrip which have some of the largest satisfaction ratings in China. Dianping, formed by the merger of two smaller companies akin to Groupon and Yelp, allows users to make lunch reservations, order food and buy film tickets through the app.
Davis:	And in terms of social news, Chinese social platforms enjoy many interactive features that are also gaining popularity among news apps. The increasingly growing app Toutiao, for example, aggregates news and features live Q&As.
Edward:	The majority of Chinese people believe Chinese social media has had a positive impact on Chinese people, the same as westerners love Western social media sites and apps.
Maynor:	As brands and agencies seek to expand into China — or to reach the Chinese diaspora across the globe — they will need to better understand the intricacies of the Chinese market and many of the unique products and services within it. I am sure our discussion will be of help for them.
Angela:	Wow, what a profound opinion!
Edward:	Exactly. But I think this discussion has lasted a long time. How about going ahead now?
All:	Okay. So much for today. See you next time.

Task 6 ▶ Translation practice

Direction: *MEDIA team are going to do Chinese-English translation, from which they can learn and compare how to express in cross-cultural way and convey the following paragraph in English accurately.*

Objectives: *To understand and master English morphology, syntax and idiomatic expressions, develop basic professional translation ability and promote English competence.*

社交媒体是一种给予用户极大参与交互空间的新型在线媒体。在当代社会中，所有国家都在利用社交媒体的力量为人民提供便利服务、改善人民的生活。社交媒体的魅力在于用户可以与任何人联系，并以文本、视频、音频等方式学习和分享自己的观点、想法，获取知识和信息等。比如，在整个新型冠状病毒感染疫情大流行期间，社交媒体为学生和教师提供了重要教育资源和教学途径，成功地帮助教师和学生转变了传统角色，学生成为自己学习的管理者，教师成为学习的辅助者。此外，社交媒体惠及几乎整个社会，从农民到教师，从学生到企业家，几乎每个人都可以从社交媒体及其意识因素中受益。社交媒体使人们能够及时获取最新信息，并可以轻松传播。同时，在社交媒体的帮助下，人们可以通过多渠道获得讯息，通过研究，判断其真实性和客观性，提高鉴别能力。

Task 7 ▶ Attending a public lecture

Direction: *MEDIA team are going to attend a public lecture delivered by Professor Maynor. Students are required to thoroughly understand the lecture, broaden the vision, elaborate on the theme, get inspiration from the lecture and do some speech activities to extend their knowledge.*

Objectives: *To train students' capability of description, expression, discussion, refutation, humor and humanistic accomplishment required by making a speech, thus, improving students' English language competence and proficiency.*

Lecture 5

Social Media, Public Discourse and Engagement in Modern China

Professor Maynor

Hello, everybody. As you no doubt remember in my previous lecture I talked to you about new media practice, addressing not only the great changes brought by new media on a basis of information technology plus its huge effect on the whole society but also its novel practice. This time, I will put emphasis on social media, which is actually is one aspect of new media.

The rapid development of communication and information technologies in the past nearly three decades has made the Internet and social media widely available to ordinary Chinese citizens, fundamentally changing the ways of communication and bringing new elements to the development of a public sphere in China. The relationship of social media with public discourse and engagement should be elaborated so as to examine how individual characteristics, such as political interest, life satisfaction, and interpersonal trust might moderate the relationship between social media usage and public participation in public discourse and activities.

This lecture will start with the discussion of the developmental stages of the Internet and social media in China. I then try to theoretically explain how social media could influence both public discourse and engagement in China. Next, we explore the effect of social media on public discourse, engagement and business practice.

The development of Internet and social media in China

Since the Internet was first introduced to China in 1994, the number of internet users has increased exponentially in the country. According to China Internet Network Information Center, China only had 1 million internet users in 1997, but this number skyrocketed to 11 million in 2005 and to 649 million in 2014. During this period, social media have gone through three developmental phases and have gradually become one of the most popular medium types in China.

Before 2005 the Bulletin Board System (BBS) was the main form of social media. Popular BBS sites included online forums with major portal sites such as Sina.com, Sohu.com and 163.com, and more specialized bulletin board sites such as Tianya and the like. Even today, BBS is still fairly popular among Chinese netizens. Between 2006 and 2008, multiple social media sites emerged where users can interact with friends and post pictures, status, and comments. Momo.com, for example, was one of the most widely used social media platforms during this phase. A chatting software QQ also became popular during this time. Since 2009, social media have entered the third phase whereby various social media applications were launched and quickly became popular among Chinese people, first Weblog in 2009, and then WeChat (an instant messaging social media platform) in 2011. WeChat has immediately attracted an unprecedentedly large number of users and become the most popular social media tool in China, followed by QQ and Weblog. Today approximately 89% of online Chinese use WeChat and other instant messaging apps, 61% use QQ, and 44% use Weblog and other microblog sites.

Social media have fundamentally changed the ways people entertain, shop and communicate with one another. Chinese use social media to obtain news, find friends' status, upload pictures, update their status, post their dairy, comments and share information, watch videos and listen to music. However, there are slight differences in the use of each type of social media. While Chinese netizens primarily use QQ and other social media sites to upload pictures, diary and to update their status, they use Weblog and other micro blogging sites to obtain news and track the status of people whom they are interested in. WeChat and other instant messaging apps are primarily used to chat with friends and get to know friends' status.

Social media and public discourse

Social media help build a public sphere where people can exchange ideas freely through "meetings, debates, dialogues and discussions". With social media, individual citizens can now easily access and gain information on various political and social issues and become more informed and rational. In addition, social media and computer networking offer "cheap, decentralized, two-way communication" and enable people to participate virtually through email lists, electronic bulletin boards, online chat groups, and the like. Therefore, social media provide a unique virtual space for citizens to engage in free and open dialogues, whereby "participants put forward and challenge claims and arguments about common problems, not resting until satisfied that the best reasons have been given and fully defended. Participants attempt to come to an understanding of their interlocutors and to reflexively modify their pre-discursive positions in response to better arguments."

To use a popular Chinese BBS, Qiangguoluntan, as an example, we find that a variety of political topics were discussed in August 2015 alone. Subscribers of this BBS had heated discussions on issues such as corruption, the anti-corruption movement, territorial disputes with Japan, pension system for migrant workers, health care reform, pollution and environmental protection, reform of state-owned enterprises, recent stock market crash, and law and constitutionalism in China. The discussions on this site are quite free and open. For instance, a discussion thread under the discussion panel of "Monitor by the People" called for ordinary Chinese citizens to use this panel to expose misconducts of government officials and monitor governmental activities. More than 200 people responded to the thread and debated on whether or not the panel can really influence politics. When a political commentary is posted on Weblog for instance, thousands of Weblog users can instantly access this post and share this post to their friends/followers. Posts can be also shared and re-shared through WeChat instantly and reach a large volume of audience within seconds. The feature of the rapid diffusion of information makes social media a unique platform for not only ordinary Chinese citizens to articulate their own problems and voice their opinions, but Chinese official media also make full use of social media to do publicity. When the initial stage of COVID-19 outbreak, the official Weibo account of People's Daily took advantage of the compatibility of Weibo platform with various media forms such as text, images, and videos to use "images+text", "videos+text", and lives streaming to report news concerning COVID-19. It has launched "People's Lives" on Weibo so that the official Weibo could promptly release the latest progress of the epidemic, follow up on the epidemic situation, and respond to social concerns. For instance, the official Weibo account of *People's Daily* reported the establishment of "Huoshen Mountain" and "Leishen Mountain" hospitals, thus enabling people to realize "cloud supervision" through live broadcast, enhancing people's confidence in overcoming the epidemic and calming their worries. Through Weibo platform, *People's Daily* timely and effectively disseminated news information to the audience. It played the role of the mouthpiece of the *People's Daily* and effectively maintained social stability, consequently, avoiding secondary harm, and playing an important role in guiding the entire population to fight against the epidemic successfully.

Based on the theorization of cyberspace's role in public discourse and the above examples, we postulate that individuals who use social media more often will be more exposed to various political information and discussions online, and therefore more likely to engage in these public online debates and political discussions. We argue that the positive effect of social media can extend to offline space and promote general public discourse. Particularly, once individuals actively use social media to engage in online discussions on certain issues, they will naturally bring the discussions to their circles of friends, coworkers, classmates and acquaintances and further discuss or debate on these issues with them. Therefore, social media usage could be positively related to both online public discourse in general.

Social media and public engagement

Not only do social media promote public discourse, they can also potentially involve individuals in public activities.

The role of information and communication technologies in public engagement is somewhat controversial. Some scholars hold that the Internet is suspected to disengage people from public matters for three reasons. First, it is likely that when people use most of their online time on shopping and entertainment, they are likely to be less involved in public matters. Second, surveillance and censorship by states and employers could discourage citizens from participating in public affairs. Finally, online communication including electronic conversations, bulletin boards, chat rooms, and virtual conferences etc. is only a poor substitute for traditional face-to-face interaction, and therefore does not contribute to healthy public engagement. Yet, contrary to the conventional prediction that the Internet disengages public participation, others believe that the Internet, especially social media, promotes public engagement. Online communication may be used to support offline relationships and keep people connected despite of geographical boundaries. Internet usage is also shown to have a positive effect on volunteering for charities.

The positive relationship between social media and public engagement perhaps resides in the mechanism of social capital. Social capital is "the aggregate of the actual or potential resources which are linked to possession of a durable network of more or less institutionalized relationships of mutual acquaintance or recognition." When individuals participate virtually through electronic bulletin boards, online chat groups, and the like, they become bound by shared problems, interests, ideologies and values and form a sense of belonging. These social media platforms bring total strangers together and maintain interpersonal ties relatively easily and inexpensively. As a result, virtual communities are formed to provide informal associational spaces, and play an important role in replacing the degraded pubic sphere of modern urban life.

Figure 5.5 Internet platform users.
Source：新浪财经头条，《用户增长在新时代必备的五大超能力》，2021-9-29，https://t.cj.sina.com.cn/articles/view.

Examples of social media facilitating social activities and maintaining social ties can be easily found in today's China. In an article titled "Cannot Say No to Class Reunions" published on *People's Daily*, a certain Mr. Wang recounted that in the past he and his classmates were only able to have an offline classmate reunion every year or every few years. Typically, someone had to make phone calls to everybody to extend the invitation and eventually confirm attendance, which was a big hassle and not effective. However, nowadays, because of the group chat function in WeChat, they can have a class reunion carnival nearly every day. According to Wang, with WeChat, now anyone can "throw" a suggestion for reunion in the group chat, which normally will result in a heated discussion and a gathering together somewhere.

Another interesting example is the square dance groups in China. In almost every city, women and men get together to dance in public squares. The square dance group started using WeChat to spread the word about their dancing group when it was first established in May 2014. Soon, their dancing group expanded from about 10 people to almost 60 people. They then used WeChat group chats to share information on group activities, competitions with other groups, as well as dancing videos. One of the dancers indicated that WeChat made their communication much more effective and they were able to connect with group members easily.

Social media also make engagement in charitable and volunteering activities much easier than before. On May 2, 2015, the Women and Children's Hospital in Yueqing City in Zhejiang province charged a 26-week pregnant woman, Ms. Chen, experiencing hemorrhage due to placenta previa. The hospital used up all AB type blood and needed more. Right after the surgery, a staff in the hospital posted a message in the WeChat group soliciting blood donation at about 4pm on May 3, which was immediately shared by doctors, nurses and staff members into their own friend circles. Within hours, more than 20 volunteers came to the hospital to donate blood. By 8 pm on the same day, the hospital collected 3100 CC AB type blood and saved Ms. Chen's life. These three examples vividly demonstrate the effectiveness of social media in engaging citizens in public activities such as networking group events, interest-based group activities, as well as charitable and voluntary activities.

The influence of China's social media on companies

For companies, the rise of social media opens opportunities to engage with consumers and, at times, avert serious problems. By ignoring social media, companies may not see a consumer-led crisis coming.

Companies can use social media to conduct consumer research, shift brand preference, launch products, and manage crises. Even monitoring online conversations can yield striking results. For example, while conducting daily online monitoring for a client, a brewing consumer is found to protest over the client's shop in Guangzhou. Early in the week, a disgruntled customer had posted complaints about customer service and announced his intention to visit the store that coming Saturday to express his dissatisfaction. Other netizens said they would join, exchanged mobile phone numbers, and discussed where to meet. By Wednesday, a group of 30 disgruntled customers had plans to meet at the store on Saturday. Because the original complainer had posted full details of his experience, the company was able to contact the customer and rectify the situation. In response, the customer announced online that he would cancel his visit to the shop. He was impressed with the direct outreach and the fact that the company listened.

An example involving a nationwide consumer recall shows how companies should use social media and speak the language of consumers. In this case, consumers had different concerns from what the company expressed in public statements about its recall. The company also posted general information about the recall, but consumers online wanted more detailed and practical information. By actively listening to consumers on BBS and other social media sites during the recall, the company adjusted its online messaging to answer consumer questions. As the recall went into full swing, the number of people visiting recall-related forums remained high, but fewer people left comments or asked questions because their questions were being answered sufficiently.

Therefore, the relationship between social media use and public discourse, engagement and business activities are interdependent on political interest, generalized trust, and life satisfaction. Before I put end to this lecture, I'd like to leave three questions for you to discuss in your online forum. Firstly, while social media are so popular with most people, especially the youth, do social media have any ill effect on the society or individuals? And How? Secondly, as a Chinese saying goes: "A man should be what he looks like." Do you like to be a "Glass man" with all your personal information transparent through social media? Thirdly, is there any possibility of social media to impact the state safety? Try on them.

So much for this lecture. Bye for now.

Task 8 ▶ Online forum and summary writing

Direction: *MEDIA team are going to launch an instant online post-talk about the lecture to appeal to more of other students who are interested in the topic to join them. This is an integrated practice of listening, speaking, reading and writing. They are particularly expected to write a summary of the entire unit.*

Objectives: *To provide a platform for MEDIA team to fully display their talents. To comb language learning with professional knowledge so as to cultivate students' professional learning, academic literacy and language competence. To realize the teaching objectives of acquiring professional knowledge through learning English language.*

Edward: Hi again, MEDIA members. What do Prof. Maynor's lecture impress you this time? This lecture did thorough analysis of social media, its practice, its participants and its influence. In one word, it helps us to clarify the main theme from its birth, its progress to its performance, from outside to inside. However, what I have to stress is that you guys should spend more time on pondering over the last three questions raised by Prof. Maynor. Can anyone understand my intentions?

Irene: Yes. Prof. Edward, I am quite willing to try my best.

Angela: I think I have a thorough grasp of this lecture. At least over 85%.

Davis: I believe practice shows true knowledge. Let's devote ourselves into practice. Practice is the sole criterion for testing truth. Can I win everyone's approval?

Maynor: Yes, Davis. To be fair, I am deeply convinced that you must have mastered most of the content. Here, I just want to reiterate Prof. Edward's proposal: among others things, please reflect on the three questions and initiate an online discussion.

Edward: So, go ahead with your online forum. Maynor and I will be ready to offer assistance at any time.

Irene: Okay, dear professors. I'd like to cast a brick to attract jade by initiating the discussion first on public discourse through social as a warm-up. Is it ok?

Davis & Angela: You are too modest. Please just go ahead.

Irene: Given that social media platforms provide open news outlets, which are integrated with active online social networks, both can now spread information faster, more widely, and more effectively. Hence, social network users are no longer just passive recipients of information, they can also create and distribute content, selectively disseminate information, and share their own opinions through social platforms. Consequently, individuals can easily find evidence that can support their existing ideas and follow those people who hold similar viewpoints, amplifying preexisting socio-cognitive biases. Recommendation algorithms further amplify these biases by predicting and delivering these contents. Thus, public discourse may represent the free speech of the public while disseminating biases. It is contradictory, isn't it?

Angela: It truly is. But the solution to such problems has found its way. The role of opinion-based confirmation bias in the diffusion of rumors and fake news has also attracted the attention of network and data scientists, and they have found a way to terminate this spreading.

Davis: There is no absolute answer. In my perspective, how the social media platforms are shaping public discourse should also be within our consideration. You know social media platforms are transforming public discourse in ways we may not understand.

Irene: Yes. This can respond to Prof. Maynor's questions concerning personal safety or the state security. Billions of people around the world get their news, debate policy, join political discussion, and connect with friends and families through social media platforms. The platforms have become the substrate of our social interactions and the means by which human relationships are formed and maintained.

Angela: Yes. The platforms disseminate the public messages, but it also determines whether their signals will be amplified, suppressed or distorted. So a social platform is not just a carrier of social media, it is an entirely new social medium.

Irene: So we need to understand how this new social medium works, how it influences its users, and how you will build your social media activity into your existing routine. Do remember that posting on social media does not mean that you will access the groups you want to engage with – you will need to work hard to make connections, and get noticed.

Davis: Absolutely. Not everyone will welcome our content, so make sure we have a strategy for dealing with any negative feedback or trolls. Social media can be a really effective part of our public engagement toolkit.

Angela: So when developing an engagement activity, it is important to consider that there are a few key things to bear in mind before developing any engagement activity. For example, who am I trying to engage with and why? Which platforms are suitable for the people I would like to engage with? Can I "piggyback" on to other events or engage with others?

Irene: Full of Philosophy! Most of us spend more time apart than ever before, so connecting online is getting increasingly crucial. Still, it's important to remember that these platforms can pose risks if we aren't thoughtful about how we use them.

Davis: Certainly. Everyone should learn to protect his or her privacy and the security of his or her social media accounts. When we post personal information on social media, we make ourselves, our loved ones and even our physical belongings a target for local and online criminals. I strongly recommend that we avoid posting names, phone numbers, addresses, school and work locations, and other sensitive information as text or in a photo.

Angela: Always keep alert. Please check and update our privacy settings frequently, so only people we know can view our posts. And we should also enable the strongest privacy options that social media sites offer, and make confirming our settings a habit. Some social media apps regularly push updates that disable settings.

Edward: Really terrific! Your discussion has covered almost all the questions raised. Although you still have more to say,

	time is limited after all. We have to shift this discussion of combining face and line to purely online forum, and invite more students to participate at the same time. I am sure you will preside well over this continued forum.
All:	Okay. Bye for now. Welcome to our online forum.

Appendix: Vocabulary for Unit 5

Listening

proliferation /prəˌlɪfəˈreɪʃn/ *n.* 激增，剧增；繁殖，增生；大量

revenue /ˈrevənjuː/ *n.* 收入，收益；（政府的）税收；税务局，税务署（the revenue）

affiliation /əˌfɪliˈeɪʃ(ə)n/ *n.* （与政治、宗教等组织的）联系，从属关系；加盟，加入

fake /feɪk/ *adj.* 伪造的，冒充的；（动作或感情）虚假的，做作的
n. 假货，赝品；骗子，冒充者；假动作
v. 伪造，冒充；假装，佯装；（尤指体育运动中）做假动作；不懂装懂

authoritative /ɔːˈθɒrətətɪv/ *adj.* 专断的，命令式的；可靠的，可信的，权威的

verify /ˈverɪfaɪ/ *v.* 核实，查证；证明，证实

stark /stɑːk/ *adj.* 荒凉的；严酷的；明显的，鲜明的；完全的，十足的；健壮的，结实的

anonymous /əˈnɒnɪməs/ *adj.* 匿名的，不知名的；不记名的，不具名的；无特色的

Reading Activity

integral /ˈɪntɪgrəl/ *adj.* 必需的，必要的；作为组成部分的；完整的；整的，积分的
n. 积分；完整

flourish /ˈflʌrɪʃ/ *v.* 繁荣，昌盛；挥动；（植物或动物）长势好，茁壮成长
n. 夸张动作；（讲话或文章的）华丽辞藻，修饰；花彩号声；（手写花体字的）花饰

thriving /ˈθraɪvɪŋ/ *adj.* 欣欣向荣的，繁华的，兴旺的
v. 茁壮成长，兴旺，繁荣

netizen /ˈnetɪzn/ *n.* 泛指一般的网民

substantial /səbˈstænʃ(ə)l/ *adj.* 大量的，价值巨大的；牢固的，结实的；基本的，实质性的；（饭菜）丰盛的；重要的，真实的；有地位的，富有的

n. 重要材料

boom /buːm/ *n.* 繁荣；流行，风靡；隆隆声；吊杆；帆桁；水栅

v. 迅速发展，繁荣；轰鸣，轰响；用低沉的声音说

flock /flɒk/ *n.* （鸟或羊等动物）群；一大群人；（某个教堂的）会众，全体教徒；（填充垫子的）絮屑，毛棉填料；（植绒用的）短绒，绒屑

v. 群集，蜂拥

mishap /ˈmɪshæp/ *n.* 灾祸；不幸事故；晦气

portion /ˈpɔːʃ(ə)n/ *n.* 一部分；一份，一客；

v. 分配

pirated /’paɪrətid/ *v.* 盗版，侵犯版权；劫掠（船只）（pirate 的过去式及过去分词）

adj. 盗版的；非法复制的

skepticism /ˈskeptɪsɪzəm/ *n.* 怀疑态度；怀疑论

switchover /ˈswɪtʃəʊvə(r)/ *n.* 转换；替换

demographics /ˌdeməˈɡræfɪks/ *n.* 人口统计资料

versus /ˈvɜːsəs/ *prep.* （比赛或诉讼中）以……为对手，与……竞争；与……相对，与……相比

tweet /twiːt/ *n.* （小鸟的）啁啾声，啾啾声；在推特网上发的帖子，微博

v. 啾啾地叫；在推特网上发微博；在推特网上（与人）发信息

segment /ˈseɡmənt/ *n.* 部分，片段；（市场）细分的部分；（水果或花自然形成的）瓣，（昆虫的）节；球缺，弓形；（直线或弧线上两点间的）段；（特定广播或电视节目的）时间段

v. 分割，划分；（细胞）分裂

passionate /ˈpæʃənət/ *adj.* 热诚的，狂热的；热恋的，情意绵绵的；易怒的

default /dɪˈfɔːlt/ *n.* 不履行，违约；默认，系统设定值；缺席，弃权

v. 违约，不履行义务；默认，预设；弃权，未到场

adj. 默认的

unvarnished /ˌʌnˈvɑːnɪʃt/ *adj.* 未涂漆的；无装饰的；无掩饰的

pseudonym /ˈsuːdənɪm; ˈsjuːdənɪm/ *n.* 笔名；假名

Lecture

skyrocket /ˈskaɪrɒkɪt/ *n.* 流星烟火；冲天火箭

v. （价格）飞涨，猛涨；（使）……猛然上涨

unprecedentedly /ʌnˈpresɪdentɪdli/ *adv.* 空前地

virtually /ˈvɜːtʃuəli/ *adv.* 事实上，几乎；虚拟地，模拟地
interlocutor /ˌɪntəˈlɒkjətə(r)/ *n.* 对话者；谈话者
reflexively /rɪˈfleksɪvli/ *adv.* 反身地
pension /ˈpenʃ(ə)n/ *n.* 养老金，退休金；津贴，补助金
v.（尤指因年龄或疾病而）向（某人）支付养老金使其退休
commentary /ˈkɒmənt(ə)ri/ *n.* 现场解说，实况报道；评注性著作，评论文；讨论，评论；说明，写照
confiscate /ˈkɒnfɪskeɪt/ *v.* 没收，查抄；充公，罚没（某物，尤指土地）
adj. 被没收的
postulate /ˈpɒstʃəleɪt/ *v.* 假定，假设；（教会法）提名（某人）任圣职，选举（某人）任圣职
n. 假定，假设；（数）公设
disengage /ˌdɪsɪnˈgeɪdʒ/ *vt.* 使脱离；解开；解除
vi. 脱出；松开
surveillance /sɜːˈveɪləns/ *n.* 监视，监察
reside /rɪˈzaɪd/ *v.* 居住，定居；存在于；（权利、权力等）属于
aggregate /ˈægrɪgət/ *n.* 总数，合计；骨料，混凝料
adj. 总计的，合计的；（种群）聚生的
v. 集合，聚集；总计达到；合计
degraded /dɪˈgreɪdɪd/ *adj.* 退化的；堕落的；被降级的
v. 分解（degrade 的过去分词）；降低……的身份；削减
hassle /ˈhæs(ə)l/ *n.* 麻烦，困难；争论，争吵；起哄，骚扰
v. 打扰，使烦恼；〈非正式，美〉争辩，争论
carnival /ˈkɑːnɪv(ə)l/ *n.* 狂欢节，嘉年华会；庆祝活动；（学校的）游园会，嘉年华会
charitable /ˈtʃærətəbl/ *adj.* 慈善的；仁慈的，宽容的；慷慨的
hemorrhage /ˈhemərɪdʒ/ *n.* [病理] 出血（等于 haemorrhage）；番茄汁
vt. [病理] 出血
vi. [病理] 出血
placenta /pləˈsentə/ *n.* [胚] 胎盘；[植] 胎座
previa /ˈpriːviə/ *n.* 前置
brewing /ˈbruːɪŋ/ *n.* 酿造；酝酿；计划
v. 酿造；策划阴谋（brew 的进行式）
disgruntled /dɪsˈgrʌnt(ə)ld/ *adj.* 不满的；不高兴的
rectify /ˈrektɪfaɪ/ *v.* 纠正，矫正；整流，把（交流电）转变成直流电；蒸馏；求曲线的直线等长

outreach /ˈaʊtriːtʃ/ *n.* 外展服务，扩大范围的服务；主动帮助

v. 超出……的限度或范围；超过，胜出；伸出双臂

adj. 外展服务的，扩大服务范围的

swing /swɪŋ/ *v.*（使）摆动，摇荡；改变（情绪、状况或想法等）；做弧线运动，转弯

n. 摇摆，摆动；（为打某人而）挥舞，挥拳；挥杆动作；改变，变化；秋千；荡秋千（板球）侧飞球

adj. 摇摆乐的；（在投票选举中）摇摆不定的

6
Unit

Weblog Sphere in China

TABLE OF CONTENTS

Unit 6 Weblog Sphere in China

Warm-up: Be proactive

Direction: *MEDIA team are going to do warm-up activities by discussing, airing their views on the topic and discovering problems.*

Objectives: *To arouse students' interest, get a preliminary understanding of relevant knowledge and prepare for the following study.*

Angela: Hi, welcome back, MEDIA partners. From now on, we're starting a new leg of our journey through Chinese microblog, a very popular social media platform with which we're quite familiar, right?

Irene: Yes. We are going to delve into Weibo in China, but I am hesitating to admit that I am quite familiar with Weibo because I only browse on Weibo or Weblog for information or for fun other than write, post or repost etc. I have never registered a microblog account. I am sorry for that.

Davis: I have opened an account but just post text or photos occasionally. That doesn't mean my lack of knowledge about how to use Weblog, instead, I am just concerned with the personal information safety as we talked last time on our online forum.

Angela: Aha, you are so cautious a guy. Actually, as long as you can apply it properly, there's no need to worry about personal safety. Common individuals often blog about whatever they love, from their experiences, thoughts, and comments on a situation, social issues, and various topics. So, you can free from doubts and misgivings and make full use of the freedom of speech brought by social media.

Irene: I see. Usually, bloggers are not compensated for their writing and do not need to obtain permission from authority or organizations before they publish their articles on the blogging platform. Would you please offer me a hand by guiding me to publish a short comment on the advantage of social media discussed last time?

Davis: What a clever girl. I'm honored to offer whatever help you need. And we can co-publish if you don't mind.

Irene: Certainly not. You took the words out of my mouth.

Angela: Wait, wait. Are you two going to exclude me?

Davis: You can rest assured that three of us will do our best together.

Irene: Exactly. Microblogging is designed to allow a form of online publishing where articles are written by either an individual or a group of individuals. We publish group paper, don't we?

Angela: Fantastic! More often than not, these blog posts reflect the author's attitudes, political stance, person interests, education levels and the like. Our opinions can be unanimous or dissenting.

Davis: Internet users visit different blogging sites mainly based on topics and fields those sites specialize in. So we need to make clear which Weblogging site is appropriate for us.

Irene: That's easy. We have Angela — an expert in this regard. He has a good command of internet-related knowledge. Leave the task to him. Agree, Angela?

Angela: I'm honored. There are several alternatives among which five blogging sites are either widely-used by the general public or influential in specific fields in China. To my knowledge, Sina Blog, Caixin Blog, Quasi-blogging platform, Consensus Website, and baijia.baidu.com are all very good sites with unique feature.

Davis: Then, it's turn for us to determine our topic and prepare a qualified draft.

Irene: Sure, let's invest ourselves in deep learning.

All: Let's go ahead to feed our mind with rich input first. See you soon.

Task 1 ▶ Listening activity

Direction: *MEDIA team are going to listen to an introduction of key concepts so as to lay the foundation for later learning.*

Objectives: *To understand the main conception, practice and strengthen the ability of listening comprehension.*

An Overview of Chinese Blogs

The Cambridge dictionary defines a blog as — a regular record of your thoughts, opinions, or experiences that you put on the internet for other people to read. Whereas Miriam Webster has two definitions — a website that contains online personal reflections, comments, and often hyperlinks, videos, and photographs provided by the writer. And a regular feature appearing as part of an online publication that typically relates to a particular topic and consists of articles and personal commentary by one or more authors.

The term "microblogging" refers to a relatively new broadcast and information blogging channel, unique for its limited number of characters per post. On microblogging platforms, users can post microblogs in the text with photos, videos, weblinks, and locations, receive posts in their news from accounts they are following, repost others' microblogs and mention other microbloggers in one's posts by tagging them.

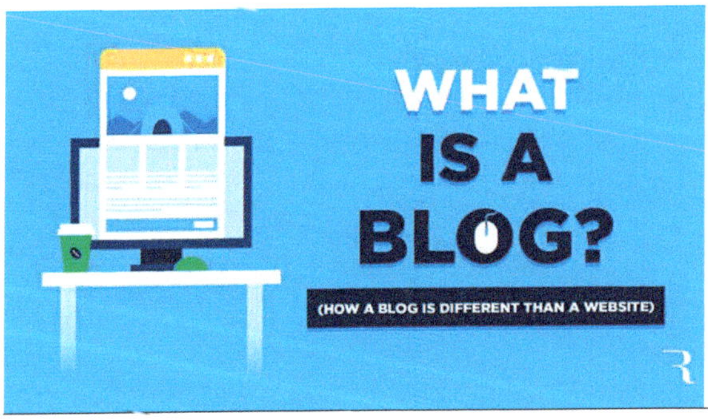

Figure 6.1 What is a blog? Source: E-Library Admin, "What is a blog?" May 5, 2022, www.google.com.hk.

Sina Corporation, one of the Chinese internet portals, released its test version of a microblogging service in August 2009. Then in April 2011, Sina Weibo names its domain weibo.com, making it stand out from other competitors by using the Chinese character for microblog. In March 2014, the name Sina Weibo was changed to Weibo. In January 2016, Weibo removed the 140-character limit for original posts, and introduced posts with words counting up to 2000 characters, though the 140-character limit still applied to reposts and comments. It offers a range of features just on its homepage starting with essential microblogging services and functions including instant messages and replies displayed below the microblogs. Weibo has integrated many features from other social networking platforms into its service. It also provides users the ability to create group discussions, which is similar to what is available in other Bulletin Board Systems (BBS). And users can also click "like" a microblog or set privacy levels of microblogs. Additionally, Weibo has designed certain functions to meet Chinese users' needs. One of those special functions is called "quietly follow", which allows users to follow other users without their awareness. The normal "follow" action causes a new follower notification to be sent to the user being followed and will be listed on his/her follower list. The "quietly follow" action results neither in notification nor the followers' name being listed as such but will permit the follower to view the person's microblog feeds. Another essential function is grouping the microblogs one follows. Weibo users can sort those they follow into groups to filter and read only the microblogs from one customized group instead of all posts by microbloggers they follow. This helps users filter information and enables flexibility of reading.

Moreover, Weibo also offers an account and identity verification service to celebrities, businesses, organizations, government agencies, and even individuals. Because of the platform's extensive popularity among Chinese netizens, the leading foreign or international media organizations, like the Wall Street Journal, have also registered their Weibo accounts.

When Weibo initially established its platform, it invited many famous Chinese celebrities to register, which then encouraged many fans to join. Besides validating institutional accounts with a Blue V symbol, and verified celebrities with a Red Star. Weibo also provides a verification service to personal-account users, which includes verification of interest, verification of their linked media, and verification of own identity. A user can apply for identity verification when he/she meets the conditions of connecting his/her account with a mobile number and a profile picture, and keeping at least 50 followers etc. Once their verification application is approved, the user's displayed name will be shown along with an Orange V logo, which indicates that account has been validated by Weibo. Any verified individual user with a monthly reading count of over ten million and ten thousand followers is also qualified to apply for the Weibo Gold V verification. These gold-verified Weibo users receive specific privileged services such as a personalized page, a "fan station" to interact with followers, and being officially promoted by Weibo to gain more followers.

In parallel with the various levels of account verifications, Weibo provides professional versions of its interface for different types of users. Apart from its common interface for individual users, it also has separate interfaces for its business version, media version, school version and government version. Each interface version is customized with extra functions and services such as information management, administrative sets, data analysis, and opinion monitoring etc. which are not available to individual users. The earlier version of Weibo contains five modules, including a management center, message center, statistics center, administrator setting and application center. Meanwhile, subsections can be added in the application center per the user's request. Weibo has been continuously updating its functions and services.

According to China Voice's "News Evening Peak" report, Sina and Weibo launched a complaint platform — Black Cat in February, 2018. Through the Black Cat Complaint Platform, users can complain about any issues that arise during the consumption process at any time, thereby achieving rights protection. On the afternoon of February 1st, the Black Cat Complaint Platform announced the status of consumer complaints received as of January 31st, and data showed that 90% of valid complaints had been matched with merchants for processing. Weibo adopted a complaint system to supplement its technological and manual censorship procedures. When users find that a post contains inappropriate information, e.g., illegal, harmful, or false information, they can click the "report" button attached to the post and submit a complaint to the Weibo administrator. Users can apply to become a Weibo supervisor and be paid for reporting complaints to the platform. The basic requirements to be approved as a Weibo supervisor include: being registered on Weibo for more than a year, holding a credit score above 80, and being registered with a verified mobile phone number.

Weibo is now the most popular microblogging service among microblogging service providers in the Chinese mainland, which benefits from its various improvements. Most people take Weibo as daily usage. Some adopt it as a source of information, or a service for information searching, and others consider it a space for self-expression and keeping personal records. The rapid advancement of high technology contributes to constant changes in Weibo function, content and users as well. Weibo content has been enriched and improved in both quantity and variety. The entertainment and marketing content has become dominant while social-political discussions declined. Such changes in function lead to the rapid growth in volume, individual accounts, institutional accounts, government accounts etc. Users changes from the middle-aged to the youth now, and from opinion leaders or public intellectuals to interest groups. Weibo enhances productivity or facilitated user interactions such as multi-media posts, live streaming videos, variable ways of commenting and the like.

In all, most users utilize Weibo as news and information source because of its immediacy and accessibility to digging for more relevant information on a news source and a wide range of topics. Some see Weibo as supplementary to mainstream media because they can interpret mainstream news and grapevine news. Hence, Weibo is worthy of its fame as China's second largest social platform.

Task 2 ▶ Listening comprehension

Direction: *MEDIA team are going to have a topic-oriented discussion to exchange their views on the listening material and challenge each other with puzzling questions.*

Objectives: *To broaden students' horizon, develop their ability to sum up the skills of answering questions and strengthen language output ability.*

Maynor: Hello, again everybody. Prof. Edward delivered you an overall review on Weblog in China through listening practice. It's likely to help to clarify the originally puzzles. So you can have a more in-depth discussion around this topic. Knowledge is endless, right?

Edward: Thank you so much for your affirmation of the above excerption. My suggestion is that you should try to imagine what will be Weibo in future. Is it possible to be replaced by other social platforms or merged by international giants? How can a company keep competitive and remain sustainable?

Maynor: These issues are far-reaching. Being students majoring in this domain, you should especially reflect on them and try to diverge thinking and put forward some creative suggestions. Of course, that's really challenging.

Angela: Thank you for your enlightening advice. In my opinion, nothing could go smoothly without obstacles. Weblog is no exception, especially when the Chinese media is going through its transformational period. With the constant progress in enterprise mergers and reorganizations, Weblog in China will be increasingly competent.

Davis: Weblogging platforms must keep doing technological innovation. High-tech is the life of smooth development, and talented people are the main force of driving the technological advancement.

Irene: This is why so many university students specialize in this subject, but interdisciplinary talents can play a greater role. I mean the integration of the operation, management, technical support, data analysis and language expression of the platform becomes more pressing.

Angela: What you said is about the future. Let's down-to-earth and do the present thing first. The equivalent of Weblog in China is Twitter in the United States. That means they both share some similarities. Twitter has a much larger market share globally than Weblog, which indicates that Weblog in China is striving for effective marketing strategies to earn larger market share.

Davis: For this, I think language service should be put to one of the top priorities so as to provide users all over the world with platforms in their preferable languages.

Angela: In addition to language, techniques to test the information diffusion in online social networks also call for attention. Techniques adopted to model the diffusion of processes based either on explanatory models or predictive models have been improving to ensure good operation.

Irene: I'd like to share the information concerning Sina Weibo network. It's said that it includes a number of features like static following network, dynamic following network, retweet behaviors with retweet content, merged retweet behaviors without retweet content, and user profile etc. But it's a shame for me, for I have little idea about these functions.

Davis: I am afraid that I don't fully understand these functions either. Angela, you will be capable of explaining these functions for us, won't you?

Angela: Well, I strongly recommend that we should study the following reading material carefully and then I assure you that you will quite understand those functions.

Irene: Really? Having read the reading excerpt, we can renew the analysis of these functions. That will be easier.

Angela: I am sure that you can. However, I hope to address that our main objective will be to understand the dynamics and model the information spreading phenomena on Sina Weibo.

Davis: To better clarify these problems, we need learn to observe the information diffusion among various platforms simultaneously subject to the availability of data.

Edward: Wow, our problems are piling up. It's time that we explored truth and solved problems by ourselves. Are you ready?

All: Yes. We're resolved to put end to all of these problems. Bye for now.

Task 3 ▶ Pre-reading activity

Direction: *This part serves as connecting link between the preceding and the following. MEDIA team are required to ponder over some problems concerning the whole unit, reflect on them and then find solutions. The answers are open-ended.*

Objectives: *To cultivate students' capability of exploring problems, develop critical thinking ability synchronously and improve expression ability.*

1. How many Weblogging sites do you know? Please give comment on at least one of them.
2. How did Sina give birth to the first Weblog in China?

3. What do you think of the future of Weblog in China?
4. Is there any possibility of getting stuck like a chip?
5. Which is the favourite feature you love to apply when blogging? And why?
6. "Weibo Event" can be regarded as one of the most popular features of Weblog. Have you ever experienced acquiring or disseminating news through Weibo Event? Please share your experience with us.
7. How does Weblog cater for its users?
8. Can you generally categorize Weblog users?
9. What effect does Weblog have on the society?
10. How was Weblog replaced by WeChat?

Task 4 ▶ Reading activity

Direction: *MEDIA team are required to read the following excerpt to obtain information, expand vocabulary volume, increase knowledge reserve, comprehend between lines, appreciate the writing style and evaluate the article.*

Objectives: *To cultivate students' capability of reading and absorbing information in a way that "eyes see quickly and brain processes quickly" to enhance reading comprehension, build up logic thinking, learn writing through reading and improve students' comprehensive quality.*

Weibo and Its Appealing Features

Weibo, or Microblog in English, is an online social networking and blogging service that enables its users to share, disseminate, get information and read text-based posts of up to 140 characters, was first introduced to China by Sina Corporation, which is the first media company that brought the concept of Microblog into China in 2009. Enlightened by the idea of some other social platform, Sina grasped the opportunity, did some innovation plus some variations, launched Microblog, and developed it as the main media production of the company. What's more, Sina conducts self-censorship, which means the company's internet supervisors will actively delete ill news or will deal with unpleasant messages according to the advices of China's Publicity Department by banning related accounts or deleting their Microblogs. Sina is doing very well with its Microblog business and enjoys over 516 million monthly active users, making it only the second largest social media platform in China after WeChat. Microblog, covering 90% market share of China's microblogging services and with a large population of audience, is forming a kind of Micro-force, which is gradually changing the situation of Chinese media and beating all other China microblogging services. Its huge success is inseparable from its favourable features.

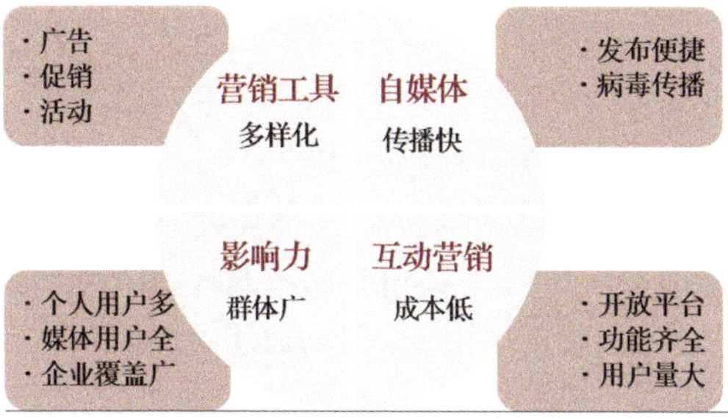

Figure 6.2 Sina Weibo features.

The threaded comments

Weibo has capitalized on the "social validation" aspect of their platform and have focused on making their comment thread user-friendly. The feature makes the feedback tracking process simpler. On Weibo, one can see comments which users properly sorted out under a tweet by just one click. Having scanned through the comment thread of the tweet, one can add his/her own comment and also mention "your @username" in his/her comment, seizing the opportunity to remind the audience about his/her company and brand or any people of clicking on the "Reply" button located on the right side of the commentator's tweet to reply to the commentator. In this way, Weibo assists corporate in increasing the level of brand awareness.

Apparently, most successful microblogging services in China, such as Tencent Weibo and Sina Weibo, all focus heavily on making user's social feedback easier in their own services. The reason is pretty easy. We humans are social animals. Therefore, we care about what others think about us, and threaded comment is really a big plus in making the entire feedback tracking process easier. Weibo makes it available for any user to skim and scan all the users' comments sorted correctly in his/her tweet with just one click with threaded comments too. How user-friendly this threaded comment feature is, as all comments and replying actions are made in a single section.

Besides, Weibo's user interface is cluttered but organized at the same time. It is just like any other Chinese websites that are link-rich. However, the platform makes use of HTML coding which is why the user interface is still far behind in terms of modern design and user experience.

Rich media

One of Sina Weibo's features that most microblogging users praise is its ability to insert rich media like images, videos, music, emoticons, and even polls without any plugin required.

This sparks a really interesting debate between bloggers. Do microblogging service really needs these features? The answer is an absolute yes. Users can probably see the images and videos pretty much existing in most tweets. Surprisingly, the rich media offers far more than users can imagine, such as emoticons and polls without plugin. It allows users use 400 emoticons to be precise! Youngsters in China have a particular interest in playing emoticons, so this is a cult feature for them. There are also fun images provided by Weibo in the image feature, which also pretty much serves like emoticons.

Figure 6.3 Sina Weibo emoticons.

You can also upload the video from your computer or just input the link from the video site, and it will show thumbnails about the video. For example, the best thing about the video feature is if you input the link from supported video sites like Youku or Tudou, you will be able to view the video without even leaving the site, a great strategy for Sina Weibo to retain the users within its website! The newest addition to the video viewing feature allowed professionals to manage video material and edit video clips, marking its latest effort to boost its booming online short video business. One more notable feature is the ability to start a poll by any user. You can put in the description, options, decide whether users can choose single or multiple options, and ultimately, set the visibility of the poll and its expiration date, really a complete and awesome feature, isn't it?

Micro topics

Micro topics is a relatively new concept in microblogging services, implemented by Weibo. It's effortless to understand. Weibo takes any tweet related to a particular topic, then creates a unique page for all users to view and discuss the particular topic. For instance, one of the hottest topics now is Russia-Ukraine conflict, so a dedicated page is created to discuss the issue. If a user likes the topic, there's a tweet box with tags added for him/her to share the topic on his/her own profile immediately, or he/she can push the link on the top of the topic's page to promote the topic to your friends.

Trends categorization

Weibo has a dedicated page for trends, literally named as Board of Fame. Being the hottest trends of last hour, or today or even this week, Weibo's Board of Fame is always prepared to tell users what trends that they really want in the specified time. Categorization is of great significance when it comes to sorting overloaded trends, and Weibo scored full marks on this part by categorizing all hottest trends into several categories such as general, sport, entertainment, finance, gaming, traveling, just about everything anyone might be interested in. In the Board of Fame, users can view the first ten hottest trends by the category, and can probably dig into more trends by click on the "Check out More" link from the respective category. Users can then view the remaining 40 hottest trends in the category or, if those trends still cannot satisfy them, they can even trackback the hottest trends by setting the date located on the right side of the page.

Verified Account & Hall of Celebrity

Verified Account is specifically created for celebrity and famous people, and they will be treated more like celebrities if they registered a verified account of Sina Weibo. It wants those celebrities to shine even more, as they might have expected, they created a dedicated page for highlighting their superstars, literally named "Hall of Celebrity". What's great about the Hall of Celebrity is its detailed categorization. Sina Weibo categorizes celebrities very well into several key categories like entertainment, sport, finance, tech, etc. Then, there are even more subcategories inside the field like entertainment, such as actors, musicians, and entertainment executives. Also, newly joined celebrities do not need to worry about their fame. They will be covered by elite users, as there is also a section that featured celebrities who just joined the world of Sina Weibo. On the page, users can either choose their favourite celebrities to follow or simply click on "Follow All" button to follow all celebrities in the particular field. Why Weibo treats celebrities so seriously is because the celebrities themselves got thousands of fans, so retaining them in Weibo is the key strategy to convert their massive dedicated fans into loyal users.

Medal reward system

The Medal Reward System is another appealing feature in Sina Weibo. It encourages users to tweet more! Everyone is a gamer by nature. Those who love to play the game enjoy earning reward that makes them proud in that particular game society. Sina Weibo has implemented a very interesting medal reward system to stimulate users to earn medals for personal enjoyment or show-off.

The entire system is not just about fun but also one of the strategic plans in Weibo's business ecosystem. Brands such as Transformers actually are partnered with Weibo to market their products by offering medals, mostly requiring users to perform certain actions like retweet about their events. This is a really neat marketing strategy for the brands as it helps to spread the event message and allows the logo of the brand to be exposed in users' profiles as a medal.

Weibo has even built a page to introduce, promote and remind users about those medals that are associated with certain events or brands.

More style templates

In microblogging services like Sina Weibo, every profile is a personal space. All hope to advertise themselves and be different from others by possessing at least stylistic templates among the entire platform. Sina Weibo provides satisfactory solution by offering over 60 chic templates, categorized into five groups which are "Newest Promotion", "Classic", "Fashion", "School" and "Events". Of course, if they are not satisfied with these templates, they can always do it themselves by using the template builder.

With the builder, users can define font colour, put custom background pictures, apply tile backgrounds and adjust the picture's alignment.

Weibo event

Weibo has a feature known as "event", which is the virtual version of a party, but still in sections as usual. The feature collects everyone's thoughts together, increasing engagement X10. The Weibo event allows you to join local events, prized events, forum events and other grand events featured on top of the page and spark Weibo messages, called Weebs.

Weibo Event is a fresh concept that Sina Weibo brought to the microblogging service, which will revolutionize people's concept about microblogging service from a place that collects everyone's thoughts together to a place that gets everyone involved and fun together!

With Weibo Event, one user is not just limited to see what other people are tweeting, but also joining events that other users are joining, sparking more tweets and fun! There're thousands of events categorized into "Local Event", "Prized Event", and "Online Event", with a few grand events featured on the top of the page. Companies or individuals sponsor most Weibo Events. So, please get ready to exchange your hard work with prizes!

This may be an eighth great feature that explains why people stay on Sina Weibo. In the past, users can only see what people are tweeting and maybe joining specific discussions, and some people will eventually get bored with this repetitive cycle. However, with Weibo Event, they gather together to involve in certain events. Thus, users don't only win prizes but also make new friends during the event. They can also promote the event to non-users, encouraging them to join Weibo for their events.

Conclusion

Overall, Weibo platforms are aimed at catering to different users, and mainly targeted to attract new users, retain elite users and encourages their users to keep exchanging messages on the platform. A brand can position itself exclusively on Weibo and customize its content as well.

Weibo, to some extent, is a channel to get the public voice heard, a path to protect individual rights, a platform to participate in public affairs. It, meanwhile, needs to concern about some negative phenomena including low quality content due to lack of professional training and insufficiency in media literacy and online abuse.

In short, Weibo is used for news and information broadcasting in addition to personal and group communications. Most Chinese mainstream media companies and organizations, government agencies, and business corporations have their official microblogging accounts on Weibo. Despite sharing the same core service of microblogging. Weibo will continually develop more functions and services to meet the specific needs of its users all over the world.

Task 5 ▶ Reading comprehension

Direction: *MEDIA team are going to launch a discussion about the reading excerpt. They are required to summarize what they learned, share their puzzles as well as their comments on the article, and try to probe into more profound issues in this domain.*

Objectives: *Learning by doing. To cultivate students' capability of finding problems, reflecting on and solving problems independently so as to improve the comprehensive ability of using language.*

Edward: Hi, everyone. I think it's an interesting article about the features of Weblog. It clearly described almost all the functions that Weblog possesses. Accordingly, you must have piled up a lot of questions. But don't worry. Just bear all of your questions in minds and discuss first to figure out the solution to each question. Then, rank your questions and then solve important and critical problems in order of priority.

Maynor: And you may also find that this article is written in a popular vernacular style, but the problems you mentioned earlier are more professional. I hope you can compare the problems expressed in technical terms you have seen before with the problems simplified in this article.

Angela: It's as sure as fate. I mentioned the technique to test the information diffusion in online social networks. Here, I'd like to explain it by using the features listed in the above article.

Irene: With Angela and Davis working hard together, we can do well comparison and simplify these terminologies including static following network, dynamic following network, retweet behaviors with retweet content, merged retweet behaviors without retweet content, and user profile etc. Am I right?

Davis: Of course. I am confident. It's a task-oriented assignment. Our objectives are as clear as crystal. Let's take action now.

Angela: The technique to test the information diffusion in online social networks is applicable to all functional maintenance. The sophisticated techniques facilitate the information diffusion, making it more fluent. And the technique is the core that ensure Weblog in leading and sustainable position.

Irene: I got it. Then how do we understand static vs dynamic following network?

Edward: The question is truly too complicated. Generally speaking, network theory and methods have been fully developed. Like other methods, the application of network tools also depends on the data type inferred by the network. Broadly speaking, the data used for network reconfiguration includes static and dynamic types. Relatively speaking, static data is easier to collect, so it is more often used to decompose complex systems. However, the network reconstructed from static data has several main limitations.

Davis: The method of using static data usually can only characterize the whole network through all samples, and cannot identify the heterogeneity between samples. The network with detailed interactive information can be applied to practical problems.

Angela: Presently, most of the related work is based on the embedding of static networks, that is, the evolution of networks over time is not considered. However, the edges, nodes and node characteristics of real networks are dynamic. That means the real world is mostly dynamic networks, whose edges and nodes are constantly changing with time. For example, the addition of new users and the generation of new friends in social networks will lead to the emergence of new nodes and edges in the network. This time series information is an important part of the dynamic network and the embodiment of the evolution mechanism. I think this is the theoretical support of the features like trends categorization, rich media, and the threaded comments.

Irene: Oh dear. It is beyond my comprehension. I am feeling like entering a maze.

Davis: I think the rest terms like retweet behaviors with retweet content, merged retweet behaviors without retweet content, and user profile are comparatively easier to understand.

Irene: "Retweet behaviors with retweet content" refers to the behavior that users republish the information published on the online social network. Users' forwarding behavior can be considered as users' acceptance and adoption of information resources obtained in online social networks. Users' perception of the usefulness of available social network information is affected by cognitive and emotional needs.

Maynor: So, the hard work pays off quickly. Irene is entering into the spirit of the character.

Davis: "Merged retweet behaviors" obviously refers to forward the message content to other friends one by one, while combined forwarding is to combine multiple messages for forwarding. The difference lies in that one-by-one forwarding cannot see the source of message forwarding, while combined forwarding can see the original sender of the message.

Angela: Finally, it's my turn to explain "user profile". It is also known as GUP (generic user profile), its basic starting point is to take users as the center to solve the problem of unified access to user data of various networks and services.

Edward: It's amazing! You reap a lot of harvest by yourselves. Your discussion is a perfect complement to the above reading material. I'm proud of you, every one of you!

Maynor: Exactly the same feeling. You've done a well job. It's time to stop for now and leave the other questions for later discussion online.

All: Okay. We're so pleased. See you next time.

Task 6 ▶ Translation practice

Direction: *MEDIA team are going to do Chinese-English translation, from which they can learn and compare how to express in cross-cultural way and convey the following paragraph in English accurately.*

Objectives: *To understand and master English morphology, syntax and idiomatic expressions, develop basic professional translation ability and promote English competence.*

微博（Microblog）是指一种基于用户关系信息分享、传播以及获取的通过关注机制分享简短实时信息的广播式的社交媒体、网络平台。微博允许用户通过Web、Wap、Mail、App、IM、SMS以及用户可以通过PC、手机等多种移动终端接入，以文字、图片、视频等多媒体形式，实现信息的即时分享、传播互动，是新近兴起的一个Web 2.0，也是一种可以即时发布消息的类似博客的系统，具有便捷性、原创性、新闻及时性等特征。它最大的特点就是集成化和开放化，微博开通的多种API使得大量的用户可以通过手机、网络等方式来即时更新自己的个人信息，通过QQ和MSN直接书写，在没有网络的地方，只要有手机也可即时更新自己的内容。微博的实时性、现场感以及快捷性，甚至超过大多数媒体，真实地反映了“媒介即信息”的时代特征。

Task 7 ▶ Attending a public lecture

Direction: *MEDIA team are going to attend a public lecture delivered by Professor Maynor. Students are required to thoroughly understand the lecture, broaden the vision, elaborate on the theme, get inspiration from the lecture and do some speech activities to extend their knowledge.*

Objectives: *To train students' capability of description, expression, discussion, refutation, humor and humanistic accomplishment required by making a speech, thus, improving students' English language competence and proficiency.*

Lecture 6

Weblog Sphere in China

Professor Maynor

I am so pleased to be talking about the sixth topic — Weblog Sphere in China. Like every one of you, I also love using this medium. It never fails to give me a very agreeable experience and a great deal of pleasure.

Weblog Sphere is a huge topic. It covers too many aspects to talk about all the details. Here, I attempt to tackle the following four to five subtopics in the hope of specifying how Weblog sphere in China originated and developed in the past decades. Some points are academic in feature, which may be hard to thoroughly understand. My suggestion is that you keep all your questions in mind for after-lecture discussion. I've got ready to offer help with whatever you feel confused.

Brief introduction

The blog, formerly known as the weblog, was introduced to the Chinese internet in 1998, not long after its appearance in the United States. At its earlier stage, blogging tools were mostly used by IT communities in China, identical to the practice in the United States. However, by the end of 2006, the number of blogs in China had reached 60 million and become a mainstream social media space for average users. By the end of 2008, the population of the Chinese blogosphere had virtually outnumbered that of the United States.

When compared to international examples, the Chinese blogosphere is young but it is catching up quickly. The importance of Chinese blogs as media, instruments for business, education, research, and channels for personal expression is becoming widely recognized. Over just a few years, its influence has been extended from the blogosphere to other parts of the Chinese internet and societies. A growing number of Chinese blog users are blogging, providing a greater variety of information and analysis than they are able to do in their official news outlets. Some Chinese academics have begun to use blogs as a platform for discussing and publicizing their research report. Some educators are using blogs to share curriculum and communicate with students. Some Chinese government officials at the local and national levels have taken blogging as a way to improve communication with the broad masses of the people.

Figure 6.4 Blog. Source: 赵彦彬，《和你聊聊博客的发展史》，2020-10-01, https://www.sohu.com/.

Technologically, the Chinese blogosphere is identical with other blogospheres, though minor differences do exist due to cost and intellectual property right constraints. The Chinese blogosphere has developed its own characteristics under Confucian sociocultural tradition. Increasing interest among Chinese and overseas scholars in the phenomenon of Chinese blogs has resulted in a number of publications in the past few years. The majority of the early research in blogs in Chinese also focused on the applications of blogging for educational and commercial purposes. Inside China, some of these studies have explored, for example, how blogs can improve second language teaching and learning, for bettering school literacy education, and for facilitating communication between teachers and students. Other studies have discussed the prospective application of blogs to businesses in terms of marketing and public relations. These studies are either introductions to blogs as a whole, or reflective descriptions and commentaries of blogs and certain blog phenomena.

However, some research is rather dubious in that their aim of featuring "blog research" is actually for gaining currency through branding their contribution to blogs such as several pioneering Chinese bloggers, mass media and new-born profit-driven internet research labs. Aside from the credibility of this kind of research, there is also an overt neglect of the fact that Chinese blogs have increasingly become a culturally and linguistically significant phenomenon and entity, which is worth in-depth research.

In recent years, research on the social impact of blogs upon Chinese society has also risen. Some researchers argue that the emergence of blogs in the Chinese internet has been revolutionary as it has helped blur the boundaries between the public and private sphere, leading to a state of so-called "carnival". They contend that the popularity of blogs in the Chinese internet may reflect the public's growing discontent with the elite discourse that has dominated Chinese media both online and offline. Researchers have addressed the effect that blogs may have had on certain social practice. And still others have principally seen blogs as a better window, medium, and channel than the traditional mass media, for understanding Chinese society and its evolving social networking systems, which provides reporting, Chinese cyberspace, perspectives from across the geographical, political and social spectrum, and daily recommendations of readings from the Chinese blogosphere. Though not purely research-oriented, the news and analysis consist of a useful database for researching Chinese blogs, especially those blogs with political orientations.

Translation and social elitism

To understand the Chinese blogosphere requires an understanding of how elitism operates in the notion. It is known that the original formation of the blog was propelled by the grassroots desire for active and meaningful social participation but the blog's inroad to the Chinese Web sphere was initiated and constructed by elite social groups. These are the people who had earlier access to the web spheres than the average Chinese and who had the capacity to capitalize on these resources.

The early online log channel started from Sina — one of China's portal websites. The early blog features were usually entertainment celebrity blogs, intellectual celebrity blogs, touching emotional blogs, self grassroots blogs, and so on. Since 2006, Sina Weibo has been organizing celebrity blogs, including well-known figures from the cultural and entertainment industry, cultural and educational circles, and the news industry. Yu Hua, Yu Qiuyu, Feng Jicai, Liu Zhenyun, Zhang Haidi and other well-known domestic writers all have their own Sina blogs.

Following Sina blog, NetEase Blog was officially launched in 2006. In addition to possessing the characteristics of general blog products, NetEase Blog is more powerful in terms of functionality. The homepage of the blog can display various modules such as friends, about me, photos, music player, etc. In addition, blogs have also introduced powerful tag search functions, including logs, images, music, author search, and more. In 2018, NetEase Blog officially ceased operation. In addition, various blog platforms such as Sohu Blog, Tianya Blog, and Blog Bus are also in vogu in China.

Hence, the trajectory of the Chinese blogosphere, from its very beginning, was a top-down momentum. Instead of a movement for the powerless to question and challenge the powerful, it was manipulated by elite groups to maximize their gains in whichever ways were possible. The use of blogs has since erupted among average internet users, consequently leading to the so-called grassroots movement of Chinese blogs. Still, attempts to reinstall, restore, and reinforce elitism into the blog-like social networking media were visible from the translating practice of the original English term of blog into Chinese and have never waned ever since. During the early days of the Chinese blogosphere, three translations of the term "blog" were used interchangeably, namely, *wangji*, *wangzhi*, and *boke*, each of them as a text indexing certain social intentions and actions. The first two names are literal translations of blogs with minor differences. *Wangji* was a shortened name for *wangluo riji* describing the blog as online or web diaries. In addition to the denotation of *wangji*, *wangzhi*, a shortened name for *wangluo rizhi*, places an emphasis on the possible role that blogs may have for personal development and attainment through blogging. It is known that the Chinese character *zhi* has another layer of meaning of setting personal goals besides recording activities and events.

Besides, the third translation *boke* has little semantic relevance to the blog. It is neither a literal nor a free translation of blog. Rather, it is a coinage of two seemingly different characters. The first character *bo* refers denotatively to being learned, knowledgeable, to the academic degree Doctor of Philosophy or *boshi xuewei* in Chinese, or academics with a PhD degree who would be regarded as social elites responsible for authoritative knowledge production and interpretation. The pronunciation of *bo* is roughly close to the sound of the first letter of blog. The second character *ke*, following the translation fashion of other internet terms such as hackers (*heike*), geeks (*hongke*), and wikipedia contributors, is known in Chinese either as distinguished guests of the powerful or professionals. Without providing adequate background knowledge, *boke* can easily conjure up an image among blog newbies of elite professionals who enjoy authoritative status in certain fields.

Disputes over the translation of the term blog into Chinese Putonghua were heated among the pioneers. Although the first two versions appeared earlier, they were outnumbered soon by *boke* and have become largely invisible in the Chinese blogosphere and the web sphere. From a historical perspective, naming an object or a phenomenon is a complex issue and can incur profound consequences. In Confucian text such as *Lunyu*, inappropriate naming in its very extreme can impair personal wellbeing and national solidarity. It is evident that the preference of *boke* over the other two names implies a stronghold of Confucian elitism and the victory of the elite over the ordinary in the Chinese blogosphere from the very outset. The elitist imperative permeates the development of the Chinese blogosphere and blogs via the translation of the term, the popularity of blog columnists, the attention to celebrity blogs, and the promotion of so-called grassroots blogs. The resistance to the populist from the elites is manifested in every possible aspect of the Chinese blogosphere. Such phenomenon may be common.

Entertainment and tabloidization

Another distinctive feature of the Chinese blogosphere is its concentration on entertainment and its trend towards tabloidization.

The Sina blog service provide the eighteen channels or tags labelled entertainment, sports, culture, women, IT, finance, automobiles, real estate, education, games, military, constellation, cooking, interior design, babysitting, health, photos, and e-magazine etc. by which the content of blogs is linked to wider communities. Among these popular tags, many of them are about entertainment celebrities, and other tags are related to entertainment, sports, foods, and travel. No channels or tags are entitled politics, current issues or affairs. In fact, on the homepage of the Sina BSP, there is also one sub-channel entitled "point of view" (*guandian*), which includes blog entries which discuss certain political and social issues.

During the early time, a small proportion of Chinese blogs seemed to be designed for providing miscellaneous ends. Generally, visiting the homepage of many of Chinese BSPs might give an impression that entertainment-oriented blogs were prevailing the Chinese blogosphere. On many BSPs such as Sina BSP, the entertainment section was the most popular teeming with celebrities, gossips, tabloid news, and the like. For example, the number one popular blog on Sina BSP is *Laoxu boke*, whose owner was an entertainment celebrity famous for her singing, writing, acting, and directing. Her blog was then not just a personal blog but a hub for her fans to express their admiration for their star and at the same time exchange information and develop communities related to her stardom. It was also a place where she presented her relationship with her fans and other parties such as film producers, agents, and colleagues to the public, consequently creating a space for group or team promotions instead of just promoting an individual pop star.

Personal blogs used to be further exploited by fans, a newly emergent occupation in free market China, for disseminating material to the tabloids about the celebrities. By publicizing celebrities' private lives, tabloid magazines, journals, and websites, they made profits while celebrities retain and expanded their publicity, consequently leading to a win-win situation, regardless of some so-called urge for privacy protection.

The prevalence of entertainment and tabloid content in the Chinese blogosphere may correspond with China's continuing economic prosperity in the past four decades as well as Chinese people's demand for lifestyle change such as leisure and holidays.

However, with time going, Chinese official Weibo platforms account for a large proportion. Weibo, as a square style social media, has always been the main battlefield for disseminating information and guiding public opinion on major natural disaster events. Those media who fully make use of Weibo will be easy to come into prominence. For example, during the "July 20" rainstorm in Henan, People's Daily Weibo platform showed the characteristics of intensive reporting, a large proportion of original microblogs, wide coverage of content, diverse forms of expression and other communication characteristics, which played a role in timely broadcasting information, providing comprehensive services and guiding public opinion. It effectively played the role of the mainstream media microblog in guiding public opinion in major natural disasters by giving play to the advantages of the mainstream media, actively participating in agenda setting, building a microblog communication matrix, achieving multi-subject interaction, doing a good job in information "gatekeepers", timely curbing rumors and other public opinion guidance strategies.

Portalisation and commercialization

In alignment with the prevailing tabloidization, the quest for profit or commercial interest is another driving force that has changed the landscape of the Chinese blogosphere at an early stage. Portalisation is the tendency of bloggers to redevelop their blogs into personal web portals. An individual blog, instead of simply publishing personal updates, syndicates a number of services such as websites, chat rooms, forums, journals, conferences that may potentially transform blogs into commercial organizations. In fact, portalisation is especially popular with celebrities, public figures and A-list bloggers. Take Professor Jin Canrong as an example. Being a well-known public figure, he is operated as part of the blogger's own personal web/blog portal. His blog portal includes his profile and a hyperlink to his blogsite, online chat service, a bulletin board system, and a fan community of 2.652 million followers and fans He frequently enjoys up to 14.959 million likes and reposts for his every article or video show in the blog. On June 7, 2023 when the college entrance examination kicked off, Jin expressed his views on the composition proposition of the college entrance examination. He thinks although the college entrance examination essay can allow various heroes to unleash their talents, we still hope that the exam essay topics can be friendly to candidates, preferably close to social reality, in line with normal logic, rather than being eccentric, in order to facilitate candidates to showcase their talents. His viewpoint immediately gained praise and support from tens of thousands of people and made it on the hot search list. Besides, his judgment and comments on the international situation have played a role in inspiring the national fighting spirit. Due to the dissemination speed and coverage of Weibo platforms, the official Weibo account of the Office of the Spokesperson of the Ministry of Foreign Affairs was officially launched at 15:44 on May 20th, 2019 and the first Weibo post was released stating that "the fewer words, the greater the matter" according to the official account of Bloomberg News. Lu Kang, Director General of the Information Department of the Ministry of Foreign Affairs and Spokesman of the Ministry of Foreign Affairs, told netizens in the first video distributed on Weibo: The Weibo account of the Spokesperson's Office of the Ministry of Foreign Affairs is officially online, please pay attention! As of 10:00 am on the second day (21st), the official Weibo account of the spokesperson office of the Ministry of Foreign Affairs has released 8 Weibo posts and quickly attracted over 350000 followers. As the main social media platform, Weibo has become an important medium for guiding the mainstream ideology of the internet. Weibo, with its advanced technology, such as algorithmic personalized recommendation systems, pushes the latest information and caters to the consumer psychology of the public, forming a huge user base. In addition, in response to public events, key hotspots, and crisis events, timely public opinion monitoring is carried out to actively intervene in hot topics, timely control public opinion emotions, promote harmonious development at the social level, guide the public to form correct thinking patterns, and cultivate a healthy public mentality. All those may well speak why many official media start their Weibo accounts.

Individual bloggers' interest in portalising their blogs is directly influenced by their BSPs. The majority of Chinese BSPs have been developed from web portals such as Sina (www.sina.com.cn) and Sohu (www.sohu.com). Consequently, these BSPs may have many features in common with the web portals with which they are associated. Such a way of providing blogging services is a strategic move to enlarge the web portals' market share through simulating content, consumers, and consequently the market. Blogs hosted on these BSPs are consequently encouraged to develop their own personal portals when their popularity reaches a threshold, for realizing various purposes such as profit and popularity.

Commercial interest is another driving force that has shaped the development of the Chinese blogosphere and blogs. By providing blog services, BSPs not only expand their market share but also compete for customers. Bloggers in this sense have little common ground with traditional customers. They are the customers of certain BSPs as receivers of their hosting and other content services. However, rather than paying their BSPs for hosting services, bloggers contribute their time and energy to creating content in return, not just for themselves but also for their BSPs, in line with respective regulations, customer agreement, or the code of conduct. In particular, bloggers are requested to allow their BSPs to access their registered information. Blogs, including their owners, become an asset of their BSPs and even, possibly, their products, depending on their capacity and BSPs marketing plans. An alliance, then, is formed, especially among certain powerful groups of blogs. The sections on those BSPs, for example, are not simply a collection of tags or themes. On the contrary, they could be seen as a way to brand the blogs according to their content and influence. Understandably, the more influence a blog has, the more buying power it brings to the BSP. That blogger, clearly, would have more power in bargaining with the blog service and more incentives to offer to the

BSP for better service as well as financial return. The dissolving or blurred border between business and customers then complicates the traditional understanding of commercialization.

Female bloggers' presence

Apart from the above-discussed features, the most remarkable feature was the predominant influence of female bloggers at the early stage of the Chinese blogosphere. Although blogs were introduced to the Chinese web sphere by several male bloggers in 1999, the most well-known blogs by 2006 were mostly authored by female bloggers. It was only at the end of 2006 that a number of male blogs began to emerge in the Chinese blogosphere.

Two hypotheses may account for this phenomenon. First, early blogs were considered personal journals or diaries that are seen as feminized. Some research, for instance, indicates that more women than men preferred keeping diaries and revealing their experiences, emotions, feelings, and desires. Although the reliability of some such findings could be problematized, to some extent, they offer alternative interpretations of women's dominance in the early phase of the Chinese blogosphere to the mainstream account. Second, blogs provide Chinese women an unprecedented space for voicing their identities and subjectivity.

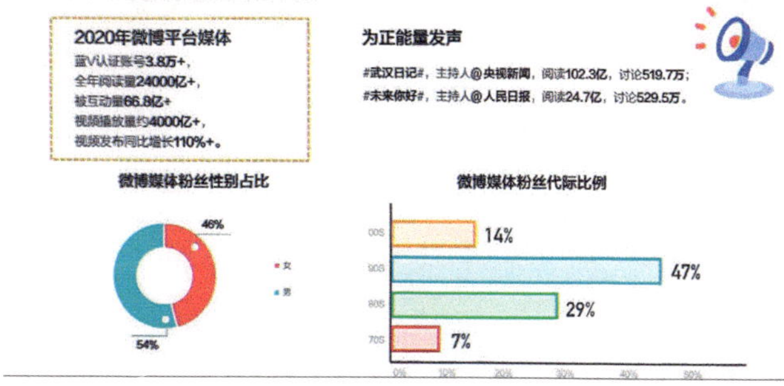

Figure 6.5 The overview of weibo media. Source: 微博2020用户发展报告：女玩家大量进入游戏世界_生活 www.sohu.com/a/455464833.

Concluding remarks

Up to now, I have summarized the essential characteristics of Weblog Sphere in China from the above five dimensions on the basis of facts. Next, I'd like to further analyze the root of Chinese Weblog Sphere tentatively.

The long tradition of Confucian elitism has profoundly shaped the course of the Chinese blogosphere, which provides an alternative for the revival of not only the Chinese language but also of other semiotic means while preserving the history and resource of the Chinese languages. Chinese blogs and their aggregation as a blogosphere are primarily valuable for research into the Chinese web sphere and society.

More significantly, the nature and infrastructure of the blog has welded the Chinese blogosphere into an unprecedented world for business in which the division between enterprises and their customers has become almost invisible. Every blog is a potential product carrying a certain brand name, be it the name of a blog service provider or even an abstract name such as happiness. The blogosphere, therefore, is creating internet syndicate through content while at the same time making such agglomeration an unlikely occurrence given the diversity of Chinese bloggers and the divergence among them.

It seems that Chinese blogs are becoming increasingly web portal-like, featuring content such as entertainment, and personal details, while at the same time avoiding interest in sensitive political issues. Factors such as economic growth have had a direct impact upon Chinese bloggers' lifestyle representations. Other factors such as political correctness may implicitly affect the content of Chinese blogs and their way of blogging. Considering the critical function of blogs as a space for personal and collective expression, the tension between institutional surveillance and bloggers' resistance plays an important role in shaping the Chinese blogosphere and the characteristics of blogs.

In short, the formation of weblog sphere should be connected with its culture. So I will end up this lecture with the following questions for you to reflect on. First, how does Confucius culture affect the name of Chinese weblog or weibo? Second, who do you think are the owners of weblog, why? Finally, why do Chinese women predominate weblog in early period? How do you account for such phenomenon? I must admit that these questions are very hard ones. I have been grappling with them for a long time, and I don't think am yet able to come up with good solutions. I appeal, therefore, to you for better solutions. So much for today. See you.

Task 8 ▶ Online forum and summary writing

Direction: *MEDIA team are going to launch an instant online post-talk about the lecture to appeal to more of other students who are interested in the topic to join* *them. This is an integrated practice of listening, speaking, reading and writing. They are particularly expected to write a summary of the entire unit.*

Objectives: *To provide a platform for MEDIA team to fully display their talents. To comb language learning with professional knowledge so as to cultivate students' professional learning, academic literacy and language competence. To realize the teaching objectives of acquiring professional knowledge through learning English language.*

Edward:	Hi MEDIA members. I am well convinced that you must have grasped enough concerning Weblog through an overall review ranging from its features or functions, some terms of technology to the particular section of Weblog etc. Prof. Maynor's lecture further strengthens your understanding of microblogging. I also benefit a lot.
Maynor:	I'm flattered. What I'm truly happy is my students' efforts and agile thinking. Besides the questions I left by the end of the lecture, you're also expected to reflect on questions like: Whether you can associate Weblog with academic research? Have you ever thought of using Weblog to do social survey? How about collecting data through Weblog? In one word, I hope that your discussion can extend as much as possible.
Irene:	I got it. We will examine the impact of microblogging on society, interpersonal communication, academic exchanges and entertainment activities from a broader cultural perspective.
Davis:	We can try to analyze whether researchers have used data from Weibo and how. Weibo, after all, is China's second most popular social media platform. It undertakes a variety of research projects and provides resources for researchers to seek chance to use Weibo as a tool for social research.
Angela:	That will be a valuable discussion. I firmly believe that Weibo is of a sign of the important social media platforms. An obvious indicator is that in April 2019, the National Library of China announced that it will archive all public posts on Weibo for non-commercial uses. This move will have a profound influence on digital-heritage retention and

it is estimated that more than 200 billion textual posts and 50 billion pictures will be stored, as well as data relating to the sentiments underlying these posts. Hence, we have reason to believe that microblog can be used as a research platform to do social surveys, questionnaires, obtain data, and find references and so on.

Irene: It's heard that in a study about emotional states on Weibo, two experimental pioneers used BDP, a free online tool to help users deal with databases, to visualize the flow in polarity over time and quickly detect the location of peaks and wanes in the general population's emotional state.

Davis: We all have known Weibo Events, which actually is another tool for data visualization. It allows users to study the spread of information and how accounts gain their popularity on Weibo.

Irene: It seems the features were endless bubbling. Why don't we sort the muddle in our heads first so that we can correctly expound the correlation between Weblog platform and users' research through it?

Angela: I think so. The lecture actually consists of four parts. Each part tells us what Weblog platform do and who are the leading users. For example, the topic of the first part is "translation and social elitism", in which we know although grass roots began posting whatever they hoped to say on Weblog platform, finally elites became the dominant.

Davis: Right. From the second part, we can judge the youngsters are the main roles. And the third part indicates how useful Weblog platform is for all business people.

Irene: And the fourth part takes woman bloggers as main theme. Accordingly, Weblog platform is totally a sweet pastry and is loved by everyone ranging from average persons to elites in all fields.

Edward: This is why Prof. Maynor hopes you make an attempt to relate Weblog platform to academia, for we are all belonging to this field. Doing research will be interwoven with your career.

Angela:	Definitely. To my knowledge, some researchers are doing analysis about the penetration of Weibo content, focusing on from its targeted audience to potential audiences. They then classify the reposting on the microblog to different layers.
Davis:	There are also researchers who investigated the interaction model between the rover account and social media users, to find out how to balance the personified mood with scientific knowledge about the exploration of the universe.
Irene:	And it's reported that a group of researchers used Sina Weibo data to analyze misinformation. They found that only 2% of their sample contained misinformed treatment options.
Angela:	In the context of Covid-19, lifelogs preset an enormous opportunity to develop an online history, which can then be used in similar ways to understand the spread of virus and its social effects.
Maynor:	How timely and valuable such studies are. So, we can safely conclude that Weibo has a powerful ability, due to its large sample size, to study and track sentiment, affective states, online behaviors, and communications within the Chinese socio-cultural context.
Edward:	At the same time, it is worth noting that in so doing, it also highlights risks and controversies surrounding online privacy and safety, which surround such research. As social media research on the social network gathers pace, how these issues will be addressed and resolved remains an open question.
Irene:	So, let's share all these question with our online members.
All:	Okay. So much for today.

Appendix: Vocabulary for Unit 6

Listening Activity

tagging /ˈtæɡɪŋ/ *n.* 标记；锻尖；（带有文字或符号的）涂鸦
v. 加标签于；附加；把……称为（tag 的现在分词）

release /rɪˈliːs/ *v.* 释放，放走；把（动物）放生；解救；公布，发布；发行，上映；表达，发泄；释放，排放（物质）；解除（职务或工作），解雇
n.（人或动物的）释放，放出；排放，泄漏；表达，宣泄；解脱，轻松感；放松的机会；新发行的东西；公开，发布；公映

domain /dəˈmeɪn; dəʊˈmeɪn/ *n.* 领域，范围；领土，势力范围；（因特网上的）域；（函数的）定义域；地产

notification /ˌnəʊtɪfɪˈkeɪʃn/ *n.* 通知；通知单，通知书；通告，布告

validate /ˈvælɪdeɪt/ *v.* 批准，确认……有效；证实，确认；使生效，使具有法律效力；证明有……价值，认可

parallel /ˈpærəlel/ *adj.* 平行的；相似的，同时发生的；（计算机）并行的；并联的
n. 相似的手法，共同点；相似的人（或物）；（地球的）纬线，纬圈；（印刷）平行符号
v. 与……相似；与……同时发生；与……并行；与……相当
adv. 与……平行

interface /ˈɪntəfeɪs/ *n.* 界面；（计算机设备之间的）连接，接口；（学科或系统间相互影响或衔接的）边缘区域，接合部位
v. 连接；相互联系，相互交流（interface with）

subsection /ˈsʌbsekʃn/ *n.* 分段，分部；细分；小部分

facilitate /fəˈsɪlɪteɪt/ *v.* 使更容易，使便利；促进，推动

Reading Activity

enlighten /ɪnˈlaɪtn/ *v.* 阐明，指导；教导，启迪

thread /θred/ *n.* 线；细线，线状物；思路，贯穿的主线
v. 穿线于，使穿过；将（珠子等）穿起来；穿行，曲折穿过；用手指梳理（尤指头发）

capitalize /ˈkæpɪtəlaɪz/ *v.* 用大写字母书写（或印刷），把……首字母大写；为（开办或发展企业）提供资金；（将资产或股票）变现，使资本化

commentator /ˈkɒmənteɪtə(r)/ *n.* 现场解说员，实况播音员；评论员

corporate /ˈkɔːpərət/ *adj.* 公司的；法人的；共同的，全体的
n. 公司，集团

clutter /ˈklʌtə(r)/ *n.* 杂乱的东西；杂乱
v. 乱堆，塞满；使（脑子里）塞满（乱七八糟的事）

insert /ɪnˈsɜːt/ *v.* 插入，嵌入；（在文章中）添加，加插
n. 插入物；（尤指）插页，附加页；（电影等的）插入镜头

emoticon /ɪˈməʊtɪkɒn/ *n.* 表情符号，表情图示

poll /pəʊl/ *n.* 民意调查，民意测验；选举投票，计票；投票数；投票点（the polls）
v. 对……进行民意测验（调查）；获得（票数）
sparks /spɑːks/ *n.*（船或飞机上的）无线电通信师
cult /kʌlt/ *n.* 异教，异教组织；狂热崇拜，迷信；（特定群体的）偶像，时尚；崇拜者，信徒；宗教信仰，宗教习俗
adj. 受崇拜的，热门的
thumbnail /ˈθʌmneɪl/ *n.* 拇指指甲；极小的东西；短文
adj. 极小的，极短的
retain /rɪˈteɪn/ *v.* 保持，保留；保存，储存；记住；付定金聘定（尤指律师）；留用（员工）
expiration /ˌekspəˈreɪʃ(ə)n/ *n.* 到期，（一段时间的）结束；呼气，吐气
awesome /ˈɔːsəm/ *adj.* 让人惊叹的，令人敬畏的；非常棒的，极佳的
profile /ˈprəʊfaɪl/ *n.*（人头部的）侧面（像），侧影；（某物的）外形，轮廓；（人、团体或组织的）简介，概况；纵断面，剖面；（地球表面纵断面的）轮廓
v. 概述，扼要介绍；给……画侧面像，显出……侧面轮廓；显出……的轮廓（be profiled）；（尤指用模板）铣出轮廓，使……成形
categorization /ˌkætəgəraɪˈzeɪʃn/ *n.* 分类；分门别类；编目方法
alignment /əˈlaɪnmənt/ *n.* 排成直线，摆放恰当；结盟；协调，一致；（铁路或道路的）路线；石排
elite /eɪˈliːt/ *n.* 权力集团，上层人士；尖子，精英
adj. 出类拔萃的，精锐的

Lecture

outnumber /ˌaʊtˈnʌmbə(r)/ *vt.* 数目超过；比……多
literacy /ˈlɪtərəsi/ *n.* 识字，读写能力；专业知识；精通文学
dubious /ˈdjuːbiəs/ *adj.* 可疑的，靠不住的；有疑虑的；（荣誉、名声等）不好的，不光彩的；质量不佳的
orientation /ˌɔːriənˈteɪʃ(ə)n/ *n.* 目标，定位；方向，朝向；（基本的）态度，倾向；（岗前、学前、课前等的）情况介绍，培训；适应，熟悉
overt /əʊˈvɜːt/ *adj.* 公开的，不隐瞒的
carnival /ˈkɑːnɪv(ə)l/ *n.* 狂欢节，嘉年华会；〈美〉游乐会，游艺场；庆祝活动；（学校的）游园会，嘉年华会
spectrum /ˈspektrəm/ *n.* 范围，幅度；光谱；波谱，频谱；余象
propel /prəˈpel/ *v.* 推进，驱动；推搡（某人走向特定方向）；驱使，促使

trajectory /trəˈdʒektəri/ *n.*（物体射向或抛向空中形成的）轨道，轨迹；（事业等的）发展轨迹，起落；（几何）常角轨道，轨线

erupt /ɪˈrʌpt/ *v.* 喷发；爆发，突然发生；（感情）迸发；（斑疹等）突然冒出；长牙

denotation /ˌdiːnəʊˈteɪʃn/ *n.* 指称意义，本义

denotatively /dɪˈnəʊtətɪvli / *adv.* 外延地；指示地

conjure /ˈkʌndʒə(r)/ *v.* 变魔术，使……变戏法般地出现（或消失）；想象出，设想出；使浮现于脑海，使想起；念咒召唤出（鬼魂等）

newbie /ˈnjuːbi/ *n.* 网络新手；新兵

incur /ɪnˈkɜː(r)/ *v.* 带来（成本、花费等）；招致，遭受

impair /ɪmˈpeə(r)/ *v.* 损害，削弱

solidarity /ˌsɒlɪˈdærəti/ *n.* 团结一致

constellation /ˌkɒnstəˈleɪʃn/ *n.* 星座；一群（相似的人），一系列（相似的事物）；群英荟萃，人才济济

miscellaneous /ˌmɪsəˈleɪniəs/ *adj.* 混杂的，各种各样的；多方面的，多才多艺的

tabloid stardom 小报明星

syndicate /ˈsɪndɪkət/ *n.* 辛迪加，企业联合组织，财团；报业集团；评议会特别委员会

v. 把（文章、图片、电视节目等）出售给多个媒体；把（赛马）卖给辛迪加；把……联合成辛迪加

threshold /ˈθreʃhəʊld/ *n.* 门槛，门口；阈，界，起始点；开端，起点，入门；机场跑道入口，跑道头

alliance /əˈlaɪəns/ *n.* 联盟，结盟；结盟团体，结盟国家；（人们间的）亲密关系

hypothesis /haɪˈpɒθəsɪs/ *n.* 假说，假设；（凭空的）猜想，猜测；前提（复数 hypotheses）

revival /rɪˈvaɪv(ə)l/ *n.* 复兴，复苏；再流行；（旧剧的）重新上演；（基督教信仰的）复兴布道会；（体力或活力的）重振

semiotic /ˌsemiˈɒtɪk/ *adj.* 症状的；符号学的；记号语言的

agglomeration /əˌglɒməˈreɪʃn/ *n.* 凝聚，结块；（杂乱的）一批，一群

divergence /daɪˈvɜːdʒəns/ *n.* 差异，不同；（气流或洋流的）分开处；（数）发散

7
Unit

WeChat — the Most Popular Social Medium

TABLE OF CONTENTS

Unit 7 WeChat — the Most Popular Social Medium

Warm-up: Be proactive

Direction: *MEDIA team are going to do warm-up activities by discussing, airing their views on the topic and discovering problems.*

Objectives: *To arouse students' interest, get a preliminary understanding of relevant knowledge and prepare for the following study.*

Irene: Hi, my dear partners. In the last unit, we have done a detailed discussion about microblog or Weblog from its birth, evolution, progress and influence on every aspect of the society. Today, our target will shift to another popular social platform — WeChat or *Weixin* in Chinese. As you know, WeChat is my favourite. Please leave more opportunities for me to air my view. Okay?

Angela: No problem, Irene. But I wonder why we only focus on Weblog and WeChat instead of so many other social platforms or websites when there are various social media in China.

Davis: I can quite understand it. Actually, I hope we can also involve other platforms such as QQ, DouYin (or TikTok in English), Toutiao, Douban, Xiaohongshu and Meituan or Dazhong Dianping, and the like. Among others, I regard Tencent Video as the King of Online Video in China.

Irene: Wow, you are mazing! I think the reason why we only focus on Weblog and WeChat is that they are respectively the first and second largest social websites. They represent Chinese social media from multidimensional perspective. Am I right?

Angela: Exactly to the point. I propose that we extend our discussion to more media as Davis mentioned. Then we can truly broaden our horizons and get a more thorough comprehension of Chinese social media.

Davis: As the Chinese saying goes: "Kill two birds with one stone." We can learn more through one discussion. I love video so much that I hope to share my favourite Tencent Video with you. That will absolutely please you.

Angela: Aside from Weblog and WeChat, I often use QQ to connect with my friends and families. Before WeChat, I think QQ should be the first favourite social platform for Chinese people. Up to now, most people still choose to use QQ email, paste attachments, upload files, pictures, videos etc., which need large storage space. So the prosperity of phonotape and videotape literature, net literature and photography literature impacts on and changes the original literature ecology. QQ satisfies people in this regard.

Irene: Besides the first and second social websites, I used Xiaohongshu a lot to find various information regarding daily life. It's an e-commerce platform that also has many features commonly seen on social media networks. Users can post reviews, join in on discussions, and post their own content. The contents on the platform tend particularly to focus on product photos and shopping experiences, including shopping tips, deals, and experiences from their trips. Its distinctive feature is the user generated content, where users could share reviews and their experiences to help others with their purchasing decisions.

Davis: So, Xiaohongshu is more suitable for girls, isn't it! But I still favour Tencent Video. As you probably know, the online video market in China is highly competitive. In recent years it's always come down to three major players, iQIYI, Tencent Video, and Youku. Formerly, Alibaba's Youku had dominated the online video market, but its grip has slipped in recent years. Tencent Video has now completely overtaken its competition. Tencent Video works the best when used as a more top of funnel strategy to build awareness rather than drive conversions.

Angela: I see. You mean you belong to top class, don't you? Or you just value its real strength? Anyway, either QQ or Tencent Video belongs to Tencent, which ranks first among Chinese enterprises with a company value of nearly 4.5 trillion and remains the sixth in the world. We are proud of it.

Irene: I do learn a lot from you guys. WeChat is also subordinate to Tencent. But I think Alibaba is as famous as Tencent internationally. In the 2019 Forbes Global Digital Economy 100 list, Alibaba ranked 10th. On October 3, 2019, American Fortune magazine released its 2019 "Future 50" list, with Alibaba ranking 11th. Among the top 100 Chinese enterprises of the Belt and Road Initiative, it ranks the 5th. What's more, Alibaba was selected as the model 100 brand in China brand power ceremony.

Davis: The contribution of these high-tech companies is indispensable to China's prosperity and rise. Now that Tencent is in the leading position, let's turn back to further probe into its first social platform — WeChat.

Angela: You got a point.

All: Let's step forward.

Task 1 ▶ Listening activity

Direction: *MEDIA team are going to listen to an introduction of key concepts so as to lay the foundation for later learning.*

Objectives: *To understand the main conception, practice and strengthen the ability of listening comprehension.*

WeChat: An Integral Part of Our Life

It's hard to imagine life in modern China without WeChat. The app is a trailblazing poster-child for the new internet messaging era. China is considered to be years ahead of the rest of the world in social messaging. Hail a taxi, split the bill in a restaurant, purchase a cinema ticket, invest in financial products, read the news, follow their favourite brands, transfer money to their friends, go shopping online, meet new friends nearby, all these and more can be done by Chinese within just one app: WeChat.

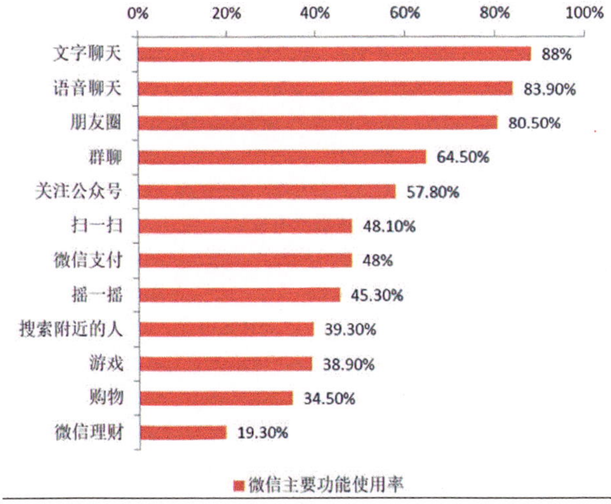

Figure 7.1 The main functions of WeChat. Source: 搜狐财经,《2017年微信小程序行业市场调研分析报告》, www.sohu.com/a/153247396_645413.

WeChat began life in January 2011 as a simple chat app with features and functionality similar to WhatsApp. It was created by a small team of just eight developers within Tencent's R&D team offices in Guangzhou. Over the following five years, WeChat grew beyond anyone's wildest dreams to become by far the most important app in China.

WeChat is often described as a super app that seemingly does everything. It allows us to order taxies, buy film tickets, play games, check in for flights, pay bills, listen to music, read news, shop for clothes or meet random people nearby. Yet despite having an amazing variety of features, the core of WeChat is still messaging. Its primary function is for communication with friends and family. This instant messaging application from Tencent, is increasingly becoming an indispensable part of the daily life in China. There has been a steady growth in the number of users and the penetration rates across all the key WeChat tools that support transactions and enhance communication.

The key reasons for WeChat's success can be summarized as follows.

Users and accounts. First of all, the traffic on WeChat is immense. WeChat enjoys 846 million monthly active users and 570 million daily active users. The average WeChat user reads seven articles per day on WeChat. 36% of users open WeChat for more than 30 times per day. 31% of WeChat users make e-commerce purchases through WeChat. Besides, WeChat is an open platform through which businesses can access WeChat's huge user base. Over 10 million official accounts opened for businesses. WeChat accounts for 35% of all time spent on mobile in China. Estimated monthly payment transactions per WeChat user is 53.

Payments. WeChat Pay has grown extremely rapid in the past two years. More than 300 million Chinese have their bank cards linked with WeChat. WeChat pay is taken in stores all across in China. In particular, peer to peer micro-payments became extremely popular on WeChat in 2015. Chinese consumers are now comfortable using WeChat for payments. It is now commonly accepted not only in most domestic stores but also stores globally. WeChat Pay sits alongside fierce rival Alipay and China's default debit & credit card system Union Pay as one of the big three payment options for Chinese consumers. Other players such as QQ Wallet also owned by Tencent, and Baidu Wallet hold margin market shares. WeChat has strategically partnered with several businesses e.g., JingDong for E-commerce, Didi Chuxing for ride hailing to provide an entire range of online stores and services baked directly into the app.

User protection. WeChat is a closed and private network which places a high priority on protecting users' information. The app carefully limits the number of unsolicited messages that businesses can send to their followers. It also does not allow businesses to directly gain access to personal information such as email address or phone number.

WeChat moments. An immensely popular feature used to share pictures and short videos with friends. Users will scroll through this stream of content to news feed. The addictive combination of switching between checking moments and chatting with friends provides the core loop. This engages users and keeps them returning to the app. Meanwhile, WeChat provides convenience by popularizing the use of QR codes in China which are now ubiquitous across print media, stores and billboards. Scanning QR codes provides a convenient gateway between the online and offline worlds, which has greatly facilitated people's life.

WeChat for business. Businesses interact with users on WeChat through WeChat official accounts. For a WeChat user, adding an official account is practically the same as adding a friend. Users can also send messages to official accounts in the same way as their friends. This creates interesting opportunities to use WeChat as a customer service platform.

Within China it's now fair to say that most companies, especially Small-Medium-Enterprises (SME) will pay more attention to their WeChat official account than their own website. Many small businesses may not even bother with a formal website. Many Chinese users have skipped the desktop era are far more comfortable and familiar with using mobile social platforms and in particular WeChat. They are more likely to find out about services or brands through their social circles or scanning a QR code than through a search engine such as Baidu.

WeChat offers an open platform for businesses to build their own apps on top of WeChat basically "apps within an app" model. Developing for WeChat is much cheaper and easier than native app development for both Android and iOS. The cost of user acquisition is also far lower than with native apps; adding an official account can be done with one click.

Possibilities on WeChat. Most businesses are using the platform for pushing promotional branded content and setting up an e-commerce store to capitalize on socially driven commerce. However, the possibilities for organizations go far beyond this. Hotels outside China even enable their hotel rooms' equipment including lights, doors, air conditioners etc. to be controlled via their WeChat official account. Even traditionally conservative luxury industry brands have been embracing WeChat e-commerce campaigns. In August 2016, Dior launched a limited edition run of 200 customizable handbags each priced at 28,000 RMB exclusively on WeChat. They sold out within one day.

Many businesses have chosen to link their in-store WIFI, their CRM and loyalty systems directly with their WeChat accounts. As the WeChat official accounts platform is open to being linked with other websites or services across the web, the possibilities are wide open as to what can be achieved.

Task 2 ▶ Listening comprehension

Direction: *MEDIA team are going to have a topic-oriented discussion to exchange their views on the listening material and challenge each other with puzzling questions.*

Objectives: *To broaden students' horizon, develop their ability to sum up the skills of answering questions and strengthen language output ability.*

Davis: Hi, guys. What do you think of WeChat? It's incredible! Finally, I see why Irene has been chasing WeChat. The reputation of the largest social media is well deserved. It's indeed an integral part of our life.

Irene: Aha, you feel passionately about it. But have you thought of how WeChat surpass Weibo to become the largest social platform? How about making clear about the difference between Weblog and WeChat first?

Angela: That's what I want to talk about. Before the existence of WeChat, Weibo is the social platform that people got connected and shared information with each other. A few of people still texted to each other through Weibo.

Davis: For WeChat, its process of standing firm and surpassing the rivals must be extraordinarily arduous. The pain point WeChat solved at first was the trouble of texting long messages, the similar function as Weibo. Tencent not only has made tremendous efforts but also a radical innovation. It came out with the outstanding function of sending voice message.

Irene: Yes. It was earlier than iMessage started to support voice message. Though this was a helpful function, at that time, not a lot of people were using it because it required a lot of time to be used to sending voice message to others.

Angela: WeChat launched the function called "Moment" in 2012 through the iteration, a sharing function. People share images and words in Moment. They can also like and comment on their friends' moments.

Davis: The big difference between Moment and Weibo is that WeChat users can only see the Moment and activities posted by their friends. That is to say, when one of my friends posts a moment, his friends can comment and like his moment.

Irene: However, I can only see the comments and likes made by our common friends. If I don't accept other's friend request, they would not be able to see my moments, likes and comments. This function makes Moment a more private sharing place compared with Weibo. We can be free of personal information disclosure.

Angela: And later on, WeChat started to have more and more functions as introduced in listening part, including Official Account, Money Transfer, Service Account and so on. With Official Account, companies found a new way to promote their brands and products. Official account is a function allowing individuals and companies establish their own media platform to post articles. It works like a blog site.

Davis: Not only brands can have official account, but individuals can also register official accounts if they want to run their own media. This provides great convenience for users.

Irene: It is the case. With the rise of official account, placement of advertisement is changing. More and more people who enjoy writing found a way to generate profits through official accounts. It is becoming an industry. For example, there are a lot of fashion blogs on WeChat Official Account. In this way, both platforms are interwoven each other.

Angela: When they have enough followers, fashion brands will invest bloggers in order to let them write articles to promote their products. Thus, information in different platforms flows reciprocally to attract different users with different purposes.

Davis: When WeChat launched financial functions, people can go out with only a smartphone. The development of WeChat Wallet was convenient and prevalent that my parents together with their peers no longer brought their wallets when going to supermarket. They paid with WeChat wallet by scanning a QR code and confirming with Touch ID. This function can be used in almost every store and market in China.

Irene: As mentioned in the listening part, even in some foreign countries, stores and supermarkets accept payment through WeChat wallet.

Angela: The success of WeChat is not random. With its iteration in functions, it makes our life much more convenient. At the same time, its social function makes people addicted to it.

Davis: Sure. According to the WeChat Influence Report, 94% of WeChat users use WeChat every single day. It does become a part of our life. But to date, not everyone writes blog.

Irene: So, all things have two sides. With all those different functions, WeChat can collect a lot of data from its users, such as the amount of money transferred, songs or films preference of a certain age range etc. This is why Prof. Maynor required discussing safety or security hidden in social media.

Angela: In all, both WeChat and Weblog can be a great database for social science research if big data is needed.

Davis: What a discussion. I think we are collecting the information about WeChat and Weblog by comparing the difference. Ha-ha.

Irene: Now, let's continue to dig out more information about WeChat.

All: Okay. See you soon.

Task 3 ▶ Pre-reading activity

Direction: *This part serves as connecting link between the preceding and the following. MEDIA team are required to ponder over some problems concerning the whole unit, reflect on them and then find solutions. The answers are open-ended.*

Objectives: *To cultivate students' capability of exploring problems, develop critical thinking ability synchronously and improve expression ability.*

1. Why do you think WeChat can become an integral part of our life?
2. Please describe two to three functions of WeChat that you use most.
3. Try to exemplify how WeChat assist companies in developing their market.
4. What is WeChat-Public-Account? How does it appeal to the public users?
5. What kind of media can poorer areas and poorer consumers gain access to? What did WeChat do for this group of people?
6. How did WeChat become so popular with brands and marketers?
7. Can you imagine the future of WeChat?
8. How do you understand Multipurpose Application of WeChat?
9. Please explain the possible detrimental effect of WeChat.
10. Try to interpret WeChat usage from a societal perspective.

Task 4 ▶ Reading activity

Direction: *MEDIA team are required to read the following excerpt to obtain information, expand vocabulary volume, increase knowledge reserve, comprehend between lines, appreciate the writing style and evaluate the article.*

Objectives: *To cultivate students' capability of reading and absorbing information in a way that "eyes see quickly and brain processes quickly" to enhance reading comprehension, build up logic thinking, learn writing through reading and improve students' comprehensive quality.*

WeChat: Present and Future

Popular with the public

WeChat (*wēixìn*, micro-message) was first released by the Chinese multinational company Tencent Holding Limited in January 2011. With currently more than one billion monthly active users, it has become one of the most important applications on smartphone in China. WeChat presents a multipurpose smartphone application, going beyond the features offered by its counterpart WhatsApp popular in Western countries. The multipurpose platform WeChat integrates a variety of services such as messaging, socialization, and mobile payment services, and steadily expands its functionality by integrating new services such as city services allowing users to book transportation or to pay for traffic fines in China's metropolitan areas. In the context of social media use, the core functions of WeChat include messaging services with other users and sharing photos/videos via the function of Moment . WeChat offers free video and voice call features and a large range of emoticons to emphasize the emotional state of the users as well.

It is of importance to mention that the social media part of this smartphone application represents only one relevant aspect of WeChat. Indeed, WeChat must be seen in broader terms than "just" being social media. From a different angle, WeChat can be seen as a platform to acquire various information. The function of WeChat-Public-Account enables users to get any kinds of information when they follow a distinct public account. In fact, increasing organizations, like enterprises, universities, and governments, have utilized a WeChat-Public-Account as a channel to transmit information to specific users and interact with them.

Figure 7.2 WeChat users. Source: 秦王会，《微信时代，流量思维必死，用户思维永生》，http://www.qinwanghui2016.lofter.com/post/1e575bc1.

Another new appealing feature was added to WeChat in January 2014, with the inclusion of the Red Envelope (*hóngbāo*) function. This function mirrors the Chinese tradition to exchange monetary gifts via a red envelope in particular during the Chinese Spring Festival. This red envelope function became immediately so successful that more than 768 million individuals participated in sending and receiving red envelopes during the six-day Spring Festival holiday in 2018. Additional numbers on WeChat behavior have recently been reported underlining the importance of WeChat. In September 2017, 902 million individuals logged in daily to WeChat and 38 billion messages have been sent over this platform every day. The average user spent 139 mins each month on the app to call and 68 million videos have been posted each day in 2017. These numbers reflect that WeChat has become an integral part of everyday life for many users.

The current user base of WeChat is still primarily teens and young adults, accounting for 60% of users between the ages of 15 and 29. The average number of friends these users have on WeChat is about 128. The peak buying times on the app for those in this age demographic are 10am and 10pm, and the most popular items purchased in September 2015 were phone battery packs, fall clothing, and selfie sticks. On average, male shoppers spent one third more than female shoppers per month on the app. The average user reads one book a month and the most popular articles read and searched from vary by age. Older WeChat users primarily focused on health and wellness, middle-aged users focused on national news, and younger generations focused more on pop culture and entertainment gossip. Users appear to be most active on the app during the summer and appear to be happiest and most receptive to branding during Spring Festival and Mid-Autumn Day.

WeChat is the leading social media app among social media users in China and reaches across China, not just in major cities on the east coast of China. The penetration rates, the rise in WeChat use, and, correspondingly, the drop-in rate of all other sites exceed 10% penetration.

This means that users are engaged in the app, viewing content constantly and offering a constant source of touch points for brands and marketers. The app integrates users' digital presence into one place, making it far easier for brands to interact and communicate with targeted customer bases on a regular basis. It is changing the way Chinese businesses and global businesses entering, or doing business in Chinese markets, promoting themselves and furthering their brands.

Appealing to business

WeChat has also changed the way businesses market to consumers. Prior to the Internet and app connecting, businesses in China had a difficult time accessing all consumers. Those in cities could be reached via traditional product placement and promotion tools, but those outside cities were much harder to reach. Poorer areas and poorer consumers did not have access to televisions or other sources of media. Additionally, big data information was not available to businesses, particularly to poorer segments. As the Internet and mobile technology became more prevalent, brands were able to better access the poorer communities in China and reach greater audiences. Similarly, underpopulated areas were finally able to purchase goods they previously could not due to the lack of infrastructure and retail locations in rural parts of Chinese. The Internet and mobile technology have created a whole new means of connecting with all

Chinese citizens of all ages, incomes, and social classes. It has changed the way businesses can connect with and market to customers. Social media platforms, and specifically, WeChat, has further transformed this communication channel and has now made it possible for brands to not only reach all customers and potential customers, but also to target marketing and promotions to the right segments of these people in an informed and efficient way.

Figure 7.3 WeChat appealing to business.
Source:《做生意的，如何才能用好微信朋友圈宣传？》2017-05-03, www.sohu.com.

Brands and marketers in China can use WeChat differently than they use any other tool for interacting with customers. WeChat bring brands and marketers a completely brand-new experience. For example, where Starbucks could post an offer for all users on WeChat, it could theoretically also allow a user to inquire after their gift card balance, place a favourite drink order, find the nearest store without having to specify intent, or receive a promotion tailored to drink preferences based on the weather in that city. WeChat basically takes the functionality of a brand's personal application and puts all of those personal apps in one platform. Customers do not need to switch from one to another platform then to a cafe app and so on. All can be done in one place. Because WeChat offers this functionality, the interaction with the customer is able to be more personalized, detailed, interactive, and thus more likely to convert to monetary transactions which can also be done on the app. This is not the only way that brands can interact with customers using WeChat. WeChat, like other high volume social networking sites, has endless data on the users of the app. It knows a user's age, location, purchasing habits, family and friend network, employment status, and major life events. This data is a goldmine for brands that, rather than looking to send mass promotions, are looking to send targeted marketing campaigns to the right people. WeChat's largest demographic is the set of users aged 18-45, a notoriously difficult group to reach. Using the data from WeChat, brands can target messaging and promotions directly to the target market with little to no effort. It does this and holds the user in one place to see a promotion and act on it. And all of this information concerning who sees the promotion, and who acts on it, can flow directly back to the brand. This is not all done in purchased advertisement space, but is given freely as functionality for account developers for brands.

Because this service is easy and functional for all businesses, the companies using WeChat are not just large-scale global businesses, but small and medium-sized businesses as well. Walking around any city in China, one can see that almost all businesses like retail space or even some kiosks have QR codes, which makes it easy to access a company's WeChat site and interact with it immediately. Brands can reach their target markets with a scan of a phone.

Many global brands are already using WeChat as a means of communication with customers and releasing large-scale promotion campaigns. One of WeChat's early campaigns was signed with BMW. It wanted to target only affluent, educated people in the so-called first and second tier cities. People who did not fit the targeting criteria saw ads for soda and smart phones instead. People who did fit the category saw BMW ads pop up on their Moments page. The highly-anticipated opening to WeChat's own platform was noticed by many people, and they also noticed the blatant targeting. While BMW's brand soared immediately after the campaign, it soon received a backlash, as people failing to see BMW's ads appearing in their news feeds began referring to themselves as losers. Since then, WeChat has learned a lot about mobile marketing, and has avoided major controversy.

Traditionally, offline retail has been the main source of traffic, but it has also brought difficulties to Brand management. Due to distance barriers and dispersed contact points within the store, it is not possible to achieve higher quality traffic especially for luxury goods. The customer service is crucial for every brand. Therefore, the value chain provided by the WeChat ecosystem has become an important factor in promoting seamless connection between online and offline services for international brands. Research has found that 80% of famous international and fashion brands have shopping mini programs, and 28% of brands have developed omni-channel linkage mini programs. For example, the fashion clothing brand Raflauren, consumers can conveniently participate in offline activities/services through small programs, including coffee order, AI try on, product recommendation, online ordering and offline picking up. Users can also enjoy services without leaving the home, further expanding the consumption scene.

At the same time, the WeChat ecosystem is constantly enriching the functional matrix suitable for international brand marketing, such as creating high-end brand zones. It's reported that 99% of famous brands have developed high-end brand zones on WeChat, with targeted features and marketing links that make it easier for customers to facilitate online transactions.

Currently, connecting WeChat to the SCRM system is also a major trend. According to surveys, 30% of international brands have achieved seamless integration between mini programs and the SCRM system. Through the drainage of a series of online contacts, legal tracking and collection of behavioral data, and the integration of SCRM's unique marketing automation system, the data center provides deep insight and intelligent layering of the scoring system, personalized management and differentiated precision marketing are carried out for customers. Systematic incubation will greatly enhance the user's lifecycle and unleash their long-term value potential. Another example shows that Cartier is committed to providing consumers with visual customized recommendations, providing detailed gift selection guidelines for different scenarios, and providing differentiated services for packaging, customization, and delivery.

Figure 7.4 WeChat marketing. Source: 烽火台博客，《最新的微信营销scrm营销自动化话题》，www.parllay.cn/blog/1.

Other brands have used the app to grow their user bases and reach a larger base of consumers. For instance, in 2014, during the Chinese New Year, British Airways launched a WeChat campaign to broaden its audience. It welcomes users to connect with the airline via WeChat and promised to send a special New Year's gift to the first 2014 users that connect with it on WeChat. This campaign garnered the brand over 10,000 new connections on WeChat, growing its British Airways brand awareness and widen its reach to consumers in China. Still another example is Pepsi that used a similar format to widen its reach. Pepsi called on invited users to connect with the brand to send customized messages to friends and family branded as Pepsi by using the Pepsi jingle. This had a dual marketing effect for Pepsi as it made new users connect with the brand on WeChat, increasing its penetration of key user groups, and also spread awareness of Pepsi to these users' friends and family, further broadening this base of the use and awareness.

These creative campaigns all take advantage of WeChat in different and exciting ways to promote their brands. These campaigns were unique only to WeChat and such achievement could not be repeated in the same way currently by applying any other app or social media platform. Those campaigns point out a direction for the future of social media marketing and WeChat itself.

Bright future

The future for WeChat appears strong as a marketing tool for brands and as a global platform. WeChat is slowly morphing into an operating system to rival iOS and Android. In the coming years, WeChat plans to introduce "mini programs," which are apps within the app. This will eliminate the need for users to download apps outside of WeChat on their phones. Another benefit is that this will keep the user in WeChat's environment for even longer than currently. Users will never need to leave the WeChat world, because the apps they need will be within WeChat's environment. This feature will be especially useful for smaller businesses with limited resources to build their own external apps and gain app awareness in iOS and Android. More brands and businesses will have access to new ways to connect with users and to market to the target groups within WeChat.

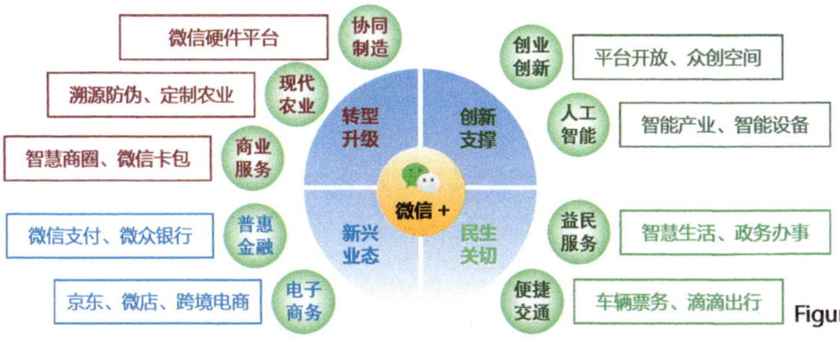

Figure 7.5 WeChat influence.

A move that will put the super app in direct competition with rivals Byte Dance and Kuaishou will be video and livestreaming. The future of China's ubiquitous messaging and social media app WeChat will be video and livestreaming. Video expression will be a major theme for the next 10 years of content generation. The do-everything app's current short video feature or channels will make video an easy way for everyone to express themselves, not just online celebrities and key opinion leaders.

However, the future is not limited within just short video. The exploration of livestreaming also goes under way. A small group of content creators has been able to access the livestreaming function in beta mode. As Angela Zhang put it: "Livestreaming has been in development for many years, but most people still view it from the perspective of e-commerce." Although the current version of WeChat does not have standalone livestreaming portal, the feature could be available via the app's next update.

In the future, livestreaming will be the way how people express themselves. WeChat's channels have already laid the foundations for future livestreaming functions.

Next feature worth mentioning is WeChat Mini Program, which is an ecosystem of mobile apps embedded in WeChat with daily active users reaching 400 million. Transactions via Mini Programs doubled from 800 billion yuan in 2019, thanks to a number of industries from retail to transportation and travelling swarming to the channel that supports payment. By the end of 2020, over 100 million users had made at least one purchase via Mini Programs. This has fueled the number of Mini Programs used per capita to rise by 25 percent from the levels in 2019, with average transaction value of each user surging nearly two-thirds.

Mini Programs have also shouldered the responsibility of COVID-19 prevention and control in China. Over 800 million people have used an official Health Code Mini Program for checking their health status as they enter public places, while some 550 million have used another digital travel card in the program that provides an overview of their itinerary in the past two weeks.

According to Xue Xu, IDC senior market analyst, WeChat's new feature will be particularly beneficial to startups and SMEs, since it will be much lower cost and much easier to use WeChat's provided resources to build an app. Established or mature companies which have already amassed a big number of users may not find it necessary to build another app in WeChat because they already have a wide user base. This new feature shows great promise for WeChat. However, thus far, WeChat has failed to expand globally. Most experts believe that the app's founders understand China and the Chinese market well but whether they are able to have enough data and understanding of global markets to make the app succeed as well. This means that WeChat needs to understand other markets and create the same positive word of mouth that has made it such a success in China. Still, it is clear that in the Chinese market, WeChat dominates and presents a unique opportunity for global businesses looking to do business in China. It also demonstrates many opportunities for competitors to learn from WeChat's success.

Task 5 ▶ Reading comprehension

Direction: *MEDIA team are going to launch a discussion about the reading excerpt. They are required to summarize what they learned, share their puzzles as well as their comments on the article, and try to probe into more profound issues in this domain.*

Objectives: *Learning by doing. To cultivate students' capability of finding problems, reflecting on and solving problems independently so as to improve the comprehensive ability of using language.*

Edward: Hello again, MEDIA team. I am quite impressed by your above discussion about the features of WeChat. And you also elaborate about how different is WeChat from Weblog and the like. I am convinced that through this reading, you can further expand what you know about WeChat. You may continue to carry forward your research spirit to explore the influence, development and future of WeChat from an even broader perspective.

Maynor: In addition to what Prof. Edward's advice, I'd like to add a few more hints. Now that WeChat is such an influential social media, how can it be used as a bridge for sino-foreign culture exchange? Next, as the Belt and Road Initiative is a common aspiration of all countries along their routes, how can WeChat contribute to serving the strategic target? With the competition intensified in almost all industries, people suffer increasing mental pressure. How can WeChat become pressure relief device to help those to reduce stress and put people into a better mood? In short, I hope you broaden your horizons and build up critical thinking.

Angela: Oh, my goodness. Your questions themselves are pressure, dear Prof. Maynor. But luckily, your questions are in the right place with the right people.

Davis: You mean we are the right people to answer these challenging questions? You believe so much in yourself.

Irene: Yes. We should be confident in ourselves, otherwise, we are prone to stagnation. Moreover, we have laid a good foundation. Of course, we can make it. Come on, Davis.

Maynor: Dear all. Don't be so stressed. All the questions are open-ended, and I just intend to exercise your thinking ability.

Edward: What's more, you are so skilled at applying various social media besides WeChat. It's easy for you to acquire a lot of information. You are really informative. I'm looking forward to your heated debate. It must be another wonderful discussion.

Irene: Thank you for your kind encouragement. Let me initiate with a question: In the era of social media, telling China's stories, spreading Chinese voice and constructing national image are important propositions of cross-cultural communication, then how can WeChat give full play to the role of publicity on the basis of huge number of users?

Davis: What a valuable question! Telling China's stories and spreading Chinese voice mean more users from different countries can hear about China's stories and voice. China is on the third index for welcoming a large number of international students especially those from the "Belt and Road" countries flocking to yield an opportunity to study in a well matured highly ranked education system. They use WeChat too besides other apps.

Angela: I know what you mean. Those international students have to deal with transitional issues like academic challenges, social issues, language barriers, teaching style, social isolation and cultural adjustment etc. First of all, they need to integrate into Chinese culture. Their intensity of WeChat usage can help them in understanding Chinese culture as well as interpreting China's stories, thus Chinese voice will be heard internationally.

Irene: Yeah, that's an effective means of telling China's stories well. When mentioning international students, they must be experiencing culture shock while pursuing higher degrees in more specialized fields in the context of alien culture. WeChat may make society interconnected and interdependent by managing individual social relationships. The intensity of WeChat usage will be positively associated with international students' psychological well-being and similarly contributes to students' psychological development.

Davis: I can imagine how hard they experience common issues such as academic pressures, loneliness, problematic verbal and nonverbal communication, and stress. Even adjusting to the host environment is difficult because their home cultures are often vastly different from the host environment. Besides, they have less access to family & friends social support to cope with problems. WeChat acts as the connection between social support and the psychological adaptation of international students.

Angela: The WeChat usage is expected to be positively related to the social emotional adjustment and social support respectively.

Edward: Thank God. You will never let me down. No matter how difficult the problem is, it can't beat you. How I wish I could hear more of your discussions, which covered almost all the questions raised by Prof. Maynor. However, other tasks are awaiting you. The current topic of discussion can be reserved as a topic for further discussion online. Do you agree with me?

All: Yes. So much for today. See you next time.

Task 6 ▶ Translation practice

Direction: *MEDIA team are going to do Chinese-English translation, from which they can learn and compare how to express in cross-cultural way and convey the following paragraph in English accurately.*

Objectives: *To understand and master English morphology, syntax and idiomatic expressions, develop basic professional translation ability and promote English competence.*

至2021年底，微信在全球有超过12.6亿的用户，也就是说在中国除了一些少年儿童和老年人以及某些经济不发达尚未普及无线网络和智能手机的地方之外，几乎每一个中国人都是微信用户。微信每天都在为中国人的社交做出巨大的贡献。中国人已经离不开微信，中国人失去微信，世界将会怎样？然而，很多人不知道的是即使是如此强大的微信，在全球的社交软件排名中只能排名第三。这可能是因为微信是基于熟人的圈子社交，人与人之间都是强关系连接的。当你所处的关系网络中都是熟人时，当你不愿意让熟悉自己的朋友亲人知晓一些事的时候，使用微信朋友圈功能就会带来一些顾虑。为此，匿名社交将会满足人们的这一需求。这也许为未来的微信提出又一个有待改进的空间。

Task 7 ▶ Attending a public lecture

Direction: *MEDIA team are going to attend a public lecture delivered by Professor Maynor. Students are required to thoroughly understand the lecture, broaden the vision, elaborate on the theme, get inspiration from the lecture and do some speech activities to extend their knowledge.*

Objectives: *To train students' capability of description, expression, discussion, refutation, humor and humanistic accomplishment required by making a speech, thus, improving students' English language competence and proficiency.*

Lecture 7

Review on Multipurposes of WeChat Application

Professor Maynor

Hello again, MEDIA team. I am sure that you must still remember what you have discussed when finishing the lecture six — Weblog Sphere in China, i.e., the second largest social platform. I recommended you to make an attempt to relate Weblog to academic research, didn't I? And your discussion extended far beyond the lecture itself. This time, I want to satisfy your interest in the connection between social platform and academic research. So I'll deliver you an academic report on the first largest social application in China — WeChat. You must have equipped yourselves well with knowledge in this regard through listening and reading materials. Hence, here, I am going to directly analyze the following three aspects: Firstly, motivation of WeChat usage; next, detrimental effect of WeChat usage on mental health, and thirdly, a societal perspective on WeChat usage. I hope you can gain something from it.

Currently, with over one billion monthly active users, the Chinese social media and multipurpose application WeChat or Wēixìn has become one of the world's most popular social media platforms. Against this background, we need first to find out what fascinates such a huge number of people.

Motivation of WeChat usage

Early work on WeChat usage aimed at understanding motivational aspects of WeChat usage. In this context, some scholars conducted an interview, pointing out that the need for social exchange represents one of the strongest driving forces to use WeChat. This view can be supplemented by the findings of an investigation in 200 students that WeChat is also used to relax and for stress relief. On the one hand, the students of this study in particular appreciated that WeChat enables them to stay in contact with friends, and on the other hand, they also stated that their own peers encourage them to use WeChat more often. Hence, social pressure may be a driving force promoting excessive and potentially problematic use, which may result in WeChat addiction or life satisfaction. Other researchers provided evidence that motivational factors such as satisfying the need for entertainment, sociality, and information on

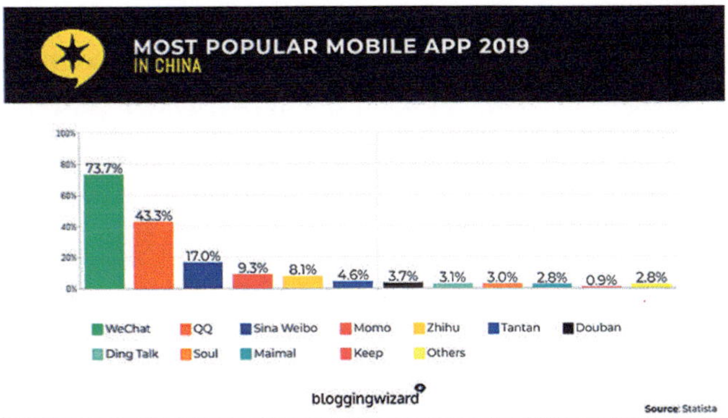

Figure 7.6.1 Increasing users of WeChat in China. Source: Adam Connell, "Latest WeChat Statistics for 2023: The Definitive List", 2023-1-1, https://bloggingwizard.com.

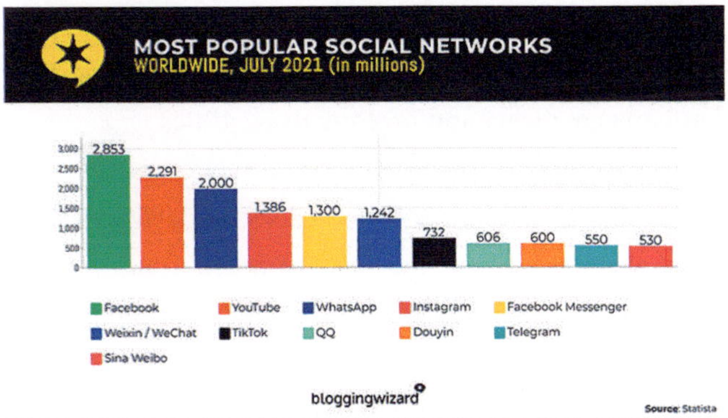

Figure 7.6.2 Increasing users of WeChat in the world. Source: Adam Connell, "Latest WeChat Statistics for 2023: The Definitive List", 2023-1-1, https://bloggingwizard.com.

WeChat impact the attitude toward WeChat, which was linked to positive word of mouth, meaning to speak positively about WeChat and its functions, whereas both the attitude toward WeChat and the variable of word of mouth were positively influenced by the factor trust in WeChat. There may exist four factors predicting WeChat usage: pastime, affection, sociability, and fashion. Although the frequency of WeChat use per week was best predicted by the pastime variable, e.g., WeChat being pleasant rest, fun, and relaxation, time spent on each session was best predicted by the factor affection, e.g., help and thank other people.

WeChat's well-known "like" function allows users to comment and like posted moments of their friends. Evidence from previous research on these social media platforms indicates that posted pictures getting many "likes" compared with posted pictures getting fewer "likes" results in stronger activity of the nucleus accumbent region/ventral striatum, hence reflecting the activation of reward-related mechanisms in the human brain. These effects might be more pronounced in adolescent users compared to older adults, possibly due to the lower top–down regulation in the adolescent prefrontal cortex undergoing maturational processes. This idea still needs to be more investigated: "only" contrasted young age groups with positive age associations and accumbent activity in the context of processing popular pictures with high vs. few "likes" in High School students. Future studies will also need to contrast younger with much older participants. For a more in-depth overview, rewarding mechanisms, self-related positive feedback, as observed for receiving a "like" may underlie the appeal of sharing pictures on WeChat. Adding to this, the following motives in a descending order were of importance to predict giving a "like" for a posted Moment on WeChat: enjoyment (hedonic gratification), providing support for another person (social gratification) and searching for information on WeChat (utilizable gratification). In line with the rewarding aspects of receiving "likes", social aspects contribute to the rewarding effects as it has been reported that receiving "likes" is self-assuring and increases self-esteem of the user. According to some aspects of psychological/neuroscientific research, the "like"-mechanism can attract and prolong usage times.

Aside from these first insights into motivational aspects of general WeChat usage, other researches attempted to explore factors that drive WeChat users' continuance intention of the app. Applying the theoretical framework of uses and gratification demonstrates that media appeal is by far of the highest importance to predict the intention to continue WeChat usage. Individuals scoring high on the psychological construct media appeal are among others known to like WeChat because it enables them to communicate with others immediately and to do this via an easy and cost-effective way. Also, the gratifications of entertainment, information, and reward significantly affect WeChat users' intention to follow the above-mentioned public accounts. Among others, the relevance of the user's satisfaction with WeChat can predict continuance intention. Meanwhile, effects of Chinese cultural factors have been paid attention to in recent years. Through introduced *guanxi*-based constructs into the technology acceptance model, affection or *gănqíng* in Chinese positively affects continuance intention to use WeChat, whereas face, with its equivalent as *mìanzǐ*, has a negative impact. For more completeness, we also point to keep investigating why persons in general discontinue with their social media use.

Detrimental effect of WeChat usage on mental health

Next, we'll focus on potential detrimental effects of WeChat usage in excessive amounts. A research demonstrates that WeChat usage itself is neither good nor bad *per se*, but that the kind of usage matters. Using WeChat to follow own interests is even associated with higher life satisfaction. In contrast, there have been a growing number of studies showing that smartphone use disorder/smartphone addiction might be associated with poorer sleep quality, because these users stick around their smartphones too long, also in the evening or at night. Interestingly, a new study observed that WeChat users have better sleep quality compared with non-users. The researcher explains the initial contradictory findings in the context of stress relieving properties of WeChat. Nevertheless, a third study did not assess problematic or potentially addictive use tendencies in the WeChat users, which might be specifically associated with negative emotions and negative sleep quality.

Recently, one more research suggests that excessive WeChat use may resemble core components of addictive behavior. A new questionnaire assesses "WeChat addiction" including the symptoms of loss of control over usage and social problems due to usage that in part resembles symptoms that characterize addictive disorders like substance-use disorders or behavioral addictions such as pathological gambling. Higher scores on this scale thus reflect more problematic and possibly addictive use. The study on integrating additional assessment of MRI-based measures of brain structure demonstrates that higher levels of "WeChat addiction" symptoms are associated with lower gray matter volumes of the subgenual anterior cingulate cortex, a key region for regulatory control and emotional conflict adaptation. These findings complement the previous findings indicates associations between the higher scores on "WeChat addiction", the lower self-control, and the higher "WeChat addiction" tendencies with a higher external locus of control. Individuals with a higher external locus of control believe that their lives are more driven by external factors such as fate or destiny. An empirical survey of 1,365 Chinese adolescents shows that higher life stress and external locus of control result in increasing risk for behavioral problems. Finally, a recent study also indicates associations between higher "WeChat addiction" and the personality trait of neuroticism, a general risk factor for psychopathology, particularly internalizing disorders including depression and anxiety. In addition, this user group additionally exhibits lower agreeableness scores, a personality trait closely linked to substance use disorders. Additional personality traits have also been shown to account for individual differences in WeChat usage, for example, posting more selfies on WeChat has been associated with higher extraversion. This kind of self-presenting/promoting behavior might additionally be associated with the personality trait of narcissism. Lastly, the personality of a WeChat user could also predict if he or she receives many "likes" on the shared Moments. In sum, personality represents an important construct to understand WeChat usage.

Figure 7.7 Excessive use of WeChat. Source: 《警惕！过度沉迷微信，大脑结构可能正在发生变化》，2018-2-2，www.whb.cn/zhuzhan/kjwz/20180202/188456.html.

A societal perspective on WeChat usage

A third area in WeChat research initially explored the impact of WeChat usage on the societal level. Western researchers are increasingly concerned about the impact of filter bubbles and echo chambers due to personalized news feeds undermining democratic processes. Among others, informing yourself via a personalized news feed, which is presented to you according to your "like" profile, might lead to biased views on the world and even radicalization, in particular if persons inform themselves only via social media about the daily news. Note that effects of such a personalized news feed on pluralistic opinions in society might differ depending on the different forms of governance across global societies.

Going beyond the already mentioned points, a good understanding of WeChat usage in Chinese participants will only be possible if psychological constructs will be investigated being closely linked to Chinese culture. Among these are concepts such as *guānxì*, as a unique feature of Chinese society, consists of different aspects covering *gǎnqíng* (affection), *rénqíng* (favour), and *xìnrèn* (trust) etc. Recent studies have paid attention to the roles of different *guānxì* (relation) dimensions exerting effects on the usage of social media. Much attention also should be paid to factors impacting different WeChat usage behavior, such as discontinuance behavior of WeChat and switching behavior to other social media. In fact, the increasing functions and more popularity of WeChat platform have already resulted in some negative phenomena, such as technology/system overload, information overload, and social overload; and have gone along with negative emotional and behavioral outcomes, such as stress, conflict, and discontinuance.

The research has also been done on an enormous popularity with the great potential in the discourse of societal areas of relevance and also using WeChat for educational purposes. Given that older generations are using WeChat in the meanwhile, the study of the WeChat platform will be of interest to get insights into a wider array of human behavior. This might be of special relevance when considering the new social credit system of the Chinese government used as a tool to develop a national reputation system of the Chinese population.

Figure 7.8 Modes of communication through WeChat.

Conclusion

To sum up, the present research report demonstrates that WeChat represents a multipurpose platform including social media functions, but going beyond this. Researchers interested in cross-cultural research on social media usage will need to take this into consideration, because this fact complicates matters when one aims to understand if same mechanisms globally can explain why humans are attracted to social media applications. Studies with respect to motivation to use the app and potential effects on well-being are also needed to address. Unfortunately, overall research report will only be hard to achieve given that some platforms are not available in all countries and certain platforms are dominating domestic markets with low chances for competitors to get a huge share of an already saturated market.

My talk today may be complicated to some degree. It's all because WeChat itself is overwhelmingly rich in content. As a closing remark, I want to leave you with some questions to ponder over, which will also assist your online discussion. Firstly, do you think it is true that smartphone usage reduces smiles between strangers? Secondly, at what levels do you think WeChat may benefit users in everyday life and may even enhance resilience due to its potential stress-relieving effects or increased social support? Thirdly, do you agree that the roles of different *guānxì* dimensions exert effects on the usage of social media like WeChat? Now it's time for us to stop. Good luck with your coming discussion.

Task 8 ▶ Online forum and summary writing

Direction: *MEDIA team are going to launch an instant online post-talk about the lecture to appeal to more of other students who are interested in the topic to join them. This is an integrated practice of listening, speaking, reading and writing. They are particularly expected to write a summary of the entire unit.*

Objectives: *To provide a platform for MEDIA team to fully display their talents. To comb language learning with professional knowledge so as to cultivate students' professional learning, academic literacy and language competence. To realize the teaching objectives of acquiring professional knowledge through learning English language.*

Edward: Well, with the lecture going deeper and deeper, I can't help but praise from the bottom of my heart. This unit provides us with rich information ranging from WeChat's history, present situation, and future to the serious competition faced by High-tech companies, impact brought by sophisticated technology, and culture transmission and so on. Prof.

Maynor's questions especially deserve commendation and warrant careful consideration.

Maynor: Thank you for your kind cooperation, Prof. Edward. I do hope that MEDIA team's discussion revolves around the problems but not limiting to these. Am I clear? I mean that you can give full play to your potential and explore more profound issues according to your knowledge structure.

Edward: Yes. You MEDIA members must have well prepared for the coming talk. Just go head. Do remember Maynor and I are always with you. Please don't hesitate to consult with us. You're truly welcome.

Davis: We are continually inspired to go ahead. Both of our tutors are highly valued. At the sight of the title, I have been turning the problem "multipurpose application" over in my mind. In my eyes, WeChat has only on purpose – social communication.

Angela: You are partially right. "social communication" is the core of any social platform. If we interpret all social media with the same answer "social communication", it sounds as if there were no differences or unique features for each specific medium. My understanding about "multipurpose application" WeChat is that the features are all that makes and shakes an app.

Maynor: Yes. Thanks to app like WeChat, messaging has transformed gradually ever since then. Multipurpose messaging apps have come out a long way and driven to the highest graphs when it comes to popularity.

Davis: I got it. "multipurpose" means the capability of meeting multiple demands. It all started with the emergence of WeChat as a small project that was initially launched in China strictly as a messenger app. Later in the world, it offered other various features along with mobile calling and multimedia sharing. These features include – WeChat stores, WeChat payments, thus multipurpose application coming into being.

Irene: Let me comb out its progress. It started with "baby steps" and covering one thing at a time. To create a faithful user base, the WeChat app team did not charge users for any features initially. The features of the app were offered to its users without costing even a coin. Later in the story of WeChat mobile application, the features of WeChat games and WeChat payments were added. When more features were added in the app, the app was not limited as a messaging app anymore, it became a platform to flourish businesses.

Edward: Well done, Irene. Clear and accurate. With the time and technology moving ahead, WeChat kept releasing new features to give an edge to competitions. The success of any application relies upon the list of capabilities. WeChat owes its success to its abundant functions like multimedia comparability, video chats, end-to-end encryption, cloud storage, sharing location and so forth.

Maynor: This is why WeChat has been in the limelight and has an edge over competitions in the app industry. WeChat offers a smooth user experience and comes with various robust features in one single app. This app has so much to offer on one single plate and is believed to be the future of communication and smartphone.

Angela: Wow, the topic itself tells us so much. I am considering another question: whether the users of the same App in different context may experience differently?

Davis: I think there exist differences, but the similarities prevail over differences, otherwise, how WeChat could be among the top social media.

Irene: Reasonable. What do you think is the greatest benefit to mankind by WeChat?

Angela: What harms human most in the last three years?

Davis: Covid-19 ranks the first, of course.

Irene: So contribution of WeChat in the anti-epidemic of Covid-19 is the most that I hope to express here. Mentally, psychologists offer twice-daily psychological counseling delivered via WeChat video communication. Officially, management personnel at various levels utilize WeChat groups to provide daily updates regarding the epidemic and related policies to ensure that patients received external information in a timely manner, to alleviate panic and anxiety etc.

Angela: Sorry to cut in. I know personalized WeChat tips are also offered on the basis of the actual situation of each patient. These included reminders delivered through WeChat about important issues, such as medication regimens, work and rest, meal times and diet, self-protection like washing hands and wearing a mask, and appropriate in-room exercise.

Davis: Doctors can offer daily relaxation therapy to guide patients through deep breathing, muscle and whole-body relaxation training via WeChat phone sessions. Relaxing music can be played via WeChat to improve physical and mental comfort and reduce anxiety.

Edward: Wonderful! It seems that I need a lot of time to digest the information you provide. It's time for us to interact with online learners, isn't it?

Irene: Gee, thanks for reminding.

All: See you next time.

Appendix: Vocabulary for Unit 7

Listening Activity

trailblazing /ˈtreɪlbleɪzɪŋ/ *adj.* 开拓性的
n. 开拓
v. 开拓（trailblaze 的 -ing 形式）

hail /heɪl/ *v.* 赞扬，欢呼；呼喊，招呼；下冰雹；（大量物体）像雹子般落下（或击打）
n. 冰雹；雹子般的一阵；招呼（某人）

split /splɪt/ *v.* 分裂，使分裂（成不同的派别）；分开，使分开（成为几个部分）；（使）撕裂；分担，分享
n. 裂口，裂缝；分离，分裂，分歧；（尤指钱的）分配，份额；区分，不同；（婚姻、感情、工作关系的）结束
adj. 分裂的

immense /ɪˈmens/ *adj.* 极大的，巨大的；非常好，极好；无边无际的
default /dɪˈfɔːlt/ *n.* 不履行，违约；默认，系统设定值；缺席，弃权
v. 违约，不履行义务；默认，预设；弃权，未到场
adj. 默认的
debit /ˈdebɪt/ *n.* 借记，借方；借项，借款
v. 记入（账户）的借方，借记；（从银行账户中）取款
margin /ˈmɑːdʒɪn/ *n.* 页边空白；差额，幅度；盈余，利润；边缘，非主体部分；保证金，押金
v. 给……加上边；预付定金，交押金
scroll /skrəʊl/ *n.* 长卷纸，卷轴；一卷古书（或公文、文件）；（绘制或雕刻的）涡卷形装饰；（视频显示器屏幕上为查看新资料而设的）显示滚动装置
v. 滚屏，滚动；使像纸卷合（或打开）那样移动
loop /luːp/ *n.* 环形，环状物；循环胶片，循环磁带；（程序中）一套重复的指令；回线，回路
v. 使成环，使绕成圈；成环形运动；执行计算机指令
ubiquitous /juːˈbɪkwɪtəs/ *adj.* 普遍存在的，无所不在的
skip /skɪp/ *v.* 蹦蹦跳跳地走；跳绳；不做（应做的事等），不参加；跳过，略过；快速转移，骤然转换（话题）；悄悄溜走，突然离开；打水漂
n. 蹦跳；（计算机）跳跃（进位），跳行
conservative /kənˈsɜːvətɪv/ *adj.* 保守的；保守派的；（衣着）守旧的，传统的；低估的；保守党的；不愿冒险的，谨慎的
n. 保守者，因循守旧者；保守党党员，保守党支持者

Reading Activity

metropolitan /ˌmetrəˈpɒlɪtən/ *adj.* 大都市的；本土的；（与）宗主国（有关）的
n. 大城市人，都会居民
inclusion /ɪnˈkluːʒn/ *n.* 包含，包括；包含物，包括的人；认同感，归属感
underline /ˌʌndəˈlaɪn/ *v.* 在……下面画线；强调，突出
n. （尤指为强调）下划线；（动物）下体轮廓
selfie stick *n.* 自拍杆
correspondingly /ˌkɒrəˈspɒndɪŋli/ *adv.* 相应地，相对地
prior /ˈpraɪə(r)/ *adj.* 先前的，事先的；优先的，更重要的；在前面的（prior to）
n. 〈美，非正式〉犯罪前科；小修道院院长；大修道院副院长；托钵会会长
segment /ˈsegmənt/ *n.* 部分，片段；（市场）细分的部分；（水果或花自然形成的）瓣，（昆虫的）节；（直线或弧线上两点间的）段

v. 分割，划分；（细胞）分裂

prevalent /ˈprevələnt/ *adj.* 盛行的，普遍的

tailor /ˈteɪlə(r)/ *n.*（尤指男装）裁缝；蓝鱼（Tailorfish 的简称）

v. 定做（衣服）；迎合，使适应

kiosk /ˈkiːɒsk/ *n.* 凉亭；公用电话亭；报摊

affluent /ˈæfluənt/ *adj.* 富裕的，富足的；丰富的

n. 富人

criteria /kraɪˈtɪəriə/ *n.*（评判或做决定的）标准，准则，尺度（criterion 的复数）

blatant /ˈbleɪt(ə)nt/ *adj.* 喧嚣的；公然的；炫耀的；俗丽的

backlash /ˈbæklæʃ/ *n.*（尤指对政治或社会事件的）强烈反应，反对；（机械的）反冲，反作用；（机械部件间的）间隙，轮齿隙

garner /ˈɡɑːnə(r)/ *vt.* 获得；储存；把……储入谷仓

n. 谷仓

morphing /ˈmɔːfɪŋ/ *n.* 变形

embed /ɪmˈbed/ *v.*（使）嵌入， 把……插入；深信，使深留脑中；（计算机中）内置；栽种；派遣

n. 随军记者

swarm /swɔːm/ *n.* 一大群（移动中的昆虫）；（移动着的）一大群人

v.（昆虫）成群飞行；（人）蜂拥，涌动；挤满，云集；成群地包围

amass /əˈmæs/ *v.* 积累，积聚

Lecture

detrimental /ˌdetrɪˈment(ə)l/ *adj.* 有害的，不利的

n. 有害的人（或物）

sociality /ˌsəʊʃɪˈælɪti/ *n.* 社会性；社交；好交际

nucleus /ˈnjuːkliəs/ *n.* 原子核；细胞核；核心，中心；神经核；（彗星的）核

accumbent /əˈkʌmbənt/ *adj.* 横卧的；斜靠着的；依状的

ventral /ˈventrəl/ *adj.* 腹侧的；［解剖］腹部的

n. 腹鳍

striatum /straɪˈeɪtəm/ *n.* 纹状体，终脑的皮层

adolescent /ˌædəˈles(ə)nt/ *n.* 青少年

adj. 青春期的；不成熟的

cortex /ˈkɔːteks/ *n.* 皮层，（尤指）大脑皮层；（植）皮层

accumbent /əˈkʌmbənt/ *adj.* 横卧的；斜靠着的；依状的

descend /dɪˈsend/ *v.* 下来，下降；下倾，下斜；降临，来临；降低身份，堕落；衰落，陷入

hedonic /hiːˈdɒnɪk/ *adj.* 享乐的；快乐的；快乐论的
n. 快乐论
gratification /ˌɡrætɪfɪˈkeɪʃ(ə)n/ *n.* 满足，令人喜悦的事物
per se /ˌpɜː ˈseɪ/ *adv.* 本身，自身
resemble /rɪˈzemb(ə)l/ *v.* 像，与……相似
pathological /ˌpæθəˈlɒdʒɪk(ə)l/ *adj.* 病理学的；病态的；
由疾病引起的（等于 pathologic）
symptom /ˈsɪmptəm/ *n.*（医）症状；（大问题的）迹象，征兆，征候
anterior /ænˈtɪəriə(r)/ *adj.* 前面的；先前的
cingulate /ˈsɪŋɡjʊlɪt/ *adj.* 有色带的；（昆虫腹部）有色带环绕的
neuroticism /njʊəˈrɒtɪsɪzəm/ *n.* 神经质，［心理］神经过敏症
psychopathology /ˌsaɪkəʊpəˈθɒlədʒi/ *n.* 精神病理学
extraversion /ˌekstrəˈvɜːʃən/ *n.* 外向性；外倾性
narcissism /ˈnɑːsɪsɪzəm/ *n.*［心理］自恋，自我陶醉
bubble /ˈbʌb(ə)l/ *n.* 气泡，泡沫；经济泡沫；
v. 冒泡，沸腾；发出冒泡的声音；忙碌，活跃；兴奋，激动；（情绪、感情等）涌动
radicalization /ˌrædɪkəlaɪˈzeɪʃn/ *n.* 激进，激进化
pluralistic /ˌplʊərəˈlɪstɪk/ *adj.* 兼职的；兼管数个教堂的

Unit 8

Media Convergence: Path and Practice

TABLE OF CONTENTS

Unit 8 Media Convergence: Path and Practice

Warm-up: Be proactive

Direction: *MEDIA team are going to do warm-up activities by discussing, airing their views on the topic and discovering problems.*

Objectives: *To arouse students' interest, get a preliminary understanding of relevant knowledge and prepare for the following study.*

Edward: Hello, MEDIA team. This is the last unit with a very fresh topic: media convergence. I wonder how much you know about this conception, which has lasted for almost two decades since its inception. However, how the true practice, the path to develop and the solution to current problems are going still remains open to discussion. So my advice is that we elaborate this topic from a 360-degree omni-directional perspective, am I right?

Maynor: I strongly approve of Prof. Edward's proposal. I hope that you prepare this unit with these issues in mind: Why media convergence is important? Do you know anything about 3Cs of media convergence? Are there any advantages of media convergence? I assume that these can be of some help to you.

Irene: Thank you, my dear supervisors! For me, this concept is a little alien. I do hope we can start with its notion, its implication and its influence so that we lay the foundation for the latter learning.

Angela: So, let me launch the discussion by airing my view about the importance of media convergence. It is important because it blends content, communication technologies and computer networks together, thus leading to the immediate transformation of many established industries, services as well as work practices, and through all these, new forms of content are born.

Davis: Specifically, media convergence actually transforms the modes of communication, news reporting, and journalism, in short, media journalism. It leads to cross-media since a huge amount of content is now being accessed through portable devices. For instance, news organizations no longer simply rely on print media or AV transmission.

Irene: I seem to understand something. Maybe, I can understand it in this way: Many new media forms are born like news portals, podcasts, news feeds, blogging, websites and mobile applications, while the newly converged media platforms provide online access to the archives, and endless opportunities for users to comment on the story or provide links to relevant materials. Is that so?

Maynor: You got it, Irene. You know communication across the world has evolved with the advent of technology and media. There are now several ways to exhibit your work, voice your opinions on issues and spread knowledge and information globally. The phenomenon related to these is called media convergence. People sometimes name it 3C media convergence. Please go on with it.

Edward: Convergence means integration. Just think about the correlation between the merging of different types of mass media like traditional media, print media, broadcast media, new media and the Internet as well as portable and highly interactive technologies. The linkage is through digital media platforms.

Angela: I got it. Digital media platforms result in the combination of communication, computing and content as all three are integrated through technology. 3C is the abbreviation for communication, computing and content. How do you think of my interpretation?

Davis: Great, Angela. A word reveals the secret. I'd like to exemplify what is media convergence. Nowadays, every one of us applies the converged media in our daily life. That is a Smartphone. It blends together various media, i.e., print media (e-books, news apps), broadcast media (streaming websites, radio, music apps) as well as new media (the

Internet) into a single device that performs various functions from calling and texting to photography, videography, and gaming, and the like.

Irene: As clear as crystal. You gave a vivid description. I think I fully understand it now. As we take endless advantages of a smartphone, its advantages must be engraved in our minds.

Maynor: Good job. So far, you've spent around 15 minutes to cover the preliminaries. Why not go on with more profound knowledge?

Edward: I'm convinced that you will be well prepared about the following listening part. Right? Come on.

All: Okay. We'll not let you down. See you soon.

Task 1 ▶ Listening activity

Direction: *MEDIA team are going to listen to an introduction of key concepts so as to lay the foundation for later learning.*

Objectives: *To understand the main conception, practice and strengthen the ability of listening comprehension.*

Media Convergence: Concept and Effect

It's important to keep in mind that the implementation of new technologies doesn't mean that the old ones simply vanish into dusty museums. Today's media consumers still watch television, listen to radio, read newspapers, and become immersed in movies. The difference is that it's now possible to do all those things in one device through the Internet, be it a personal computer or a smartphone. Such actions are enabled by media convergence, the process by which previously distinct technologies come to share tasks and resources. A cell phone that also takes pictures and video is an example of the convergence of digital photography, digital video, and cellular telephone technologies. An extreme, and currently nonexistent, example of technological convergence would be the so-called black box, which will combine all the functions of previously distinct technology and would be the device through which we'd receive all our news, information, entertainment, and social interaction.

Figure 8.1 Converged media.

Media convergence refers to content that is made available through multiple forms, formats, and access points on multiple platforms. Network convergence refers to a single network infrastructure that handles and distributes multiple types of media. The IoT is a system of interrelated devices that transfer data over a network among connected devices without requiring human-to-human or human-to-computer interaction.

Kinds of convergence

But convergence isn't just limited to technology. Media theorist Henry Jenkins argues that convergence isn't an end result as is the hypothetical black box, but instead a process that changes how media is consumed and produced. Jenkins breaks convergence down into the following five categories.

Economic convergence. It occurs when a company controls several products or services within the same industry. For example, a single company may have interests across many kinds of media in the entertainment industry. Rupert Murdoch's News Corporation is involved in book publishing. Through his company News Corp, he is the owner of hundreds of local, national, and international publishing outlets around the world, including in the UK (*The Sun* and *The Times*), in Australia (*The Daily Telegraph*), and in the US (*New York Post* and *The Wall Street Journal*) take newspapers as the main business. It is the same with Colorado Rockies that is famous for sports program, while Fox is well known as broadcast television. And FX, National Geographic Channel is cable television based. The 20th Century Fox is so popular with audiences all over the world, its films are at the top. Myspace used to be the biggest social networking site and so forth.

Organic convergence. It is happens when someone is watching a television show online while exchanging text messages with a friend and also listening to music in the background — the "natural" outcome of a diverse media world.

Cultural convergence. It covers several aspects. Stories flowing across several kinds of media platforms is one component, for example, novels that become television series, radio dramas that become comic strips, and even amusement park rides that become film franchises. The character Harry Potter exists in books, films, toys, and amusement park rides. Another aspect of cultural convergence is participatory culture — that is, the way media consumers are able to annotate, comment on, remix, and otherwise influence culture in unprecedented ways. The video-sharing website YouTube is a prime example of participatory culture. YouTube gives anyone with a video camera and offers an internet connection the opportunity to communicate with people around the world and create and shape cultural trends.

Global convergence. It is the process of geographically distant cultures influencing one another despite the distance that physically separates them. Nigeria's cinema industry, nicknamed Nollywood, takes its cues from India's Bollywood, which is in turn inspired by Hollywood in the United States. *Tom* *and Jerry* cartoons are popular on Arab satellite television channels. Successful American horror movies *The Ring* and *The Grudge* are remakes of Japanese hits. The advantage of global convergence is access to a wealth of cultural influence. Its downside that some critics posit is the threat of cultural imperialism, defined by Herbert Schiller as the way developing countries are attracted, pressured, forced, and sometimes bribed into shaping social institutions to correspond to, or even promote, the values and structures of the dominating center of the system. Cultural imperialism can be a formal policy or can happen more subtly, as with the spread of outside influence through television, movies, and other cultural projects.

Technological convergence. Technological convergence, in general, refers to the trend or phenomenon where two or more independent technologies integrate and form a new outcome. One example is the smartphone. A smartphone integrated several independent technologies — such as telephone, computer, camera, music player, television (TV), and geolocating and navigation tool — into a single device. Echnological convergent devices share three key characteristics. First, converged devices can execute multiple functions to serve blended purpose. Second, converged devices can collect and use data in various formats and employ machine learning techniques to deliver enhanced user experience. Third, converged devices are connected to a network directly and/or are interconnected with other devices to offer ubiquitous access to users.

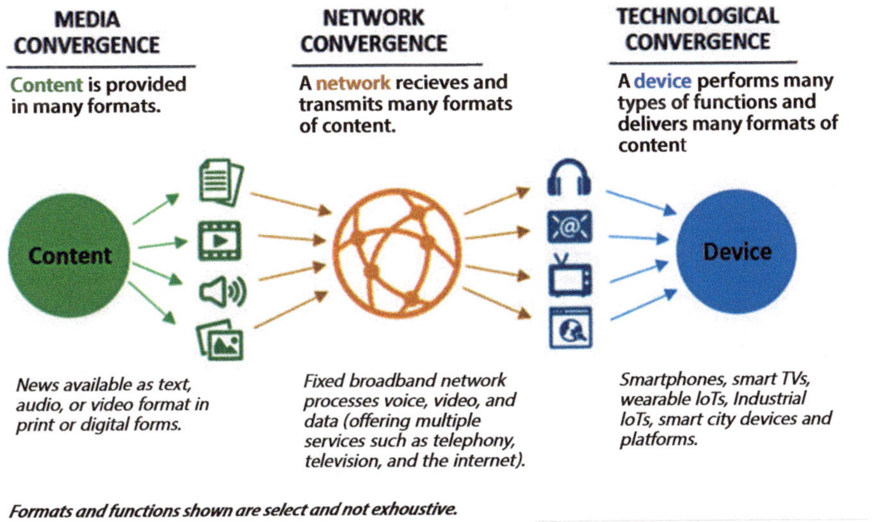

Figure 8.2 Technological, media, and network convergences. Source: Suzy E. Park, "Technological Convergence: Regulatory, Digital Privacy, and Data Security Issues", 2019-05-30, https://www.everycrsreport.com.

In other words, technological convergence is a concept whereby merging, blending, integration, and transformation of independent technologies leads to a completely new converged technology. This broad, complex concept encompasses a wide range of technologies, including IoT and smart home devices. When a converged technology emerges, it often replaces single-function technologies or renders them obsolete. In this sense, technological convergence can be viewed as a progression or evolution of technology.

Effects of convergence

Jenkins's concept of organic convergence is perhaps the most telling. For many people, especially those who grew up in a world dominated by so-called old media, there is nothing organic about today's media-dominated world. As a *New York Times* editorial recently opined, "Few objects on the planet are farther removed from nature — less, say, like a rock or an insect — than a glass and stainless-steel smartphone." But modern American culture is plugged in as never before, and today's high school students have never known a world where the Internet didn't exist. Such a cultural sea change causes a significant generation gap between those who grew up with new media and those who didn't.

A 2010 study by the Kaiser Family Foundation found that Americans aged 8 to 18 spend more than 7.5 hours with electronic devices each day — and, thanks to multitasking, they're able to pack an average of 11 hours of media content into that 7.5 hour. These statistics highlight some of the aspects of the new digital model of media consumption: participation and multitasking. Today's teenagers aren't passively sitting in front of screens, quietly absorbing information. Instead, they are sending text messages to friends, linking news articles on social media, commenting on social videos, writing reviews of television episodes to post online, and generally engaging with the culture they consume. Convergence has also made multitasking much easier, as many devices allow users to surf the Internet, listen to music, watch videos, play games, and reply to e-mails on the same machine.

However, it's still difficult to predict how media convergence and immersion are affecting culture, society, and individual brains. In his 2005 book *Everything Bad Is Good for You*, Steven Johnson argues that today's television and video games are mentally stimulating, in that they pose a cognitive challenge and invite active engagement and problem solving. Poking fun at alarmists who see every new technology as making children stupider, Johnson jokingly cautions readers against the dangers of book reading: It "chronically under stimulates the senses" and is "tragically isolating." Even worse, books "follow a fixed linear path. You can't control their narratives in any fashion — you simply sit back and have the story dictated to you... These risks instilling a general passivity in our children, making them feel as though they're powerless to change their circumstances. Reading is not an active, participatory process; it's a submissive one."

According to Nicholas Carr, *The Shallows: What the Internet Is Doing to Our Brains* is more pessimistic. Carr worries that the vast array of interlinked information available through the Internet is eroding attention spans and making contemporary minds distracted and less capable of deep, thoughtful engagement with complex ideas and arguments. "Once I was a scuba diver in a sea of words," Carr reflects ruefully. "Now I zip along the surface like a guy on a Jet Ski." Carr cites neuroscience studies showing that when people try to do two things at once, they give less attention to each and perform the tasks less carefully. In other words, multitasking makes us do a greater number of things poorly.

Whatever the ultimate cognitive, social, or technological results, convergence is changing the way we relate to media today.

Task 2 ▶ Listening comprehension

Direction: *MEDIA team are going to have a topic-oriented discussion to exchange their views on the listening material and challenge each other with puzzling questions.*

Objectives: *To broaden students' horizon, develop their ability to sum up the skills of answering questions and strengthen language output ability.*

Maynor: Hello, everyone. I'm deeply impressed by this leading-in listening provided by Prof. Edward. It is truly comprehensive and in-depth. I am sure that you must have gained a lot from it. As your tutor, I really hope to provide you with some shortcuts to explore more profound issues in this regard.

Davis: Of course, you can. Actually, every time you and Prof. Edward drew a sketch map of the area to show us the way so that we are always on the right path. We truly appreciate what you have done for us.

Irene: Exactly. Your questions are just like route signs for us. The process of answering your questions is the process of our acquiring knowledge.

Edward: We're so honored. Let me go on drawing another road map for you. First, you should clarify the typologies of media convergence, then you may take the influence of media convergence on society into consideration, and finally, what fields do you think the future career in media will cover? Why?

Maynor: You need to weigh up those questions carefully. As long as you can find solutions to these questions, you are meant to have a good grasp of the knowledge concerned.

Angela: Thanks heartily. From my standpoint, the types of media convergence mainly make up of technologies and media forms. For instance, the Internet together with multimedia integrated into one medium form, where people can read, watch and listen etc. as they like. Those contents were originally distributed in different forms.

Davis: Sure. Media convergence facilitates all these activities. Media convergence is an umbrella term that can be defined in the context of technological, industrial, social, textual, and political terms.

Irene: I see. Indeed. The main types of media convergence actually cover three categories: technological convergence, economic convergence and cultural convergence.

Angela: It is easy to understand technological convergence, which, academically speaking, describes the layers of abstraction which enables different technologies to interoperate efficiently as a convergent system.

Davis: Technological convergence is the combination of computing, communication, and content around networked digital media platforms. That is what Prof. Maynor called "3C".

Irene: It can convert existing media into a digital form of technology, for example, viewing a book online (e-books, kindle). We have compiled some of the basic fundamentals of technological convergence below: Technologies convergence is when new technologies are created that mostly take over or get upgraded from past technologies and perform the same task but in a more advance manner. For example, people used to listen to music by radio, but now the technological convergence has evolved into the stage when majority use smartphones.

Angela: In all, technological convergence is the tendency that technology sometimes evolves towards performing a similar task. But I am puzzled how cultural convergence happens in media convergence?

Davis: Oh, this concept of media convergence occurs when two or more cultures adopt each other's traits and become more alike. Those increasing similarities between cultures are related to beliefs, consumer brands and media.

Irene: But I don't think culture convergence only limit to beliefs, brands or so. It involves at least two typologies: one is acculturation, meaning when weaker among two cultures adopt traits from more dominant culture, e.g., Indians mostly speaking the English language. The other is assimilation: When original traits of weaker culture are completely erased and replaced by traces of more dominant culture, e.g., war immigrants no longer speak the native language.

Angela: Irene's explanation is philosophical. Besides, economic convergence is still a pendent problem awaiting us to deal with.

Davis: To my knowledge, just like the general definition of economic convergence suggests that countries with lower GDP are going to grow faster than countries with higher GDP, the economic media convergence allows a single company to target larger interest groups through various kinds of media.

Irene: To sum up, the key features of economic convergence are that in economic convergence large companies use old and new media to their advantage by selling merchandise or the rights of the product. Next, it is the horizontal integration of the entertainment industry companies such as Sony, AOL. Time Warner now has an interest in film, TV books, games,

	and the Internet, music real estate, etc.
Angela:	Hi guys, we can't linger on one issue all the time. There are still other two questions are awaiting us. We are far too inefficient. I just hope to add one more about the relation between future career and media convergence: I believe that media convergence will touch upon a broader field including editors, reporters, travel Journalism, columnists, correspondents, staff or freelance writers, photojournalists, proofreaders, news analysts, critics, cartoonists, illustrators and high-tech engineers etc.
Irene:	So, our major or our specialty will be more popular. This can account for one aspect of influence brought by media convergence.
Davis:	From the social angle, media convergence has proven beneficial for small and large businesses both as well as have provided people with the rapid accessibility and availability of information and content at the touch of the screen. It has also made communication better thus making our society more globalized.
Maynor:	You are really good students with extraordinary self-study abilities. I rejoiced to appreciate what you've done each time.
Edward:	So do I. Time is flying, and the time for our discussion is coming to an end. You are going to do more reading and more reflection on the issue.
All:	Okay. Bye for now.

Task 3 ▶ Pre-reading activity

Direction: *This part serves as connecting link between the preceding and the following. MEDIA team are required to ponder over some problems concerning the whole unit, reflect on them and then find solutions. The answers are open-ended.*

Objectives: *To cultivate students' capability of exploring problems, develop critical thinking ability synchronously and improve expression ability.*

1. Please give an example to demonstrate what media convergence is.
2. How has media convergence led to universalization of popular culture?
3. How does media convergence affect society?
4. What are the major disadvantages of media convergence and why?
5. Why do central leaders attach so much importance to media convergence?
6. What are the current problems about media convergence in China?
7. Can you draw a blueprint for future media convergence? Please try to describe it.
8. Why is media convergence regarded as a national strategiy?
9. How can China's media convergence be realized in the near future?
10. Please take an example to explain how to tell China's stories well in the context of media convergence.

Task 4 ▶ Reading activity

Direction: *MEDIA team are required to read the following excerpt from a research on media convergence by Xie Wanying in 2021, to obtain information, expand vocabulary volume, increase knowledge reserve, comprehend between lines, appreciate the writing style and evaluate the article.*

Objectives: *To cultivate students' capability of reading and absorbing information in a way that "eyes see quickly and brain processes quickly" to enhance reading comprehension, build up logic thinking, learn writing through reading and improve students' comprehensive quality.*

On the Feasible Path of Media Convergence in China

Background

The logic of media behavior has been changed with the development of technology and the popularization of Internet, which reflects the integration of technology and media. In 1999, the concept of media convergence was first introduced into China, leading to great changes in China's media ecosystem. In 2013, the Third Plenary Session of the 18th Central Committee of the Communist

Party of China mentioned that promoted the integrated development of traditional media and new media for the first time. The year 2014 is known as the first year of media convergence in China. In 2019, our state found that it is an urgent task for China to make use of the achievements of the information revolution, promote the in-depth development of media convergence, expand and strengthen mainstream public opinion, and consolidate the common ideological basis for the united efforts of the whole Party and the whole people. In 2020, the central government officially incorporated media convergence in China's 14th Five-Year Plan and 2035 vision.

Under the leadership of the Communist Party of China, Chinese media have the thought of political communication with Chinese characteristics. Our government pays high attention to the political communication and public opinion. A series of new ideas and viewpoints are put forward, which reflect the concept of people-centered political communication of Chinese mainstream media. Traditional policy transmission is unable to meet people's increasing demand for political information acquisition. The pattern of Political communication in China has been constantly expanding. China's new path of political communication has been gradually constructed.

Figure 8.3 2020 中国经济媒体融合发展高峰论坛在京召开 . Source: 中国市场监管报官网，2020-12-28.

Current problems

The political communication of Chinese media in the media convergence era currently faces some challenges, such as the confusion of public opinion field, the obvious port diversion problem and the problem of "hollowing out of talents". In the current media convergence era, the network space presents decentralized distributed architecture. The period of social public opinion is compressed. Weibo, WeChat and other social media are getting more and more involved in political communication, producing the confusion and the false political information to some extent though such media promote the prosperity of media industry and facilitate intercommunication. Media convergence makes public opinion and content more diversified and brings new challenges to political communication. Next, there are obvious problems such as port shunting and uneven progress of media convergence. Traditional media is successively entering in Weibo, WeChat, Tik Tok and other social media platforms to open new media accounts. Some convergence of traditional media and new media failed to take the modes of convergence operation into consideration. Traditional media and new media ports sing different tunes, resulting in port diversion, poor integration effect, product asynchronism, inconsistent content phenomenon, and even zombie platform. It is difficult to break the convergence circle for the general public. Last but least, the problem of "talent hollowing out" technology promotes the development of media convergence. While liberating the mechanical labor of political journalists, technology brings unprecedented challenges to the production of political news. Traditional mass and broadcast models could not satisfy all the public. Facing the complicated, high speed, massive and fragmented false political news in the media convergence era, it is hard for traditional political media talents to instantly screen information from the perspective of journalism.

The feasible path of media convergence

In view of the above possible problems, it is suggested that Chinese media make full use of big data to monitor political public opinion, build full media matrix and make political communication professional talent team with full media thinking in order to promote the development of political communication in the media convergence era.

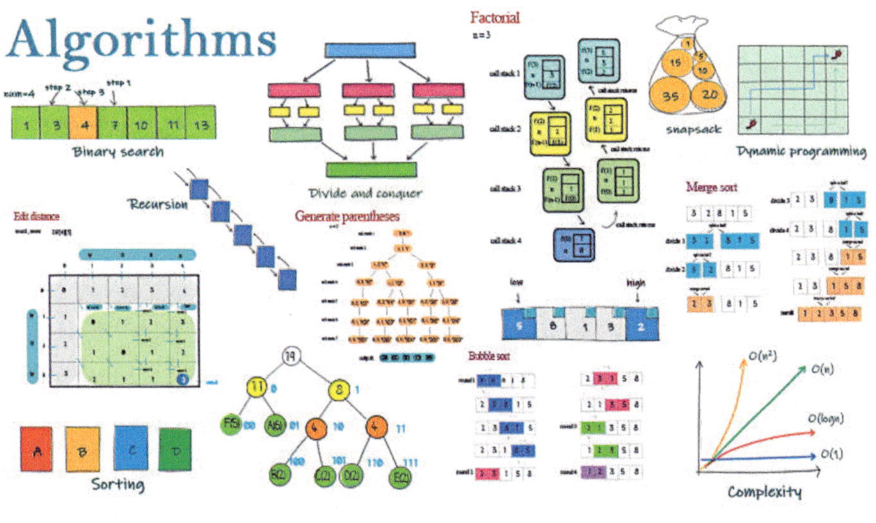

Figure 8.4 La Vivien. Source: Algorithm types and algorithm examples, 2022-07-18, www. lavivienpost.com.

Algorithm utilization

Big data can be made full use of to regulate political public opinion. Algorithm is not only a core technology of new infrastructure, but also a new form of rights. Algorithm penetrates into all levels of the political field, promotes the reform of political communication and brings new opportunities and risks. Therefore, algorithm technology can improve the monitoring mechanism of big data, define the scope and construct the framework of political communication.

Firstly, intelligent recommendation technology with the integration and complement of multiple algorithms should be developed to ameliorate the accuracy of political information. Algorithm rules, such as the rules of editor selection and those of quality manuscript recommendation in line with the mainstream of society, should be well formulated. Secondly, various types of text data should be judged from semantic analysis, text emotion analysis and other aspects with advanced means such as big data to timely monitor the flow of political information. Thirdly, the cause of the political public opinion events should be carefully analyzed with deep learning technology. The processing mechanism of political public opinion should be established to improve the ability of early warning, public opinion supervision and public opinion reaction. The construction of network integrated management system should be strengthened in order to make real-time feedback, make quick response to the political public opinion and guide the correct political opinion. Lastly, the human-machine cooperation database of political public opinion should be built to accurately grasp the trend of political public opinion.

Same-frequency resonance

All-media matrix should be efficiently created. The integrated support strategy should be implemented and the internal operation mechanism of media should be optimized in order to establish an all-media system featuring extensive consultation, joint contribution, sharing and unity, and build an all-media matrix with resonant frequency. Political news product service and information service products are complemented each other, in order to realize the full convergence between upstream and downstream, traditional media and new media, content and operation. The content on various media such as Weibo and WeChat should be connected by innovating the acquisition, production and publicity path of news content, strengthening the correlation of transmission mode and handling all ports connection. Adhere to the principle of transition and integration, media convergence will realize from plus to convergence.

Talent cultivation

The most fundamental is to build a professional talent team of political communication with all-media thoughts. Consensus is reached that we should build a political ideological team with political competence, high skill as well as realistic and innovative capability. First, the introduction and management mechanism of political communication talents with all-media thinking need to be established. Then, the talent incentive system and mechanism may be bettered with the introduction of political communication talents strengthened to stimulate the endogenous vitality. Next is to cultivate the compound political communication talents with technical and innovative thoughts so as to build a professional and versatile all-media political communication talent team. Third, setting up well-planned training system to reserve force including high-tech professionals in computer communication technology, mobile new media technology, new platform construction, maintenance and operation to form larger number of political communication talents in the development of media convergence. Finally, attention ought to be paid on the cooperation between the media and universities, encouragement of learning new technologies to adapt to the transformation and upgrading of media.

Objectives

Facing the situation of in-depth development of media convergence, Chinese media should find the way of media convergence with Chinese characteristics. Political communication would constantly bring forth new ideas in the wave of in-depth development of media convergence in the future. Chinese media convergence will innovate the political communication by innovating the way of media political communication, building up the media discourse system and communicating the political communication content in the story-telling way.

I. Method innovation

It is natural that Chinese media should break the time and space barriers of conventional political communication, build a new platform for political communication, innovate the way of political communication, enrich the forms of content presentation, construct the three dimensional and diversified political communication system, and maximize the use of political resources.

Political communication in the media convergence era takes ultra-high definition (UHD) video news as the mainstream trend, which provides new development opportunities for UHD video news. The combination of various new technologies improves the upstream and downstream speed of video, bringing revolutionary changes to all aspects of UHD video content from collection, production, pushing and streaming, all of which was called the new video era. UHD video should also be combined with traditional graphic to form new high-definition live TV screen scenarios such as new media formation of multiple element fusion with "technology + video + news". Only when the form of content presentation and the audience's political participation plus subjective initiation are enriched and enhanced, can higher-quality political communication service be really provided for audience.

3R, 3D, VR, AR and interactive reality technologies are becoming increasingly mature, resulting in immersive news experience to audiences. Immersive news refers to a form of political news production, allowing audience to get the first-person experience of events or situations described in political news. Under such situation, audience would be able to restore the real-time scene of political news. The 360-degree panorama perspective make it available for the real-time sharing and switching of political news scene to interact each other, hence raising the audience ratings of political news. In the future, political news will transfer from planar space to three-dimensional space, virtual space and multidimensional space, thus, realizing the combination of reality and virtual space. The highlight of the value of scene will make the audience completely immersed in three-dimensional and multi-dimensional space. The Web 3.0 era will further make immersive political news perfect. The era of "news for everyone" is coming.

II. Media discourse construction

The solutions to the problems involving innovating the language style of Chinese mainstream media for political communication, enhancing the feedback and interaction mechanism, and constructing the media discourse

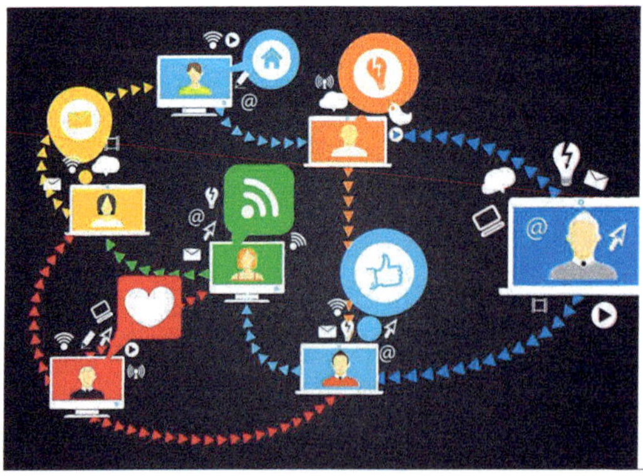

Figure 8.5 Media discourse construction. Source: 肖博文，《关于传统主流媒体融合的几点思考与建议》，2020-12-01，www.sohu.com.

system with Chinese characteristics need to be put to the priority. Our government hold that China should strengthen the construction of discourse system, create new concepts, new categories and new expressions integrating China and the rest of the world, and enhance China's voice in the international arena. Chinese media should follow the mass line to the greatest extent, stay close to life, serve the general public and make political information transparent and political language understandable. Audiences should timely feedback political information with media, express self-cognition and opinions and build a systematic media discourse system with Chinese characteristics. It has gradually reached a consensus to build a philosophical discourse system with Chinese characteristics. What kind of discourse to choose and how to choose discourse for the transmission of political civilization need to be deeply studied.

III. Story-based content

The communication of political content in a story-telling way should be the guiding direction of Chinese media political communication. The ways of interpreting news and individuating narrative scenes change traditionally serious political topics into daily news report, which make political communication more influential and appealing. The goal to improve the audience's understanding and acceptance of political news will come true in the near future.

Conclusion

In the media convergence era, China's traditional media and new media will adhere to the correct values, seize the opportunities for media convergence to further develop, embrace new technologies to complement each other. The deeper and comprehensive media convergence will drive Chinese media to keep on exploring new paths of the convergence development of political communication with complementary advantages, resource integration and sharing accommodation. The rapid advancement of China's digital media will unswervingly promote the development of the media convergence in the future. The wide application of new technology is pushing Chinese media to transform from the convergence media to the wisdom media, which symbolize completing deep development with overall upgrading of media convergence and speeding up to enter the new pattern of political communication in the media convergence era.

Task 5 ▶ Reading comprehension

Direction: *MEDIA team are going to launch a discussion about the reading excerpt. They are required to summarize what they learned, share their puzzles as well as their comments on the article, and try to probe into more profound issues in this domain.*

Objectives: *Learning by doing. To cultivate students' capability of finding problems, reflecting on and solving problems independently so as to improve the comprehensive ability of using language.*

Edward: Hello, there. What do you think of this reading excerpt? It is actually extracted from an academic thesis on media convergence by XIE Wanying in 2021. It tells us how important media convergence is and why our central leaders attach so much significance to it. It also shows us a blueprint for the future of media convergence. Of course, the bright future can't come true itself. Each of us should contribute to the ideal goal as much as we can.

Maynor: Sure, it is. You needn't care too much about the research method such as survey or questionnaire etc. You should focus on the information acquisition. After all, this paper offers you enough about why media convergence causes so much attention, and how media organization can implement the initiative of the central government and the like.

Edward: And you'd better also highlight on whether media convergence brings disadvantages to the society though it has benefited us so much. Meanwhile, please ponder over why the mode of political communication should transform and why?

Irene: I see. From the shortened paper, I obtain a lot of information, but I'm also puzzled by some problems. I'm now eager for the discussion.

Angela: Preparation has already been made for me. I am eager to discuss why central leaders focus so much on media convergence, and why it is an urgent task for China to promote the in-depth development of media convergence, expand and strengthen mainstream public opinion, and consolidate the common ideological basis for the united efforts of the whole Party and the whole people.

Davis: It fully illustrates the necessity and urgency of media integration. You know when compared with the old media, the converged media can be much more subversive. Being digitized and distance-insensitive, whatever news can more easily penetrate through national borders. News reports about what has happened in one place can be circulated around the globe within seconds. People's acquaintances are just a click or a dial.

Irene: So, to some extent, media convergence means discourse power. In such context, Chinese media should build up and improve its political communication to enhance political guidance and the cultural heritage of political discourse, create diversified and three-dimensional images of party leaders, and enhance the political participation of the audience so as to innovatively improve the effect of political communication.

Angela: Exactly. Media convergence makes the boundary between the foreign and domestic blurred. What regulators can do to prevent undesirable communication or to fend off harmful content is not clear at this point. Hence, the nation-state is apt to lose part of its jurisdiction over the regulation of media, and part of its influence over the shape of domestic mediascape. So, it is inevitable that international unfriendly people find the opportunity to spread rumors to discredit the state and the Party. That is absolutely not allowed.

Irene: But sometimes, challenges create opportunities. Chinese media can take advantage of the 3C media convergence to improve the Party's publicity education work so as to propagandize the Party's ideas and course policies to people, thus heightening people's trust in the Party and government. Media should consolidate Marxist guiding status, hold high the great banner of socialism with Chinese characteristics, follow the path of development of socialism with Chinese characteristics, spread political and mainstream values, and vigorously promote core socialist values.

Davis: The mainstream media has kept on enhancing the cultural foundation of political discourse. In recent years, metaphors and allusions with strong characteristics of China's political and cultural are often reported in the press, revealing Chinese cultural confidence, strengthening Chinese cultural background and telling good China's stories to people all over the world.

Angela: The manageability of the converged media should be able to assure the security of transported content and effectively unify content security and technology development to guarantee the stability and unity of the country and meet the demands of building a harmonious society.

Edward: So, don't you sense any disadvantage?

Irene: Yes, I do find some disadvantages. While the advantages of this form of convergence focus on content integration, faster access and international reach, disadvantages highlight the impact of convergence on consumers as well as technology.

Maynor: Yes. Will you like to specify how to affect consumers and technology? Please go ahead.

Irene: It is difficulty in assessing consumer responses and reactions which are scattered across diverse converged platforms. And...

Angela: And it calls for more competition for consumer's time and attention with various media platforms in one device. So the result is audiences often feel overwhelmed with massive amounts of information overloaded.

Davis: The older generation and the disabled sections of the community find it hard to learn the digital skills to use different types of media, while youngsters or high educated people highly rely on technology and the Internet, thus giving birth to communication gap.

Maynor: How about the proneness to cyber-attacks and malfunctioning?

Davis: That's more harmful.

Edward: You had a rich discussion. Next, you're to attend Prof. Maynor's lecture. The lecture-oriented discussion will be more exciting.

All: So much for this discussion. See you later.

Task 6 ▶ Translation practice

Direction: *MEDIA team are going to do Chinese-English translation, from which they can learn and compare how to express in cross-cultural way and convey the following paragraph in English accurately.*

Objectives: *To understand and master English morphology, syntax and idiomatic expressions, develop basic professional translation ability and promote English competence.*

媒体融合给传统媒体的内容传播提供了众多新途径，同时带来的变化也是多方面的。在管理机制上，媒体融合是为制度创新预设了可能性，为向现代企业转型提供了空间；在新闻生产上，媒体融合是信息整合的具体方式、报道形态，以多媒体素材集成报道；在传播渠道上，媒体融合是向各种平台终端强力渗透的产品，汇聚新一代受众群；在商业模式上，媒体融合是完善对传统媒体广告之外的市场布局。媒体融合平台提供多媒体产品，通过电视、广播、互联网、手机、户外电子公告牌等多渠道，分销这些产品从而满足用户个性化需求，实现用户价值。此外，媒体融合的进展也不断促进了新闻从业者信息获取方式的改变，促进了采访报道方式、新闻发布方式、新闻理念等的诸多变化，加快了从传统媒体从业人员向新媒体领域的转行的进程。

Task 7 ▶ Attending a public lecture

Direction: *MEDIA team are going to attend a public lecture delivered by Professor Maynor. Students are required to thoroughly understand the lecture, broaden the vision, elaborate on the theme, get inspiration from the lecture and do some speech activities to extend their knowledge.*

Objectives: *To train students' capability of description, expression, discussion, refutation, humor and humanistic accomplishment required by making a speech, thus, improving students' English language competence and proficiency.*

Lecture 8

Telling China's Stories Well in Converged Media Context

Professor Maynor

Hello, MEDIA Team. Welcome to this last lecture of our series: Chinese Media — A window to Chinese Civilization and Culture. As the hours go speeding on, our series of lectures is coming to an end. What I propose to do for today is to jointly look forward to the future of China's media convergence era. I will address the contemporary Chinese media and its advancing trend. Besides the review of the background of media convergence, I'd like combine with China's national conditions to talk about the importance of media convergence and feasible paths of media integration. Why do we consider telling China's stories well and having Chinese voice heard internationally as strategic measures? Ultimately, can you imagine what will be the prospect of Chinese media convergence? Let's commence on from the context of media convergence.

The context of media convergence in China

Broadly speaking, media convergence in any context is about integrating technologies of information and communications, various forms of media content, and computer networks, for which some scholars now use the abbreviation "3C" to represent communication, computing and content. In the context of China's media revolution, media convergence can be referred to media convergence as a national strategy.

The topic of media convergence has been discussed in China for at least two decades. The term first appeared in the newspaper *People's Daily* in 2007, in an article marking the tenth anniversary of the launch of *Peoples Daily Online.*

The article "Interactivity" was published and effused. It is the interactivity between the paper and the website and between the online and the offline that has realized news horizons for media convergence between the *People's Daily* and *People's Daily Online*. Through the 2000 and 2010, much discussion was focused on the transition of traditional media, such as newspapers and television, to accommodate the new reality of digital media and of emerging social media platforms. Then more and more articles mentioning "media convergence" were appearing in the Party's flagship paper. The notion of media convergence has become central to the discussion of the Party's leadership of the media and its guidance of public opinion.

In the text of the 14th Five-Year Plan, released in March 2021, a section on "Improving the Public Culture Services System" explicitly gives media convergence priority, which means the deep convergence of media should be greatly promoted by strengthening the new mainstream media. Media convergence mainly includes the process of remarking the Party-led media system in the 21st century digital world.

Following the release of Opinions on Accelerating the Promotion of Deep and Integrated Media Development on September 27, 2020, the China New Media Conference was held in November 2020, both with the main theme "media convergence". Opinions spelled out a range of actions to be implemented at all levels and at all departments in China in order to create an omni-media communication system with assurances provided by innovative management.

The most fundamental is that media convergence for the mainstream media can be appealing to wider audiences in an era of digital media proliferation, hence, ensuring that the Party' dominant ideology which can permeate throughout social media and commercial websites and accounts.

Our main media should put publicity and interpretation of Chinese characteristics to top priority. The first essential misson is to clarify the historical traditions, cultural accumulation, and basic national conditions of each country and ethnic group because their development paths will inevitably have their own characteristic; The next is to explain clearly that Chinese culture embodies the deepest spiritual pursuit and richest nourishment, which can speak why the Chinese nation can keep going on its continuous growth and development; The third is to make it well known that our excellent traditional Chinese culture is a prominent advantage of the Chinese nation and also our deepest cultural soft power; Finally, our media should make great efforts to articulate clearly that socialism with Chinese characteristics is rooted in the fertile soil of Chinese culture. It reflects the willingness of the Chinese people, and adapts to the development and progress requirements of China and the times. It also has a profound historical origin and a broad practical foundation.

Media convergence as national strategies

The report of the 20th National Congress of the Communist Party of China pointed out: "From now on, the central task of the CPC is to unite and lead the people of all ethnic groups in the country to comprehensively build a strong socialist modernization country, achieve the second centennial goal, and comprehensively promote the great rejuvenation of the Chinese nation with Chinese path to modernization." Focusing on the central task of the Party, serving the overall situation of the work of the Party and the country, and promoting economic and social development is the most fundamental responsibility of publicity and ideological work, It is also the main battlefield and direction of old media and new media. In recent years, Old media has actively used new media to innovate communication methods, built a multimedia integration platform, built a multi-level and multi-form new media product pattern of common development, and formed a cross departmental, cross terminal, cross channel financial media production pattern.

To promote the integrated development of old media and new media, it is necessary to move from the additive stage to the integration stage as soon as possible, from "you are you and I am I" to "you are me and I am you", and then to "you are me and I am you", and strive to create a number of new mainstream media. In recent years, traditional mainstream media have continuously transformed production processes, enriched reporting methods, promoted technological upgrades, and led innovative development with internet thinking. The main national media have conducted comprehensive exploration and innovation around media forms, operating mechanisms, content production, discourse systems, and achieved remarkable results. People's Daily, Xinhua News Agency, China Media Group and other major central news organizations accelerated the in-depth integration of old media and various emerging media in terms of content, channels, management, etc., gave full play to the advantages of content resources, and actively expanded publicity positions, not only consolidating their position as the center of traditional news and public opinion, but also expanding the influence of Old media into cyberspace. Many local media have actively participated in the wave of media convergence, exploring the development laws of new media, and continuously launching new media platforms and products with their own characteristics, presenting a good development trend. The path to media convergence reflects in the following aspects.

I. Accelerating the full construction of an omni-media communication system

Create a comprehensive national system at four levels. That is from the center to the province and from city to countryside. That means integrating content production and distribution through advancing communication technologies and forms resource-intensive and high-level coordination. Take the Internet as the principal battleground and recognizes that mobile-based and video content is an increasingly dominant trend. The roles of Party media and commercial media. Party media should set the tone of mainstream public opinion, meaning Party-led messaging, and commercial platforms should principally serve as channels with their technologies and other advantages aiding the transmission of mainstream public opinion. In the course of the media convergence, content innovation, form innovation, and means innovation are all important, but content innovation is fundamental. Content production is the core competitiveness and skill of media. No matter how the media format changes or how communication methods improve, content production can only be strengthened, not weakened. In the process of integration and development of all media, facing the complex situation of increasingly diversified social thoughts, content production must adhere to the correct orientation, adhere to promoting Core Socialist Values, highlight mainstream values in the complexity, and effectively guide the direction of public opinion.

II. Adhering throughout to correct guidance of public opinion

The correct guidance and value orientation of public opinion is the soul of news and public opinion work. And the overarching priority of media management in the midst of technological transformation is becoming more clearly here than we have perhaps seen in some time. The development of convergence may bring a change in the forms of the media, but regardless of what kind of media, whether these are mainstream media or commercial platforms, whether they are online or offline, and whether they are small-screen or large-screen, there is only one standard in terms of guidance. There is no land outside the law, and there are no public opinion enclaves. While convergence is a priority in consolidating the Party's leadership over the message, Xu is very clear here that the weakening of the Party's leadership in the name of convergence must be completely eradicated, and the risk of capital controlling public opinion must be resolutely prevented.

III. Focus on expanding the production capacity of high-quality content

In the current Internet Age, with the proliferation of information, ordinary information is no longer scarce, but high-quality content with profound ideas, original insights and authoritative content is still scarce. So high-quality content should be highly valued. Whether the media can attract the masses, and whether they can lead public opinion, the consensus is ultimately up to whether the content is good enough. Creating a flood of information that spreads positive energy and to emphasize positive publicity turns to urgent mission for national media. All the media should make efforts to design more good programs that integrate ideological and artistic elements together, and create more popular and entertaining programs as well. By strengthening the excavation and processing of information resources, deepening the cultivation of information content, exploring the connotation of information, sorting out and elucidating the spirit and principles contained in information, professional content production is carried out to create high-quality professional content with profound ideas and distinct perspectives, ensuring the accuracy, comprehensiveness, and objectivity of media reports.

IV. Actively seizing the high ground of communication technology

Media convergence is a media transformation brought on by technological innovation. Technologies like 5G have driven transformation to stay on top in terms of guiding public opinion and ensuring the dominance of the Party as mainstream. Promoting media integration with new technology requires old media should seize the technical outlet with a strong sense of urgency to create new advantages in media communication. When aiming at new technologies and trends, the national media should also focus on the layout and reshape the overall situation, strive to build a Big data information resource platform, intelligent production and communication platform, take a powerful data platform as the basis for running various businesses, effectively improve the processing speed and communication efficiency of news information, and maximize the diversified needs of users. They should timely and fully utilize new technologies such as 5G, mobile internet, Internet of Things, artificial intelligence, etc., and plan according to the situation, respond to the situation, and follow the trend, so that the light of technology can illuminate the path of media integration and development.

V. Resolutely advancing deepening reforms

To advance and harness the media transformation form, a technical perspective is of course not enough. The situation requires that the party remake the human mechanisms of media development and control. It will no longer be sufficient, for example, to have one leader on the traditional media side and another on new media side. That will lead to "two skins" approach. Patchwork approaches and temporary fixes must give way instead to more comprehensive solutions on the management side, which involves of course both content production, distribution and the policing of current guidance. The Party's management of the media is the fundamental guarantee for adhering to the correct political direction. Promoting the integration and development of media as an important part of publicity and ideological work in the new era must be under the leadership of the Party, adhere to the correct political direction, stand firm in political stance, firmly promote the Party's theory, line, policy, decision-making and deployment of the Party Central Committee, firmly promote the Party Central Committee's major analysis and judgment on the situation, firmly maintain high consistency with the Party Central Committee, and firmly uphold the authority and centralized and unified leadership of the Party Central Committee. No matter how the public opinion environment and communication methods change, the integrated development of media must reflect a clear political and value stance, and must always adhere to reflecting the Party's propositions and the people's voices, as well as reflecting the mainstream values of society. Adhering to the leadership of the Party and adhering to the correct political direction, the integrated development of media can stand high, stand stable, and go far, gathering positive energy for the development of the Party and the country.

China's story convergence

The national strategy of media convergence is Party-led digital transformation, which is an ambitious project with far-reaching implications not just for speech and information inside China, but for the global conversation on a range of issues touching on China's ever-broadening interests from security to 5G, from diplomacy to trade and investment and from health to human rights and democracy.

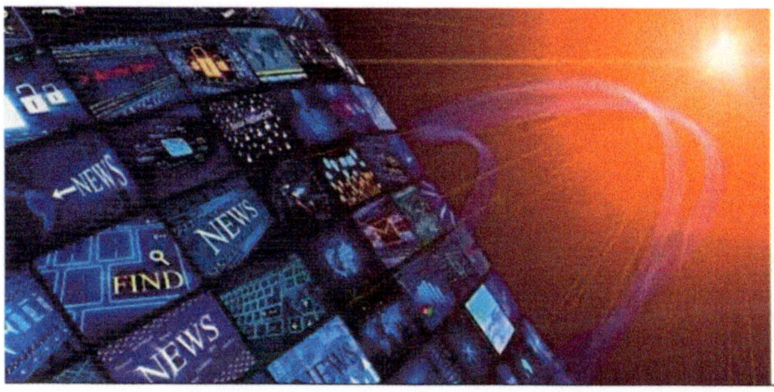

Figure 8.6 Story convergence.
Source: 盛夏财经，《浅谈中国媒介生产融合》，2022-07-05，https://baijiahao.baidu.com.

Our Party's Central Committee and the State Council have been aware that China must expand its "discourse power" internationally by telling China's story well, which essentially means shifting global narratives to suit the objectives of China. As the key to the transformation of domestic media control, media convergence is at the heart of the re-envisioning of external publicity and influence. In 2016, an article published in the *People's Daily*, addressing the creation of "a new mainstream media" wrote that, innovative expression and telling China's stories well require promoting the integrated development of traditional media and newly emerging media and preventing losing none of opportunities.

An article in *China Social Science Daily* is exploring the expansion of

China's international discourse power against Western dominating opinion. Under such circumstance, telling China's stories well and enhancing the dissemination capacity of China's international discourse will raise new expectations for media convergence.

According to a report from local Hunan media, the Party's mainstream media must persist in using offense as defense in transmitting China's voice. Our media must strive to increase the territory occupied in the field of international communication and fight with a "combined punch" in echoing policy-making on communication as a "public opinion struggle".

Telling China's stories well

In the past 70 years since the founding of New China, the Chinese people have created the miracles of rapid economic development and long-term social stability. Insightful people around the world have expressed admiration for what has been achieved.

Shaping global narratives for telling China's stories has become the key mission of Chinese media, especially mainstream media. The work of media communication is the work of creating people's thoughts. Invisible publicity is the most brilliant communication. As the spring breeze and rain can water everything and bring life, telling China's stories well can touch people's deep hearts. In this sense, converged media development arouses people's awareness of the news communication laws, which is self-reflection and self-improvement of media personalities through the drive of new technology.

Chinese media should actively participate in shaping international discourse by telling China's stories well. They should actively strengthen the construction of Chinese foreign narrative system, use innovative ways to tell China's stories to the world and enhance the affinity of Chinese cultural communication to make the image of contemporary China more appealing to the people in the world. The contemporary Chinese story has had different focuses at different times. At the founding of the People's Republic of China in 1949, the story talked about revolution, and the independence of Chinese people from foreign powers. After reform and opening up, the narrative arch followed the Chinese economy's takeoff. In the new era, the narrative has been about China's development and the rejuvenation of the Chinese nation.

Poverty alleviation is an integral part of the third narrative, facilitating its realization and demonstrating its achievements. It involves multiple perspectives and fits in the international dialogue. It reflects the joined efforts of contemporary Chinese people. It is a story about the development of science and technology in modern China, the revitalization of traditional Chinese culture, and its deep reforms that brought new development opportunities to the world. It presents a comprehensive image of China to the world as being traditional, modern, and global.

In 2020, the COVID-19 pandemic has complicated global public opinions of Chinese enterprises, making it particularly important to rebuild their image overseas. To more actively respond to the concerns of the international community about the novel coronavirus outbreak, our media need to use various forms to make our voice heard in a timely manner, narrate our fight against the epidemic, clearly explain our positive actions and progress in epidemic prevention and control, and promote our vision of a community with a shared future for mankind. Besides, Sports events provide a diversified global platform for displaying corporate images. Enterprises can tap into the global audience's common passions to effectively bring down ideological barriers and better communicate the image of Chinese enterprises as good actors and China being a responsible major country. The 2022 Winter Olympic Games is another good opportunity to reach out to global audiences and brands and uplift the image of Chinese enterprises and their country as a whole.

When we are gaining the ability to tell China's stories well with converged media development, our stories will truly touch the hearts and souls of the people across the world. The media should enable to win the understanding,

Figure 8.7 Telling China's stories well. Source: Fu Ying, "Shape Global Narratives for Telling China's Stories", *China Daily* (Global version), Apr. 21, 2021.

respect and recognition of international audiences through penetrating analysis, appealing ideas and persuasive arguments. Based on the profound and enduring values of the Chinese culture, our media should also adhere to the spirit of humility, inclusiveness and learning from others, and employ a plain, down-to-earth narrative style to convey what is happening in China, and make objective judgments on what is happening outside China, thus, forming a narrative style with Chinese characteristics that gives China a distinctive voice that can be heard and understood in international discourse. Only by this way, can China present in front of the world with an even clearer and more vivid and amiable image. Our new mainstream media and new media groups can reveal a true, civilized and amiable China to the world.

Task 8 ▶ Online forum and summary writing

Direction: *MEDIA team are going to launch an instant online post-talk about the lecture to appeal to more of other students who are interested in the topic to join them. This is an integrated practice of listening, speaking, reading and writing. They are particularly expected to write a summary of the entire unit.*

Objectives: *To provide a platform for MEDIA team to fully display their talents. To comb language learning with professional knowledge so as to cultivate students' professional learning, academic literacy and language competence. To realize the teaching objectives of acquiring professional knowledge through learning English language.*

Edward: Hi, MEDIA members. Finally, we come to the last task of the last unit. The theme of this forum is quite popular with us as we can access this sort of information from various media. Such information fuels you with energy and encourages you to be more patriotic and confident. So, what is it?

All: Telling China's stories well.

Maynor: Ha-ha. This time, Edward and I will both participate in your discussion rather than just offering guidance. Here, I'd like to propose some questions for your online forum:

(1) From the reading excerpt plus your discussion above,

we all deeply acknowledge the importance of media convergence. We may also be aware of why central leaders attach so much importance to it. Then comes my question: How can we tell China's stories well in the context of media convergence?

(2) It is well accepted that storytelling is the best way of international communication. Then, in what way should China converged media innovate and improve the discourse system in order to enhance the international discourse power?

(3) How to strengthen media integration so as to create multiple communication channels?

Edward: Please ponder over these questions and reflect on them. They are truly wide-ranging and most thought-provoking. If I may, I would like to add a question to his very comprehensive list. I believe that all of us must still remember that we have expounded the soft power and media at the very beginning. Here, I can't help thinking whether you will associate storytelling with the China's image and soft power? I know it's a rather rigorous demand, but I really think it is worthy of your consideration.

Irene: Thank you so much for your kind suggestions, dear professors. I assure you that we won't let you down, right?

Angela & Davis: We surely won't. We are an invincible team!

Davis: Guys, I am eager to express my view first about why we must tell China's stories well. As everybody knows, China has a long history of five thousand years, and the stories handed down by the Chinese nation over the past five thousand years are certainly rich and colourful. However, the implicit national characteristics and the objective environment with complex context have made it difficult for the Chinese media to tell China's stories well, as is wished. As a result, some Western countries dominate the position of international discourse, which led to the international community's understanding and cognition of China limited to the dislocation of individual Western media comments and reports.

Maynor: Terrific. Your excellent answer also accounts for why we should tell the story of socialism with Chinese characteristics, the Chinese dream, the Chinese people, the excellent Chinese culture and the peaceful development of China. Through China's stories, people across the world can see clearly China's image and policy.

Davis: I give you a thumbs up, dear Maynor. The content of the story is also the message conveyed by media. In this digital age, it is difficult to imagine a pipeline without good oil, or a superhighway without qualified cars. Similarly, if information contained in the story can't spread authentic and rich Chinese culture, it ceases to be meaningful. Content is at the core of the story, and its importance will heighten as channel capacity multiplies. Whoever owns both rich content and the super technique to transmit will dominate the creation and distribution of converged media.

Edward: Now let's turn to the path to telling China's stories well. We should adapt to the new communication pattern of "globalization, popularization and full media" strategically. We are to shift from international communication to global communication, from publicity thinking to storytelling thinking, from dispersion and imbalance to pluralistic coordination in theme, and from position consciousness to scene consciousness in space. We should dare to speak out at the first time, be good at speaking out, make an objective, authentic and authoritative interpretation, and provide the timeliness and credibility of the state-owned media by making full use of digital convergence.

Angela: I'd like to have a trial on the third question on the way to strengthen media integration. In the era of big data, industry changes triggered by technological changes have brought new opportunities and challenges to cultural communication, and users' needs become an important change factor. In the media convergence context, we should strengthen the comprehensive application of big data modeling and algorithms, regularly analyze the essence and direction of user needs, constantly feed back, guide information production, and further improve the effectiveness of communication.

Irene: Too professional, Angela. Well, for me, I know that China has drawn up a national technological innovation strategy in its long-term national interest. Digital convergence together with the continuous rapid increase in the services of mobile, broadband and internet provides a chance for technological innovation. China has made it clear to support enterprises as the mainstay of technological innovation.

Edward: Don't you think it worth talking over the storytelling and China's soft power? What China stand for globally? With China's growing influence in the world, China has a conscious desire to tell China's stories well. How do you understand the correlation between China's commitment to telling its own story, China's image and soft power? These perceptions may be an illustration of China's interpretation of soft power and its long-term soft power strategy.

Angela: It deserves wider discussion. Media also play a vital role in shaping, communicating and attracting public opinion through positive characterization of China, its state, society and development in the media convergence context.

Davis: Telling China's stories well can be a part of China's "going global" strategy. All mainstream media should enhance the coverage and generate potential favourable influence on the world opinion through storytelling.

Irene: Telling China's stories well can create a beautiful and amiable image of China. Digital convergence integrated with rich cultural resources can certainly appeal to a larger audience overseas and communicate the narrative of peaceful and responsible China and resultantly that would assist in countering perception of the so called "China threat" in Western countries and bring a positive image for China.

Maynor: Perfect. And China's story telling may form a sort of confrontation with the Western narrative dominated media, but will become a proactive drive to expand the outreach of Chinese media together with its influence and image.

Edward: All in all, telling China's stories well is a powerful starting point for building up the national image and strengthening external communication, plus an effective measure to highlight the international voice and enhance the cultural soft power.

Maynor: Wow, the last discussion is the longest one. It seems that everyone has much to say and everyone is nostalgic for the time when we studied and discussed together. So am I.

Edward: However, there is no feast that never ends in life. Our discussion has been open to online learners. Let's look forward to the next chance to study together. We have to say good-bye for now.

All: Good bye.

Appendix: Vocabulary for Unit 8

Listening Activity

cellular /ˈseljələ(r)/ *adj.* 由细胞组成的，细胞的；（电话系统）蜂窝状的，蜂窝式的
n. 移动电话

hypothetical /ˌhaɪpəˈθetɪk(ə)l/ *adj.* （基于）假设的，假定的
n. 假设命题，假设陈述

strip /strɪp/ *v.* 除去，撕掉（外皮或表层）；夺去，剥夺（地位，权力，财产）；脱衣服；表演脱衣舞；为（奶牛）收奶；拆卸，拆开（机器、车辆或引擎）
n. （纸、金属、织物等）条，带；带状地带；商业街；脱衣舞；连环漫画；飞机跑道

annotate /ˈænəteɪt/ *vi.* 注释；给……作注释或评注
vt. 注释；作注解

remix /ˈriːmɪks/ *v.* 合成；再混合（音乐录音）；（用调整安排不同音轨的方法）制作（已录制音乐的）修改版；重新搅拌
n. 调整版录制音乐，重新合成版

participatory /pɑːˌtɪsɪˈpeɪtəri/ *adj.* （体制、活动、角色）参与式的

cue /kjuː/ *n.* 暗示，提示；（戏剧或电影中的）尾白，提示；（台球等的）球杆；线索

v. 提示，暗示；用球杆击球

posit /ˈpɒzɪt/ v. 假设，认定；建立在（假说）上（posit sth. on）；安置，放置
n.（哲）假想

stainless /ˈsteɪnləs/ adj. 不锈的，防锈的；无污点的；（人，名声）纯洁的，无瑕的
n. 不锈钢

episode /ˈepɪsəʊd/ n. 一段经历，一段时期；（电视剧或广播剧的）集，一集

immersion /ɪˈmɜːʃn/ n.（做某事的）专心，投入；浸没，浸泡；沉浸式语言教学法;（基督教的）洗礼，浸礼

chronically /ˈkrɒnɪkli/ adv. 慢性地，经常复发地；长期地，习惯性地；严重地

instill /ɪnˈstɪl/ vt. 徐徐滴入；逐渐灌输

passivity /pæˈsɪvəti/ n. 被动性；被动结构；无抵抗

erode /ɪˈrəʊd/ v. 侵蚀，腐蚀；削弱，降低

scuba /ˈskuːbə/ n. 水下呼吸器，水肺；带水肺潜水
adj. 使用水肺的，有水下呼吸器的

ruefully /ˈruːfəli/ adv. 可怜地；悲伤地

zip /zɪp/ n. 拉链，拉锁；〈非正式〉速度，活力
v. 用拉链扣上，拉开拉链；（使）迅速移动；压缩（电脑文件）
adj.（袋，包等）用拉链扣住的

neuroscience /ˈnjʊərəʊsaɪəns/ n. 神经科学

Reading Activity

consolidate /kənˈsɒlɪdeɪt/ v. 使巩固，使加强；合并，统一

ideological /ˌaɪdiəˈlɒdʒɪk(ə)l/ adj. 思想体系的，意识形态的

shunting /ˈʃʌntɪŋ/ n. 分路；转线
v. 分路；拖延（shunt 的 -ing 形式）

diversion /daɪˈvɜːʃn/ n. 转向，转移；绕行路，支路；转移注意力的事物，分心的事物；消遣，娱乐

asynchronism /æˈsɪŋkrəˌnɪzəm/ n. 不同时；异步性

zombie /ˈzɒmbi/ n. 僵尸，还魂尸；无生气的人，麻木迟钝的人

fragmented /frægˈmentɪd/ adj. 支离破碎的，分裂的
v.（使）支离破碎，（使）分裂（fragment 的过去式和过去分词）

matrix /ˈmeɪtrɪks/ n. 矩阵；模型；社会环境；矩阵转接电路；线路网，道路网；精细材料；交叉结构

algorithm /ˈælgərɪðəm/ n.（尤指计算机）算法，运算法则

manuscript /ˈmænjuskrɪpt/ n. 手稿，原稿；手抄本，手写本
adj. 手写的

semantic /sɪˈmæntɪk/ *adj.* 语义的；语义学的
unity /ˈjuːnəti/ *n.* 团结，统一；整体性，统一性；统一体
resonant /ˈrezənənt/ *adj.* 洪亮的，共振的；共鸣的
adhere /ədˈhɪə(r)/ *v.* 黏附，附着；遵守，遵循（规定或协议）；拥护，持有（观点或信仰）
endogenous /enˈdɒdʒənəs/ *adj.* [生物]内生的；内因性的
versatile /ˈvɜːsətaɪl/ *adj.* 多才多艺的，有多种技能的；多用途的，多功能的
barrier /ˈbæriə(r)/ *n.* 障碍，壁垒；障碍物，关卡；分界线，屏障；大关，界限
ultra-high /ˈʌltrə haɪ/ *adj.* 超高的
scenario /səˈnɑːriəʊ/ *n.* 设想，可能发生的情况；剧情梗概；场景
fusion /ˈfjuːʒ(ə)n/ *n.* 融合，结合；核聚变；混合音乐；融合菜肴；熔化；融合物
immersive /ɪˈmɜːsɪv/ *adj.*（计算机系统或图像）沉浸式虚拟现实的
panorama /ˌpænəˈrɑːmə/ *n.*（陆地或海洋的）全景，全貌；全景画，全景摄影；（某一主题或系列事件的）概论，综述；万花筒，各种人物，多样事物
unswervingly /ʌnˈswəːviŋli/ *adv.* 坚定不移地

Lecture

effuse /ɪˈfjuːz/ *vt.* 流出；涌出；泻出（过去式 effused）
vi. 流出；涌出；泻出
accommodate /əˈkɒmədeɪt/ *v.* 为……提供住宿；容纳，提供空间
spell /spel/ *n.* 一段时间；（疾病突然的）一次发作；咒语，符咒，着魔
v. 拼写，拼缀出（单词）；拼作，拼成；招致，意味着（通常指坏事）（过去式 spelt 或 spelled）
omni-media 全媒体
hostile /ˈhɒstaɪl/ *adj.* 敌对的，怀敌意的；强烈反对的；敌人的，敌方的
n. 敌对分子
infiltration /ˌɪnfɪlˈtreɪʃn/ *n.* 渗透；渗透物
metamorphosis /ˌmetəˈmɔːfəsɪs/ *n.* 变形；变质
allusion /əˈluːʒ(ə)n/ *n.* 暗指，影射，典故
harness /ˈhɑːnɪs/ *v.* 控制并利用；（把动物）拴在一起（或拴到某物上）；给（马）套上挽具；连接，串联
n.（马的）挽具，马具；系带，吊带；日常工作
pliable /ˈplaɪəb(ə)l/ *adj.* 柔韧的；柔软的；圆滑的；易曲折的
overarching /ˌəʊvərˈɑːtʃɪŋ/ *adj.* 首要的；支配一切的；包罗万象的
v. 成拱形（overarch 的 -ing 形式）
resolutely /ˈrezəluːtli/ *adv.* 坚决地；毅然地
enclave /ˈenkleɪv/ *n.* 飞地，（某一人群的）聚居地；（喻）与周围人群（或地

方）有着不同特征的人群（或地方）

eradicate /ɪˈrædɪkeɪt/ *v.* 根除，消灭

proliferation /prəˌlɪfəˈreɪʃn/ *n.*（数量的）激增，剧增；（细胞、组织、有机体的）繁殖，增生；大量

ultimately /ˈʌltɪmətli/ *adv.* 最终，最后；根本上，最主要地

patchwork /ˈpætʃwɜːk/ *n.* 拼布工艺（品）；拼凑之物
adj. 拼缀的，拼缝的

requisite /ˈrekwɪzɪt/ *adj.*〈正式〉必需的，必要的
n. 必需品，必要条件

envision /ɪnˈvɪʒ(ə)n/ /ɪnˈvɪʒ(ə)n/ *v.* 想象，预想（现在分词 envisioning）

arch /ɑːtʃ/ *n.* 拱门；拱顶；足弓；拱形物
v.（使）成弓形，拱起
adj. 淘气的，调皮的；傲慢自大的；主要的

rejuvenation /rɪˌdʒuːvəˈneɪʃn/ *n.* 恢复青春，恢复活力；恢复活力；回春，更生

alleviation /əˌliːviˈeɪʃn/ *n.* 减轻，缓和；镇痛物

pandemic /pænˈdemɪk/ *adj.*（疾病）大规模流行的
n.〈正式〉大流行病

References

Alexander, R. Galloway. What is new media? Ten years after the language of new media [J]. *Criticism*, 2012, 53(3): 377-384.

Alvaris, F. Twitter vs. Weibo: 8 things Twitter can learn from the latter [J/OL]. *Social Media*, 2021. https://hongklat.com/blog (accessed 30/03/2021)

Anderson, C. W. Practice, interpretation, and meaning in today's digital media ecosystem [J/OL]. *Journalism & Mass Communication Quarterly*, 2020, 97(2): 342-359. https://doi.org/10.1177/1077699020916807 (accessed 02/09/2020)

Anonymous, Beauty and its perceptions: A deep dive into China's current social media landscape [OL]. https://china.usc.edu/beauty-and-its-perceptions-deep-dive-chinas-current-social-media-landscape (accessed 09/08/2020)

Arina, Muresan. Chinese strategies in cultivating soft power [OL]. https://www.IGD.org.za InFocus (accessed30/03/2021)

Arjun, Kharpal. Everything you need to know about WeChat – China's billion-user messaging app [OL]. https://www.cnbc.com/2019/02/04/what-is-wechat-china-biggest-messaging-app.html? (accessed 20/02/2019)

BÁEZ GARCÍA, Gara. China's "peaceful rise": Political legitimacy as a soft power strategy [J]. *Opinion Paper. IEEE*, 2020, 133.

Bean-Mellinger, Barbara. Introduction of print media [OL]. http://bizfluent.com (accessed 02/09/2018)

Bonnie, S. Glaser and Melissa, E. Murphy *Soft Power with Chinese Characteristics* [OL]. http://csis-websitc-peod.s3.amazonaws.com. (accessed 09/09/2019)

Bonnie, S. Glaser and Melissa, E. Murphy. *Soft Power with Chincse Characteristics*, EBSCO, 2009.

Brokaw, Cynthia. The origins of the modern Chinese press [J]. *China Information*, 2008, 22(3): 517-519.

Cara, Wallis. New media practices in China: Youth patterns, processes, and politics [J]. *International Journal of Communication*, 2011 (5): 406-436.

Carminati, Daniele. The state of China's soft power [OL]. http://www.e-ir.info/ (accessed 03/07/2020)

Chen, Nan, *et al*. Analysis on communication influence of official microblogs [J/OL]. *Discrete Dynamics in Nature and Society*, 2021. https://doi.org/10.1155/2021/6672944 (accessed 11/12/2021)

Chen, Liang. How has China's home-grown social media WeChat changed the traditional media landscape? [R]. Reuters Institute Fellowship Paper, University of Oxford, 2016.

Crampton, Thomas. Chinese social media: The same, but different [OL]. http://www.chinabusinessreview.com (accessed 15/02/2018)

Di Bao (ancient Chinese gazette) [OL]. https//en.m.wikipedia.org (accessed 02/03/2018)

Si, Si, Expansion of International Broadcasting: The Growing Global Reach of China Central Television [R]. Reuters Institute for the Study of Journalism, July, 2014.

Freedman, Des. Paradigms of media power [J/OL]. *Communication Culture & Critique*, 2015, 8(2): 273-289. https://doi.org/10.1111/cccr.12081 (accessed 03/04/2019)

Freedman, Des. *The Contradictions of Media Power* [M]. London: Bloomsbury Academic, 2014.

Garrison, Jean A. China's prudent cultivation of "Soft Power" and implications for U.S. policy in East Asia [J]. *Asian Affairs: An American Review*, 2005, 32 (1): 25-30.

Guo, Ping. Telling China's story well in a new converged media structure [N]. *People's Daily*, 19/08 /2014.

He, Wei. WeChat now an integral part of daily life in China, says survey [N]. Chinadaily.com.cn (accessed 02/03/2022)

Herbert, Stephen. *A History of Early Film* [M]. London: Routledge, 2000.

Hu, Yong & Chen, Lei. From the journal online media and global communication [J/OL]. *Online Media and Global Communication*, 2022, 1(1): 124-163. https://doi.org/10.1515/omgc-2022-0009 (accessed 11/12/2022)

Humphreys, Peter & Simpson, Seamus. Media convergence: Paths and constructs [OL]. https://www.elgaronline.com/downloadpdf/9781781008980/09_chapter1.xhtml.pdf (accessed 18/03/2018)

Jenkins, H. The cultural logic of media convergence [J]. *International Journal of Cultural Studies*, 2004, 7(1): 33-43.

Jia, Lianrui & Han, Xiaofei. Tracing Weibo (2009–2019): The commercial dissolution of public communication and changing politics [J]. *Internet Histories*, 2020, 4.3: 304-332.

Khillar, Sagar. Difference between social media and traditional media [OL]. http://www.differencebetween.net/technology/ (accessed11/4/2020)

Kopecka-Piech, Katazyna. Media convergence concepts [J/OL]. *Media Studies*, 2011, 46(3): 1-19. https://www.academia.edu.media(accessed 12/05/2020)

Lamont, Ian. The rise of the press in Late Imperial China [R]. Survey of Publishing, from Text to Hypertext, Harvard University Extension School, 11/2007.

Lehman-Wilzig, Sam & Cohen-Avigdor, Nava. The natural life cycle of new media evolution: Inter-media struggle for survival in the internet age [OL]. http://nms.sagepub.com/cgi/content/abstract/6/6/707 (accessed 14/02/2020)

Li, Haojian & Wang, X.T. Cyber-personality and liking expression: A study from

WeChat users in China [J/OL]. *Frontiers in Psychology*, 2021. https://doi.org/10.3389/fpsyg.2021.626040 (accessed 11/12/2021)

Li, Mia Shuang. How WeChat became the primary news source in China [J/OL]. *Columbia Journalism Review*, January 10, 2018. https://www.cjr.org (accessed 18/01/2018)

Li, Xing. China's pursuit of soft power: Norm diffusion as a soft power mechanism [J/OL]. *Advances in Applied Sociology*, 2020, 10(7): 278-297. http://doi.org/10.4236/aasoci.2020.107017 (accessed 09/02/2019)

Lin, Justin. Social media has changed the lives of modern society [N/OL]. *Summit News*, March 24, 2020. http://summitpsnews.org (accessed18/02/2020)

Liu, Jianxin. The Chinese blogosphere as a site of social engagement and contestation [J]. *Fast Capitalism*, 2014, 11(1): 1-23.

Luan, Yimei. High-quality media convergence to tell China's stories well [N]. *Chinese Social Sciences Today*, 04/2021.

Macgilchrist, F. *Discourse Approaches to Politics, Society and Culture* [M]. London: John Benjamins, 2011.

McNair. *An Introduction to Political Communication* [M]. Beijing: Xinhua Press, 2005.

Mirza, M, N., Abbas, H. & Nizamani, M. Q. Evaluating China's soft power discourse: Assumptions, strategies, and objectives [J]. *Global Strategic & Security Studies Review*, 2020, 5 (4): 40-50.

Mokros, E. *The Peking Gazette in Late Imperial China* [M]. Seattle: University of Washington Press, 2021.

Montag, Christian, *Becker, B. & Gan, C.* The multipurpose application WeChat: A review on recent research [J/OL]. *Frontiers in Psychology*, 9, Article 2247. https://doi.org/10.3389/fpsyg.2018.02247 (accessed 04/06/2019)

Multhauf, Robert P. Book Review: *Science and Civilization in China. Volume V: Chemistry and Chemical Technology. Part I: Paper and Printing* [J]. *ISIS*, 1988.

Nye, Joseph S. The rise of China's soft power [N]. *Wall Street Journal*, December 29, 2005.

Patricia, A. Y., *et al.* How WeChat has changed the face of marketing in China [J]. *British Journal of Marketing Studies*, 2017.

Roberts, Marilyn. Agenda setting and issue salience online [J]. *Communication Research*, 2002, 29(4): 452-465.

Smith, Paul & Evens, Tom. The next big match: Convergence, competition and sports media rights [J/OL]. *European Journal of Communication*, 2016, 31(5). http://doi.org/10.1177/0267323116666479 (accessed 11/06/2020)

Soon, Carol & Sim, Jui Liang. Individualized and depoliticized: A study of Chaoya

Sun's *New Media in New China: An Analysis of the Democratizing Effect of the Internet* [OL]. http://scholarworks.calstate.edu (accessed 02/07/2020)

Soon, Carol & Sim, Jui Liang. Individualized and depoliticized: A study of Chinese blogosphere in Singapore [J/OL]. *JeDEM — EJournal of EDemocracy and Open Government*, 7(1): 23-45. https://doi.org/10.29379/jedem.v7i1.373 (accessed 08/06/2020)

Tang, Xuan & Zhou, Yang. Social media use and political participation in rural China: A case study [J]. *China Journalism and Communication Journal*, 2018, (1): 216-238.

Vaagan, Wallace Robert & Wang, Yu. The development of digital television in China and Norway [J]. *Intercultural Communication Studies*, 2008, XVII (3): 169-184.

Waliczko, Tomasz. WeChat – A Chinese cyber-culture phenomenon [J]. *Modern Management Review*, 2020, XXV (27): 143-155.

Wang, Xin, *et al.* Public discourse and social network echo chambers driven by socio-cognitive biases [J/OL]. *Physical Review,* 2020, 10(4). http://doi.org/10.1103/PhysRevX.10.041042 (accessed 12/06/2020)

Wang, Yuhua. How WeChat grows into a huge part of our life [OL]. https://annenberg.usc.edu (accessed 11/02/2017)

Xia, Wen. The influence of micro-blog on the cyber-political participation in China [A]. In *Proceedings of 2011 International Conference on Public Administration (7th)* (Volume Ⅰ) [C]. Chengdu: University of Electronic Science and Technology of China Press, 2011.

Xie, Wanying, Jiang, Sheng & Kakar, Allauddin. Research on political communication of Chinese media in the media convergence era [J]. *Pakistan Journal of International Affairs,* 2021, 4(4): 44-58.

Xu, Yi & Zhang, Weimin. New media's impact on China from a culture perspective [A/OL]. In Ke Xue & Mingyang Yu (eds). *New Media and Chinese Society* [C]. Singapore: Springer, 2017. http://doi.org/10.1007/978-981-10-6710-5_6 (accessed 18/09/2020)

Ye, Yonjiao, *et al.* Social media, public discourse and civic engagement in modern China [J/OL]. *Telematics and Informatics*, 2017, 34(3): 705-714. http://dx.doi.org/10.1016/j.tele.2016.05.021 (accessed 30/04/2021)

Zhang, Lixuan & Pentina, Iryna. Motivations and usage patterns of Weibo [J]. *Cyberpsychology, Behavior, and Social Networking*, 2012, 15(6): 312-317.

Zhang, Yu. Review of *Print Culture and Media in Late Imperial and Early Republican China* [J]. *China Review International*, 2017, 24(1): 1-7.

Zhang, C. *et al.* How WeChat can retain users: Roles of network externalities, social interaction ties, and perceived values in building continuance intention [J/OL].

Computers in Human Behavior, 2017, 69: 284-293. http://doi.org/10.1016/j.chb.2016.11.069 (accessed 11/06/2020)

Zhang, Xiaoling. China's international broadcasting: A case study of CCTV International [A]. In J. Wang (ed). *Soft Power in China* [C]. New York: Palgrave Macmillan. http://doi.org/10.1057/9780230116375_4 (accessed 12/02/2020)

Zheng, Chun *et al.* Why do we "like" on WeChat moments: The effects of personality traits and content characteristics [J/OL]. *Frontiers in Psychology*, 2022, 13:1-10. https://doi.org/10.3389/fpsyg.2022.772547 (accessed 11/06/2020)

Zhong, *et al. A Historical Study of Early Film Exhibition and Film Audiences* [M]. 1997.

Zuo, T. *Characteristics and Trends of News Communication Under the Trend of Media Convergence* [C]. The 4th International Conference on Arts, Linguistics, Literature and Humanities (ICALLH 2021), 2021.

段臻臻，石淑琳，刘泽凝. 主流媒体从叙事到融情的微博传播策略探究——以《人民日报》新冠肺炎疫情报道为例 [J]. 今传媒，2023（1）：4.

范红，苏筱. 新时代中国形象的多元建构与国际传播策略 [J]. 对外传播，2022(2): 67–71.

国家广播电视总局发展研究中心（编）. 中国广播电影电视发展报告 [R]. 北京：中国广播电视出版社，2018.

胡钰，王嘉婧. 中国新媒体发展：特征、趋势与调整 [J]. 中国编辑，2021（3）：10–15.

柯荣谊. 借力新媒体对外讲好中国共产党故事 [J]. 对外传播，2022（2）：12–15.

赖炜. 中外社交媒体发展历史之比较研究 [J]. 青年记者，2019（32）：20–21.

李宇. 从 CCTV4 到 CGTN：浅析中国国际电视频道的发展嬗变 [J]. 对外传播，2017（5）：34–36.

廖基添，邸报是古代报纸吗？——中国古代报纸发展线索再梳理 [J]. 新闻与传播研究，2010（1）：12–20.

刘一璟. 中外知名社交媒体传播方式对比研究 [J]. 中国报业，2016（4）：50–51.

彭冰琳. 互联网内容传播中微博影响力的探讨 [J]. 新闻潮，2021（6）：69–71.

乔亮，张婷. 新时代以媒体融合发展推动国家治理现代化研究——学习习近平总书记关于推动媒体融合建设全媒体的重要论述 [J]. 社会主义研究，2021（6）：85–92.

秦静. 2014 年中国新媒体研究综述 [J]. 新媒体与社会，2015（1）：149–167.

沈继睿. 中国古代主要媒介的归类分期和发展特点 [J]. 南阳理工学院学报，2012（1）：94–97.

舒俊. 中国文化软实力评价研究述评 [J]. 实事求是，2019（2）：62–69.

陶建杰，尹子伊. 中国文化软实力建构与国际传播策略 [J]. 南方传媒研究，2021（4）：52–58.
闫一晨. 从 CCTV NEWS 到 CGTN：论中国国际话语权的提升 [J]. 中国民族博览，2018.1.
张韬，常川，玉珍. 新媒体时代主流媒体公信力的建设 [J]. 传媒论坛，2021（5）：23–24.
张伟、刘宝存. 全球竞争时代的教育软实力：内涵、挑战与因应 [J]. 清华大学教育研究，2022（1）：87–95.
赵翀，全媒体背景下的 CCTV 发展战略研究 [D]. 衡阳：南华大学，2016.
赵淑萍，崔林，吴炜华. 构建媒体深度融合发展新格局 [N]. 光明日报，2020-12-22（6）.